DISCOVER

MORE ABOUT

GOD

FOR YOURSELF

"You need not that any man teach you:"
1 John 2:27

ALL YOU NEED IS A BIBLE, AND TO ASK FOR A LOT OF HELP FROM **HIM**

By

BRIAN H. BUTLER

Copyright © 2017 Brian H. Butler

All rights reserved. No part of this book may be used or reproduced by any means, graphic, electronic, or mechanical, including photocopying, recording, taping, or by any information storage retrieval system, without the written permission of the publisher except in the case of brief quotations in critical articles or reviews.

The English King James Version of the Bible is generally considered by most scholars to be overall the best translation despite its ancient English, and its many errors of translation which can easily be resolved by the careful, diligent student.

Quotations from the King James Version of the Bible form a large proportion of this book. The King James Version of the Bible is in the Public Domain.

The publisher of this book may be contacted by email at:

bhb@ernestworkman.com

Because of the dynamic nature of the Internet, and web addresses or links contained in this book may have changed since publication and may no longer be valid.

The views expressed in this work are solely those of the author.

Perfect bound paperback book ISBN: 978-0-9943391-5-7

eBook edition ISBN: 978-0-9943391-6-4

Library of Congress Control Number:

Typeset by Brian H. Butler

Formatted by Loveofbooks.com

Printed by Lightning Source

DISCOVER MORE ABOUT GOD FOR YOURSELF

RELIGION
v
GOD
GOD'S WORD
The Holy Bible
v

FILTER 1
The Human Mind
The carnal mind is enmity against God, for it is not subject to the law of God, neither indeed can be
Romans 8:7
v

FILTER 2
Truth mixed with error
Partial truths
False Doctrines - Idolatry
Human ideas & reasonings
v

FILTER 3
Church organisations
Priests, Ministers
Desire to control followers
v

YOU
YOUR MIND
Your Human Spirit
Deceived into believing truth mixed with error
Having the understanding darkened being alienated from the life of God through the ignorance that is in them, because of the blindness of their heart
Ephesians 4:18

THEOLOGY
v
GOD
GOD'S WORD
The Holy Bible
v

THE PURPOSE OF LIFE IS:
To learn about God from the study of His Word & to strive to be like Him. Ask for, and receive it, **GOD'S HOLY SPIRIT FLOWS INTO YOUR MIND**
The 'Light' comes on.
New Understanding floods your mind & heart.
v

NO FILTERS
PURE TRUTH DIRECT FROM GOD TO YOU
v

YOU
YOUR MIND
Your Human Spirit
Enlightened by the flow of God's Holy Spirit,
filled with the truth
The eyes of your understanding being enlightened; that you may know what is the hope of His calling, and what the Riches of the Glory of His inheritance in the saints. And what is the exceeding greatness of His Power to us-ward who believe, according to the working of His Mighty Power.
Ephesians 1:18-19

TABLE OF CONTENTS

PREFACE - How this book came to be written 1
ACKNOWLEDGEMENT 5
INTRODUCTION 7

Chapter 1
Before the 'Beginning' of all we know 9
GOD IS A BEING – ALIVE – The source of all life 9
GOD IS LOVE – Loving concern for Everything 10
Some Aspects and Qualities of God 11
GOD IS THE AUTHOR OF PROPHECY 14
GOD IS MALE AND FEMALE IN ONE 15

Chapter 2
GOD CREATED HIS SON 17
The true nature of the Word, Jesus Christ 17
The formation & Development of 'The Plan of God' 19
Biblical prophecy shows the Omniscience of God 19
Christ's birth as a man was prophesied in great
detail hundreds of years before the event. 20
Christ 'willed' to be sacrificed for us. 21
The incredible complexity of God's plan 25
All this complexity without a Designer? 26

Chapter 3
THEN CHRIST THE WORD CREATED
EVERYTHING THERE IS 29
The Word created Spirit Beings, Satan, & God's Sons 29

God Creates Good and Evil 30

God's Secret Creative Powers were used by the
Word to form all things, visible and invisible. 31

GRAVITY is one of God's Secret Powers 32

The Energy of and within matter 33

A dramatic example of the content of
God's Power in Matter 34

Particle 'science' finds ever more of God's handiwork. 35

Can the origin of the Cosmos be proven mathematically? 36

Ancient knowledge of the Constellations
and the expanding universe. 38

God's Powers are infinite. 39

AVOID 'theories', they are guesswork 40

God is the Origin of natural laws, The Lawgiver 41

Chapter 4

THEN GOD REFORMED THE EARTH TO MAKE
IT HABITABLE FOR HIS CHILDREN 43

The miracle of Light 43

What is Light? 44

The Fauna and Flora reformation of the earth. 45

Life can only come from 'Life' 46

Then the Word Created the Man and the Woman 47

All humans have a human spirit. 48

One man plus one woman make One flesh. 50

What is a Human Being? 51

God's 'Sons' on Earth 55

The Flood 62

Chapter 5
IS GOD WORKING IN THIS AGE THROUGH THOUSANDS OF DEMOMINATIONS AND .ORGS?........... 67

God works with individuals not organisations......................... 67

Are you deceived? Here is a reality check:............................... 68

No, God and Christ are not working with thousands of 'churches', how could They be?... 70

Is Christ divided? Is He working with countless Christian divisions of opinion?... 70

Anyone who is deceived, does not know they are deceived.. 71

So who is God dealing with individually and personally?... 75

God is calling individuals at this time in history 76

God knows each of the 'called' intimately, in every detail... 77

The Christianity of 'Churchianity' has lost its way because of 'Attitude'.. 80

Repentance means to change one's mind and behaviour. 88

Chapter 6
THE NATURE AND HEART OF HUMAN BEINGS 107

The heart 'attitude' in the Bible 107

The Parable of the Talents or pounds in Luke 110

The Parable of the Talents in Matthew 110

Christ will bring His reward with Him when He returns......... 111

The word Heart includes our Attitudes of Mind 111

Attitudes of heart and mind... 115

Chapter 7
THE DEVELOPMENT OF TRUE SPIRITUALITY 131

People do not learn from miracles. 135

The Glorious future of Human Beings 136

Satan has deceived the whole world. 137

Our Salvation - planned before the world began. 139

Beware of false Ministers, religions, churches 141

The Joys of the Called, their freedom in Christ 143

The Revelation of the Future 145

APPENDIX
ASPECTS OF GOD'S CHARACTER "LOVE"
TO MEDITATE ON & TO LIVE BY 149

Psalm 19:14 Let the words of my mouth, and the
meditation of my heart, be acceptable in thy sight,
O Lord, my strength, and my redeemer. 149

PREFACE - How this book came to be written

As a child, my parents used to take me to church. When I was about twelve, I was asked to give the reading which happened to be 1 Corinthians 13, known as the 'Love' chapter. I memorised it, and somehow, its content and the occasion remained with me. Although attending for many years, my whole experience could be summed up by saying, I never really understood anything. The odd parable, or the story of Jonah, but otherwise, nothing.

Once I left home at eighteen when I was called up to do my National Service in the R.A.F., I did not attend any services at all. At twenty-two, I once went to a local church, but was so unimpressed, I never went again. I had always believed in God, and thought of Him as Creator, but I really was not interested at all in any religion. Frankly, even then, I thought, like so many do, that religious activities seemed to be at the root of many of the world's problems and wars.

Then I got the 'flu. Confined to bed, I started to browse some old copies of the Reader's Digest. Some advertisements took my eye. One said in bold lettering, 'Does God Exist?'. Another offered 'Proof of the Bible'. There was no mention of a church, just the offer of some leaflets. I sent off for them.

I was taken by the style of the pamphlets, and that the writer clearly believed that the Bible was actually, really, the Word of God. Something went on in my mind, and I was very keen to learn more.

After a year or so of studying the written material and the Bible, I came to realise that there was an organisation behind it all, a church. I wrote off to them, and to cut a long story short, when I was twenty-five, I was invited to attend.

At twenty-nine, in 1964, I applied to go to the college which was run by the church, and was accepted for the four year, full time course, to major in Theology and obtain a Bachelor of Arts degree.

During my four years in college, I was privileged to take several courses with Dr. Ernest L. Martin, the Dean of the Faculty. His lectures were always riveting, and the most enjoyable as he made the history, geography, and the chronology of the Bible 'come alive' as I had never experienced in my life before.

After graduation in 1968, I was offered the opportunity to work for the College, and I gladly accepted a position in the data processing department, which was to stand me in good stead as time went on.

I also spent time with Dr. Martin between 1971-1974 after I was appointed a member of the Faculty of Ambassador College, Bricket Wood, U.K.

In 1975, My work with that church came to an end. Two years previously, in 1973, I had met and spent time with an American Chiropractor, Dr. John Blossom, who introduces me to a new concept in chiropractic, known as Applied Kinesiology (A.K.) developed by Dr. George Goodheart. For the next twenty-five years I pioneered A.K. in Britain and Europe, ran a clinic of natural health care, and taught thousands the A.K. principles of self-help health care.

In 2000, I retired after those years working in natural health care, helping the sick to work on their health and well-being, I once again turned to the study of Theology. The word Theology comes from two Greek words, Theo meaning God, and Logos meaning Word, hence Theology is the study of God's Word, the Holy Bible.

In 2013 I began an intense and in-depth study of over two hundred tapes recorded, and articles written by Dr. Martin on the fruits of his many years of Biblical research, kindly sent to me by Ken Nagele, custodian and designer of the www.ernestlmartin.com website.

Working with Dr. Martin's material for 40-50 hours a week, using the essential 'keys' to understanding the Bible that he suggested the earnest Bible student employed, I learned more in those three years than I had in over sixty years of my own personal previous study of the Holy Bible in my own strength. Since 2013 I have written well over a thousand pages of notes on Dr. Martin's Biblical doctrinal research. In my opinion this article contains the most important details of the fundamental basis of Christianity.

Excited at what I was learning about HOW to study the Bible with God's help, I wanted to share my new knowledge and approach with others. So I wrote 'Why ARE We Here?' a 438 page book which gave proof of the Authority and accuracy of the Bible, and the essential 'Keys' to a proper approach to the study of the Scriptures. Available retail as an Ebook or printed paperback from Amazon.com

In 2017, I embarked on the second volume 'The Biggest Lie and The Greatest Truth'. It addresses the lies of the 'Immortality of the soul', 'Churchianity, and the 'Theory of Evolution'. More importantly, it gives the 'Keys' on HOW to study, and grow in Grace and Knowledge, and a glimpse of the glorious future we have as Children of God.

This present book, 'Discover more about God for yourself' has come about as a result of my last five years of an ever closer relationship with my Creator and His Son, and my intense personal study of God's Word.

The realisation of the Awesome Nature of God has changed my whole view of this human life. As I have said before, previously I saw Theology in 'black and white and mono sound'. Now my view of God is in 'glorious technicolour and stereo surround sound'.

ACKNOWLEDGEMENT

In all my seventy-eight years I had often been exhorted to study the Bible, but I had **never** been taught **how** properly to study.

Dr. Ernest L. Martin, my colleague and mentor, showed me HOW to study. The first essential tool is always to begin by asking for God's help for inspiration and understanding. The wonderful Bible study 'tools' I have learned from Dr. Martin and his tapes, also form the basis of the book, 'The Biggest Lie'.

A personal note from the author:

*"I have absolutely no doubt in my mind that in this age, Dr. Martin was a (if not **the**) most remarkable teacher filled with the Holy Spirit, and that his insights and research were guided directly by God. I have found his work more inspiring than the work of any other man in my now eighty-two years.* ***But please be very clear, in no way am I 'following a man'****, but merely using his tools. I am following Christ's Word, studying the Bible for myself, with God's help".*

Dr. Martin says we never really needed him, but I feel that God has used him to help me grow in grace and knowledge by leaps and bounds using the 'tools of the trade' he recommended; compared to sixty years of a lifetime of personal study in my own strength. I truly hope that the same may become true for those who read this book.

INTRODUCTION

The purpose and goals of this book, 'Discover more about God for yourself' is to provide a resource to anyone whose 'eyes and ears' are being opened by our Father, the Almighty God.

God, by means of the flow of His Power, Holy Spirit will inspire their minds, to see the clear evidence of deception that Christ Jesus warned about in Revelation, the last Book of the Bible He wrote for our instruction.

*Revelation 12:9 And **the** great dragon was cast out, that old serpent, called **the** Devil, and Satan, which deceiveth **the whole world**: he was cast out into **the** earth, and his angels were cast out with him.*

When Christ says that Satan has deceived the whole world, He means just that.

That includes all organisations of human beings. The Governments, the Philosophers, Scientists, the Religions, all are involved in the greatest deception possible.

In the realm of religions for instance, there are over thirty thousand separate denominations of what is known as Christianity. Each one claims that their version of the truth, what they believe, teach and practice from their understanding of the Bible, is the correct one. They cannot all be right! There can only be one version of the Truth. The Holy Bible is that Truth.

The original manuscripts, inspired by Christ were the source of the Bible we have today, and they were perfect, exactly as He intended them to be.

However, all human translations contain errors, made either by translators, or by organisations which have altered the Bible to suit their own agendas.

The earnest student of the Bible need not be concerned too much about the aberrations, as it is perfectly possible, with God's help, to find a way past those errors, and be assured that what they are learning is indeed the Truth.

CHAPTER 1

BEFORE THE 'BEGINNING' OF ALL WE KNOW

Genesis 1:1 In the beginning God….

Before the 'beginning' of anything, God was. Before any 'beginning' we are aware of, and as far as we know, there was only God. There is only One God. God was, is and always will be. God is timeless.

God created 'time' for His human family to experience the lifelong process of being alive and conscious

God's name in the Hebrew language is expressed in the four letters of the verb 'to be' – YHVH. The verb 'to be' has three aspects, Was, Is, and Will be; past, present, and future. The closest English word that expresses those tenses is Eternal.

In the English language, any verb ending in –ing indicates the 'present continuous' tense. It means that the action of the verb is ongoing and continuous. So the word 'being' means 'to be' or to be existing continuously, and in God's case without beginning or end.

GOD IS A BEING – ALIVE – The source of all life

John 4:24 God is a Spirit:

God is made of Spirit Matter and Essence which is invisible and indestructible, as are all His Powers. God is Alive, has Innate Life, and has infinite Power. God's Spirit Matter has form and shape, and occupies space.

God is 'Alive' and 'Conscious' and always has been. God is the Source of all Life and Consciousness that exists in its various forms on Earth.

God is Invisible:
John 1:18 No man hath seen God at any time; the only begotten Son, which is in the bosom of the Father, he hath declared him.

Scripture, written by God, tells us that God is male and female. Humans look like God because He formed them so, and they are His children

Therefore God looks like a human being in shape, has a head, a body, and arms and legs, although God's Power would kill any human who looked at God.

Three English words that begin with the Latin prefix omni- which means all are used to describe God. Omnipotent – Almighty, all powerful; Omniscient - all seeing.

God lives in one place, however God's Holy Spirit Power is also Omnipresent and everywhere, and everything is an expression of that Power. That Power is not a person, but it takes many forms like Gravity, Centrifugal Force, Light, Electro-Magnetic Forces of Magnetism, Electricity; Radiation.

The expression and flow of God's Holy Spirit communicates directly with the human spirit of those God calls.

God is also every aspect of everything. He embodies everything we know of. He knows all, Understands all, and has all Wisdom

GOD IS LOVE – Loving concern for Everything

1 John 4:8 He that loveth not knoweth not God; for God is love.

1 John 4:16 And we have known and believed the love that God hath to us. God is love; and he that dwelleth in love dwelleth in God, and God in him.

God is Love. God is entirely Love. Everything He does is motivated by Love, a Loving concern for His entire Creation.

God's Love is all in all and is vastly different and not to be compared with Human Love which is a shadow, a limited dim reflection of God's Love.

The task of all human beings during their lifetime is to work to become more loving, and therefore more like God. This can only be done with the flow of Holy Spirit through the human mind.

Some Aspects and Qualities of God

God is Incorruptible:
Romans 1:23 And changed the glory of the uncorruptible God into an image made like to corruptible man, and to birds, and four footed beasts, and creeping things.

God is Eternal:
In the book of Isaiah chapter 44, and verse 6 God says: Thus saith the LORD the King of Israel, and his redeemer the LORD of hosts; I am the first, and I am the last; and beside me there is no God.

Psalm 90:2 Before the mountains were brought forth, or ever thou hadst formed the earth and the world, even from everlasting to everlasting, thou art God.

Revelation 4:8 …. and they rest not day and night, saying, Holy, holy, holy, Lord God Almighty, which was, and is, and is to come. 9 And when those beasts give glory and honour and thanks to him that sat on the throne, who liveth for ever and ever.

God is Immortal:

1 Timothy 1:17 Now unto the King eternal, immortal, invisible, the only wise God, be honour and glory for ever and ever. Amen.

1 Timothy 6:16 Who only hath immortality, dwelling in the light which no man can approach unto; whom no man hath seen, nor can see: to whom be honour and power everlasting. Amen.

God is Omnipotent – All powerful:

Revelation 19:6 KJV And I heard as it were the voice of a great multitude, and as the voice of many waters, and as the voice of mighty thunderings, saying, Alleluia: for the Lord God omnipotent reigneth

God is Omniscient- All seeing:

Proverbs 5:21 For the ways of man are before the eyes of the LORD, and he pondereth all his goings

Psalm 139:1 O LORD, thou hast searched me, and known me. 2 Thou knowest my downsitting and mine uprising, thou understandest my thought afar off. 3 Thou compassest my path and my lying down, and art acquainted with all my ways. 4 For there is not a word in my tongue, but, lo, O LORD, thou knowest it altogether. 5 Thou hast beset me behind and before, and laid thine hand upon me. 6 Such knowledge is too wonderful for me; it is high, I cannot attain unto it.

God is Omnipresent - Everywhere:

Psalm 139:7 Whither shall I go from thy spirit? or whither shall I flee from thy presence?

God lives in one place, but His Holy Spirit Essence is everywhere, so in that sense, God is everywhere.

God is Immutable:

Hebrews 6:18 KJV That by two immutable things, in which it was impossible for God to lie, we might have a strong consolation, who have fled for refuge to lay hold upon the hope set before us:

God is Only Wise:
Romans 16:27 To God only wise, be glory through Jesus Christ for ever. Amen.

God is Glorious:
Psalm 145:5 I will speak of the glorious honour of thy majesty, and of thy wondrous works.

God is The Most High:
Acts 7:48 Howbeit the most High dwelleth not in temples made with hands; as saith the prophet,

Psalm 7:17 KJV I will praise the LORD according to his righteousness: and will sing praise to the name of the LORD most high.

God is Perfect:
Matthew 5:48 Be ye therefore perfect, even as your Father which is in heaven is perfect.

God is Holy:
Isaiah 5:16 But the LORD of hosts shall be exalted in judgment, and God that is holy shall be sanctified in righteousness.

Psalm 99:9 Exalt the LORD our God, and worship at his holy hill; for the LORD our God is holy.

God is Forgiving
Exodus 34:7 Keeping mercy for thousands, forgiving iniquity and transgression and sin.

Psalm 51:1 KJV Have mercy upon me, O God, according to thy lovingkindness: according unto the multitude of thy tender mercies blot out my transgressions.

God is Kind
Psalm 36:7 KJV How excellent is thy lovingkindness, O God! therefore the children of men put their trust under the shadow of thy wings.

DISCOVER MORE ABOUT GOD FOR YOURSELF

God is Just:
Deuteronomy 32:4 He is the Rock, his work is perfect: for all his ways are judgment: a God of truth and without iniquity, just and right is he.

God is the Rock
Corinthians 10:4 KJV And did all drink the same spiritual drink: for they drank of that spiritual Rock that followed them: and that Rock was Christ.)

God is merciful
Exodus 34:6 And the LORD passed by before him, and proclaimed, The LORD, The LORD God, merciful and gracious,

God is True:
Jeremiah 10:10 But the LORD is the true God, he is the living God, and an everlasting king: at his wrath the earth shall tremble, and the nations shall not be able to abide his indignation.

John 17:3 And this is life eternal, that they might know thee the only true God, and Jesus Christ, whom thou hast sent.

God is Unsearchable:
Romans 11:33 O the depth of the riches both of the wisdom and knowledge of God! how unsearchable are his judgments, and his ways past finding out!

GOD IS THE AUTHOR OF PROPHECY

The Bible contains thousands of statements that foretell events that will occur long into the future. The book of Isaiah was written around 792-722 B.C. In Isaiah, many events in the life of Jesus Christ were foretold in minute detail over seven hundred years before His birth. The chances against them all being fulfilled is astronomical.

The laws of mathematics include the laws of probability. Lotteries are run on the law of probability, so that a person who "prophecies" their choice of six numbers from a list of forty-five numbers, the chance they will win has one chance in tens of millions of winning the first prize.

Each detail in any prophetical statement doubles the chances of the prediction not coming to pass. A prophecy with one detail, has one chance in two, as it will either be fulfilled or not. A prediction with two details has one chance in four of coming to pass. So it would be impossible for a lengthy prophecy that contains a large number of details to be fulfilled without Divine power.

God says: 6 Thus saith the LORD the King of Israel, and his redeemer the LORD of hosts; I am the first, and I am the last; and beside me there is no God. 7 And who, as I, shall call, and shall declare it, and set it in order for me, since I appointed the ancient people? and the things that are coming, and shall come, let them shew unto them. 8 Fear ye not, neither be afraid: have not I told thee from that time, and have declared it? Ye are even my witnesses. Is there a God beside me? yea, there is no God; I know not any.

GOD IS MALE AND FEMALE IN ONE

God is male, and has female characteristics which are personified in Sophia or Wisdom. The eighth chapter of Proverbs tells about the time **before** anything was created, as well as things after that event.

In verse 30 it tells of how Wisdom, 'Sophia' which is the Greek word for Wisdom, was with God, by Him, as one brought up with him: like a close relative, and as the Hebrew implies, was daily His delight, rejoicing in a lighthearted way always before Him; This reveals another 'side' of God, actually enjoying Himself in the company of 'Wisdom'.

Proverbs 8:1 Doth not wisdom cry? and understanding put forth her voice? 22 The LORD possessed me in the beginning of his way, **before** his works of old. 23 **I was set up from everlasting, from the beginning, or ever the earth was.** 24 When there were no depths, I was brought forth; when there were no fountains abounding with water. 25 Before the mountains were settled, before the hills was I brought forth: 26 While as yet he had not made the earth, nor the fields, nor the highest part of the dust of the world.

All these verses tell of an eonian period of time, whatever that was, before God's Son the Word was created, and before the time when under the Father's instruction the Word created all things.

CHAPTER 2

GOD CREATED HIS SON

Then in a 'beginning', God became the 'Father' when He created His only Begotten Son, the Word, from God's own Spirit Matter and made Him His Chief Executive Officer and Creator of all things.

John 1:1 In the beginning was the Word, and the Word was with God, and the Word was God.

There is only One God, and He created His Son from His Own Spirit Essence and thus the Godhead became a family of two, a Father and His Son, who was the Word which together were One God.

John 10:30 I and my Father are one.

God then appointed the Word who became Christ to be heir of all things.

Hebrews 1: God, who at sundry times and in divers manners spake in time past unto the fathers by the prophets, 2 Hath in these last days spoken unto us by his Son, whom he hath appointed heir of all things, by whom also he made the worlds;

The true nature of the Word, Jesus Christ

The awesome heritage of Jesus Christ as the Creator of all things, and Who is currently upholding all things is not represented by the world of Churchianity. Had all those religious people then and now honoured God's commandment which forbids the making of graven images or the likeness of **any** thing in connection with the worship of God, these images, statues, stained glass windows, and so on would not exist; but they do.

Producing the picture of an effete long-haired person in long robes should never have been thought of or even considered, let alone now be a feature of so many places of worship.

The truth revealed in God's Word about the nature of God's Son who became our Saviour is astoundingly different from the world's view of Jesus Christ.

Hebrews 1: Who (Christ) being the brightness of his glory, and the express image of his person, and **upholding all things by the word of his power,** when he had by himself purged our sins, sat down on the right hand of the Majesty on high:

Upholding, is Greek: Strong's **(5342)** fe>rw, — *fer'-o*; a primary verb. to "*bear*" or *carry* (in a very wide application, literal and figurative, as follows): — be, bear, bring (forth), carry,

At this and every other moment in time, under the Father, the Son of God, Christ Jesus is totally responsible for the creation and stability of our universe, all the countless Galaxies, our Solar system, and the orderly activity of all God's invisible Powers.

This is hardly consistent with the common manner in which our Lord Jesus, meek and mild is represented in the Churchianity of this world!

The function and containment of the energy that determines the nature of every atom and element, and the rock steady balance of our oddly shaped oblate spheroidal earth rotating at over a thousand miles an hour are all due to the fact that **Christ is upholding (present continuous), carrying,**

maintaining, sustaining EVERYTHING by the Word of His Power.

The details concerning this truth are so very clearly explained throughout the Scriptures.

Yet the world at large is totally unaware of this fact.

Has anyone ever heard the evidence of this incredible truth being spoken of or preached in any religious service? Rarely if ever one would think.

As we come to understand better this aspect of God and Christ's being-ness and their present continuous involvement in the entire universe, as well as in our individual lives, it will propel our minds and hearts into a vastly new appreciation of our God and our Saviour!

The formation & Development of 'The Plan of God'

Then God began an indeterminate period of planning during 'eonian times' however long that was. It was the time when God was working with and instructing His Created Son in the matters concerning the 'how's' of all the detailed plans that were to be involved with the Creation of all things.

During this time, part of God's Plan that was discussed in Heaven by God and His Son before the Creation of all things included the incredible fact that the Word would give up His position in the Godhead and become a man and be willing to die for the whole human race. The enormity and extent of this sacrifice is not something that many appreciate.

Biblical prophecy shows the Omniscience of God

The Bible contains thousands of statements that foretell events that will occur long into the future. The book of Isaiah was written around 792-722 B.C. In Isaiah, many events in the life of Jesus Christ were foretold in minute detail over seven hundred years before His birth. The chances against them all being fulfilled is astronomical.

The laws of mathematics include the laws of probability. Lotteries are run on the law of probability, so that a person who "prophecies" their choice of six numbers from a list of forty-five numbers, the chance they will win has one chance in tens of millions of winning the first prize.

Each detail in any prophetical statement doubles the chances of the prediction not coming to pass. A prophecy with one detail has one chance in two, as it will either be fulfilled or not. A prediction with two details has one chance in four of coming to pass. So it would be impossible for a lengthy prophecy that contains a large number of details to be fulfilled without Divine power.

Christ's birth as a man was prophesied in great detail hundreds of years before the event.

Here is one example of multiple prophetic details concerning Jesus Christ. In Isaiah chapter 53, it speaks of the Messiah who was to come in many specific details:

1. No beauty that we should desire Him.
2. Despised and rejected of men.
3. A man of sorrows acquainted with grief.
4. Bore our griefs and carried our sorrows.
5. Wounded for our transgressions
6. Bruised for our iniquities.
7. With his stripes we are healed.
8. He was oppressed and afflicted.
9. He opened not his mouth.

10. For the transgression of My people he was stricken.

11. He made his grave with the wicked.

12. He had done no violence neither was there deceit in His mouth.

13. Made his soul an offering for sin.

14. He poured out his soul (his life blood and water) unto death.

If we just take this list of fourteen prophetical points concerning Jesus' life, the chances of all these coming to fulfillment is one in 16,384. There are of course many other prophecies in the scriptures concerning the life of Christ, which if included would increase the likelihood of them all occurring during His lifetime billions to one against.

God says: Isaiah 53:6 Thus saith the LORD the King of Israel, and his redeemer the LORD of hosts; I am the first, and I am the last; and beside me there is no God. 7 And who, as I, shall call, and shall declare it, and set it in order for me, since I appointed the ancient people? and the things that are coming, and shall come, let them shew unto them. 8 Fear ye not, neither be afraid: have not I told thee from that time, and have declared it? Ye are even my witnesses. Is there a God beside me? yea, there is no God; I know not any.

Christ 'willed' to be sacrificed for us.

The Word was willing to give up the Power and the Glory He had as the Chief Executive Creative Director of God the Father to become a mere man. What a sacrifice! It took this enormous sacrifice to cleanse humans of all sin, so that they too could become 'heirs' of all things as God had already given to His Son.

1 Peter 1:9 But with the precious blood of Christ, as of a lamb without blemish and without spot: 20 Who verily was foreordained before the foundation of the world, but was manifest in these last times for you,

It is hard to imagine the breadth and depth of the love of God the Father, and His Son, who planned the worst event ever to occur on earth eons before it happened.

John 3:16 For God so loved the world, that he gave his only begotten Son, that whosoever believeth in him should not perish, but have everlasting life.17 For God sent not his Son into the world to condemn the world; but that the world through him might be saved.

We are saved as heirs of all things in Christ

Titus 3:7 That being justified by his grace, we should be made **heirs** according to the hope of eternal life.

Can we conceive of the feelings over eons of time that God and His Son must have had when considering the prospect of His giving up the Glory He had with the Father to become a man. Let alone the prospect of giving that awesome position away only to be despised and rejected by the human beings they had created.

Then for the Word who became Christ finally to be humiliated, tortured, beaten beyond recognition, and to suffer the double death penalty of crucifixion by the Romans, and the horrendous stoning by the Jews. His last excruciating experience was when Jesus realised that God had had to turn His back on Him because at that final moment on the Tree, He became the epitomy of sin for us and for the entire human race for all time.

Such is the Love of God and His Son for us His children.

God is Love and He wants every human being to love him and strive to be like Him. Human love is not the same as the Love of God. Humans have to work at being in a loving frame of mind every conscious moment of their lives. We have to strive against the unloving side of our nature.

Romans 5:8 But God commendeth (Greek: exhibits, shows) His Love towards us, in that, while we were yet sinners, Christ died for us.

Christ gave us the parable of the 'Prodigal Son' to show us the practical way a father shows his love for his son, and so much more how God shows His Love to the whole human race. He just cannot wait to reward the 'called' with Eternal Life at His Coming.

All humans are a type of the prodigal son, whose father was a type of God the Father.

Luke 15:11 And he said, A certain man had two sons: 12 And the younger of them said to his father, Father, give me the portion of goods that falleth to me. And he divided unto them his living. 13 And not many days after the younger son gathered all together, and took his journey into a far country, and there wasted his substance with riotous living. 14 And when he had spent all, there arose a mighty famine in that land; and he began to be in want. 15 And he went and joined himself to a citizen of that country; and he sent him into his fields to feed swine. 16 And he would fain have filled his belly with the husks that the swine did eat: and no man gave unto him.

When we leave our Father out of our lives, we forget all the blessings, privileges, and gifts He has lavished on us. As long as that situation exists, we are distanced from our Father in Heaven

Luke 15:17 And when he came to himself, he said, How many hired servants of my father's have bread enough and to spare, and I perish with hunger! 18 I will arise and go to my father, and will say unto him, Father, I have sinned against heaven, and before thee, 19 And am no more worthy to be called thy son: make me as one of thy hired servants.

Everyone needs to come to the point of 'coming to ourselves' in a state of remorse and repentance for allowing our 'ego' to 'edge God out'! This repentant state of mind is a specific spiritual gift from God, and is not available to all humankind at this time. Blessed indeed are they who God does call, and bestow that gift upon them.

Luke 15:20 And he arose, and came to his father. But when he was yet a great way off, his father saw him, and had compassion, and ran, and fell on his neck, and kissed him.

This is really interesting in that the son did not have to go looking for his father. His father was eagerly waiting for him at the gate, and looking out for him every day, hoping that he would return to the family.

Luke 15:21 And the son said unto him, Father, I have sinned against heaven, and in thy sight, and am no more worthy to be called thy son.

But like our heavenly Father, his father could not wait to bless his son and embrace him back into the family.

Luke 15:22 But the father said to his servants, Bring forth the best robe, and put it on him; and put a ring on his hand, and shoes on his feet: 23 And bring hither the fatted calf, and kill it; and let us eat, and be merry: 24 For this my son was dead, and is alive again; he was lost, and is found. And they began to be merry.

God is love, and it is God's desire for us that his children that we strive to be like Him. God's love is perfect. His One desire is to bless us and care for us. All we have to do is to respond to His call. This call has to come directly from God, no man or woman has any power to 'call' us, or to 'save' us. When we do receive that call, it is a Spiritual Gift from God.

Psalm 1:1 Blessed is the man that walketh not in the counsel of the ungodly, nor standeth in the way of sinners, nor sitteth in the seat of the scornful. 2 But his delight is in the law of the Lord; and in his law doth he meditate day and night. 3 And he shall be like a tree planted by the rivers of water, that bringeth forth his fruit in his season; his leaf also shall not wither; and whatsoever he doeth shall prosper.

Does the average churchgoer 'delight in the law of the Lord'? Do they meditate on the Law of Love day and night? Something for them to ask themselves?

Psalm 23:1 The Lord is my shepherd; I shall not want. 2 He maketh me to lie down in green pastures: he leadeth me beside the still waters. 3 He restoreth my soul: he leadeth me in the paths of righteousness for his name's sake. 4 Yea, though I walk through the valley of the shadow of death, I will fear no evil: for thou art with me; thy rod and thy staff they comfort me. 5 Thou preparest a table before me in the presence of mine enemies: thou anointest my head with oil; my cup runneth over. 6 Surely goodness and mercy shall follow me all the days of my life: and I will dwell in the house of the Lord for ever.

The incredible complexity of God's plan

One cannot even imagine the complexity of creating all the designs involved in the Plan. The creation of DNA, the unimaginable work involved in the design of millions of species, all intertwined in the unbelievably complicated and yet delicate ecological balance that ensured all could reproduce, and were part of the food chain which ensured all were fed.

Just these few outlined details must have involved an almost infinite complexity of design that is a mind-stopping thought in itself.

These eons of developing God's Plan which included the designing of human beings in all their complexity, and how they would become a part of the eventual Creation of the Greater Family of the Children God.

All this complexity without a Designer?

Everything that is made by human beings begins its life as a mental thought picture in the mind of the person. As this picture develops, the design is perfected. Then the methods involved in the physical production of the design are carefully planned. Nothing we know of in our human world came to be without a designer.

Yet the 'scientific' world argues endlessly that there was no 'Designer' of our fabulous Universe, our incredible Solar system, our Earthly home, 'it just happened over billions of years all by itself'.

If anyone said that watch on my wrist, that chair, or that motor car, or that jet plane 'just happened', one would think they were crazy, mad, or insane. People around hearing that statement would probably send for the men in white coats to take them away, ho ho, to take them away!

What a tragedy it is that so many 'educated' people accept the theory of evolution, or state that 'everything came from nothing', and thereby commit sacrilege, which is defined as 'stealing from God'.

Romans 1:20 For the invisible things of him from the creation of the world are clearly seen, being understood by the things that are made, even his eternal power and Godhead; so that they are without excuse:

The physical universe *is* the tangible evidence of God's Power. Those who deny a Designer steal His Creatorship, and commit idolatry as they worship instead the power of the Creation to create itself.

Romans 1:25 Who changed **the** truth of God into a lie, and **worship**ped and served **the creature (creation)** more than **the** Creator, who is blessed for ever. Amen.

The community of scientists, and all human beings who reject belief in God in their arrogance and pride and choose instead to believe a lie will one day come to realise their terrible mistake.

Psalm 10:4 The wicked, through the pride of his countenance, will not seek after God: God is not in all his thoughts.

God is not in their thoughts because as far as they are concerned He does not exist. How can they ignore all the evidence? Because they are 'blinded'.

Isaiah 29:14 Therefore, behold, I will proceed to do a marvellous work among this people, even a marvellous work and a wonder: for the wisdom of their wise men shall perish, and the understanding of their prudent men shall be hid.

God-rejecters may be having their 'day', but the day will come when their saying that 'everything came from nothing' or that 'everything created itself' will be regarded as total insanity.

Isaiah 29:16 Surely your turning of things upside down shall be esteemed as the potter's clay: for shall the work say of him that made it, He made me not? or shall the thing framed say of him that framed it, He had no understanding?

They may think they are 'getting away with it' when they say there is no God, no Designer, no Creator, but God sees all. When they do realise that God really *Is*, they will want to hide, but there will be no place to hide then.

Jeremiah 23:24 Can any hide himself in secret places that I shall not see him? saith the Lord. Do not I fill heaven and earth? saith the Lord.

The evidence and proof of Intelligent Design is in everything all around them right now! It fills all we know.

God is not far away from us, He is right here, using the earth as His footstool so to speak.

Isaiah 66:1 Thus saith the LORD, The heaven is my throne, and the earth is my footstool:

CHAPTER 3

THEN THE WORD CREATED EVERYTHING THERE IS

Hebrews 1:2 Hath in these last days spoken unto us by his Son, whom he hath appointed **heir** of **all things**, by whom also he made the worlds;

Human beings are destined to be heirs together with Christ our Elder Brother of all things. Incredible.

The Word created Spirit Beings, Satan, & God's Sons

Colossians 1:16 For by him (Christ the Word) were all things created, that are in heaven, and that are in earth, **visible and invisible**, whether they be thrones, or dominions, or principalities, or powers: all things were created by him, and for him:

Notice, the Word created all that is visible to us, but also He created all those principalities and powers that are invisible to us

Invisible Satan and his cohorts are at every level of government of the earth, and are still hard at work to influence and lead people astray. They encourage all on earth to ignore God in their lives, and to follow their own lusts.

Ephesians 6:12 For we wrestle not against flesh and blood, but against principalities, against powers, against the rulers of the darkness of this world, against spiritual wickedness in high places.

During the same eon that the Word created Satan, and **before** He created the heavens and the earth, he had also created other spirit beings, the many 'principalities and powers'. Christ the Word also created other 'sons of God'. We know this because of the record in Job when God was talking to Job.

Job 36:4 Where wast thou when I laid the foundations of the earth? declare, if thou hast understanding... verse 7 When the morning stars sang together, and all the sons of God shouted for joy?

These sons of God and other angelic beings that were present at the time of the Creation of the heavens and the earth, sang and shouted with joy at the incredible spectacle.

Who were these 'sons of God'? What were their activities in the past? And what are they doing now? This is covered later in Chapter 4.

God Creates Good and Evil

Part of the Plan of God was for the Word to create Satan the Adversary which He did. God is Love, Satan is the opposite.

Without light we cannot understand darkness. Without silence, we cannot appreciate sound. So without knowing 'evil', we would never be able fully to comprehend 'good'.

Isaiah 45:7 I form the light, and **create** darkness: I make peace, and **create evil**: I the Lord do all these things.

This truth may present difficulties for some 'religious' people who do not really study the Bible, but God did create evil. God the Father is in complete charge and firmly in control of the entire creation, the 'good' the 'bad' and the 'ugly'!

Jeremiah 19:3 And say, Hear ye the word of the Lord, O kings of Judah, and inhabitants of Jerusalem; Thus saith the Lord of hosts, the **God** of Israel; Behold, I will bring **evil** upon this place, the which whosoever heareth, his ears shall tingle.

God uses 'evil' to bring about the 'good' of His loving purposes. God does not 'sin' in the use of evil. He can use His laws in whatever manner He pleases to achieve His ultimate aims.

Hebrews 6:17 Wherein God, willing more abundantly to shew unto the heirs of promise the immutability of his counsel, confirmed it by an oath:18 that by two immutable things, in which it was impossible for God to lie, we might have a strong consolation, who have fled for refuge to lay hold upon the hope set before us:

God has the Authority to use evil for good, but this option is not open to human beings.

Romans 6:15 What then? shall we sin, because we are not under the law, but under grace? God forbid.

God's Secret Creative Powers were used by the Word to form all things, visible and invisible.

At the Father's direction, the Word created space, time, the heavens, the galaxies without number, the earth and its solar system using God's Invisible Secret Powers of Creation.

Deuteronomy 29:29 The secret things belong unto the Lord our God: but those things which are revealed belong unto us and to our children for ever, that we may do all the words of this law.

Some of these secret Powers are Gravity, Centrifugal Force, the Electromagnetic Spectrum, Magnetism, Radiation, and so on. These secret powers belong to God.

Scientists know of these powers, but they call them 'The Laws of Physics'. This is pure **sacrilege**, stealing the credit for those from God who used them at Creation, and are in existence forever sustaining our Universe.

Romans 1:20 For the invisible things of him from the creation of the world are clearly seen, being understood by the things that are made, even his eternal power and Godhead; so that they are without excuse:

The evidence of God's Power is in everything and is all around us, in the Creation of all things. Yet very few it seems recognise that God Designed and Created all things with His Powers.

John 1:2 The same (Word) was in the beginning with God.

God's Chief Executive Officer, His Son, the Word, the One who became Christ, created all things with the Power of the Almighty God was before the beginning of all things we know.

John 1:3 All things were made by him (Christ the Word); and without him was not any thing made that was made. In him was life; and the life was the **light** of men.

GRAVITY is one of God's Secret Powers

Modern science with all its knowledge cannot fathom Gravity. They know what it does, they know its power, but they do not understand exactly what it is. That is because Gravity is a Spiritual Power, and they are only mere physical mortals with very limited power when it comes to Spiritual matters.

The Earth just 'happens' (??) to be just the right distance from the Sun to derive the heat we need to live. The Moon orbits the Earth every twenty-eight days. The Moon also just 'happens' to be the right size and distance from the Earth for its Gravity to move the entire mass of the oceans tidally twice a day.

The tides are the rise and fall of water caused by the combined gravitational forces of the moon and sun on the oceans of the earth. The tidal cycles consist of two high tides and two low tides each day. During the time between high and low tide there is a current flow in the seas.

There is a very special purpose for the tides which are one way the health of the oceans is maintained.

The Energy of and within matter

Einstein's Theory can only be really understood by one who has studied advanced mathematics, but even then they must remember that it is just a 'theory' and theories are simply 'guesses'. Most take is as a basis from which to form more 'theories', some question it as to whether or not it is true.

Have a look at some of the impressive words used to dress up the word 'theory' to make it appear to be more 'scientific:

Assumption, conclusion, conjecture, estimate, hypothesis, supposition, deduction, postulate, thesis.

But we can learn something about the Power of God from Einstein's work. Even if it is not entirely accurate, it can give astonishing insight into the awesome Power of our Creator.

Einstein's Theory (guess!) of Relativity is expressed as $E=MC^2$ where E is energy, M is mass, and C^2 is the speed of light squared.

Simply stated, it suggests that it takes a lot of energy to make a very small amount of matter.

The energy inside the atom is huge, as witnessed by the power of an atomic or Hydrogen bomb developed from just a few grams or ounces of a uranium isotope.

From knowing this, when God through the Word created all the Matter there is, it must have taken more Energy than it is possible for humans to count or express in any terms.

A dramatic example of the content of God's Power in Matter

On the 15th February 2013 a meteorite suddenly appeared without warning in the sky over the Russian region of the Urals. Those watching saw its trail as it entered earth's atmosphere and began to burn up. The intense heat evaporated three quarters of the meteor before it hit the Earth. Around four to six tonnes reached the ground as meteorite fragments, representing just 0.05% of the original rock.

The superbolide, or super bright meteorite was also seen by millions of others around the globe.

As it burned up, hundreds of people in the town of Chelyabinsk recorded its trail on their 'carcams' and mobile phones as it hurtled towards the earth at a speed of 24,000 miles an hour. At its most intense, the streaking fireball glowed 30 times brighter than the sun, leaving people on the ground below with skin and retinal burns.

Directly beneath the meteor's path, the shockwave that occurred some moments after it struck was powerful enough to knock people off their feet. Windows were shattered in more than 3,600 apartment blocks, and a factory roof collapsed. In the local library in Yemanzhelinsk, 30 miles away, at least 1,210 people were treated for injuries, most from falling building debris and flying glass.

The weight and size of this piece of rock containing about 10% of iron varies in accounts. An average estimate was that it was about 20 meters wide about the size of a large lorry and weighed about 20 tons.

Cosmologists hurried to the site where it landed to find and secure samples of the approximately five tons that hit the earth left after it burned up for research.

Earthquake sensors around the world picked up infrasound waves as lumps hit the ground. The largest single piece, weighing around 650kg, punched a seven metre-wide hole in ice 70cm (2'4") thick on Lake Chebarkul, and was recovered from the lakebed.

As this small meteorite hit the earth, it is estimated that the rock exploded with the energy it contained of around 500 kilotonnes of TNT. This is **33,000 times** the power of the bomb dropped on Hiroshima in August 1945 which exploded with the yield of 15 kilotons of TNT! ! !

Since that 20-40 ton tiny meteorite contained 33,000 times the energy of the atomic bomb of the type dropped on Japan, consider this for a moment. Reflect on the size and weight of the Earth which is 5.972 sextillion (1,000 trillion) metric tons, and ponder how much of God's Energy it took just to make our Planet.

Then let your mind imagine how much of God's energy the Word, Christ Jesus used and released when He created the universe and its innumerable galaxies of uncountable stars. Has that blown all the fuses in the computer in your mind? It has mine. No wonder some think that the universe started with a Big Bang! It probably did, and we know Who Caused it.

The awesome Power of the Almighty God is totally beyond our comprehension. How it is possible for intelligent (?) men to think that all the matter of the universe made itself is beyond all reason. It is because the human mind is open to influence by Satan who is insane to think that he can actually thwart God's Plan in the final analysis.

Particle 'science' finds ever more of God's handiwork.

The 'scientific world' is now struggling with the recent discoveries of the many particles that apparently exist in every atom. A Hydrogen atom was originally thought to contain 'subatomic' particles of a nucleus and a single electron orbiting that nucleus.

Humans have never understood where the energy that sustains that rotation 'inside' each atom comes from. They cannot because it is one of God's secret things!

Only a few decades ago previous scientific thought suggested that there were three basic subatomic particles: Electrons, protons, and neutrons. With the advent of the electron microscope and other amazing devices like the new huge particle accelerators, more particles were 'discovered'.

These three components of atoms are now believed to be present in many different combinations and configurations in 'ions' which are perhaps the electrical charge associated with atoms.

Scientists now grapple with many 'new' particles they have 'discovered' which of course have been there all the time!

Now scientists apparently are able 'to see' Alpha particles, Beta particles, Beta' or electronic emission particles, Beta+ or positron particles, and many more. It appears that there are yet many more like 'Quarks'. 'Quarks' seem to appear to come and go! Scientists cannot actually 'see' all of these particles, but can only deduce that many of these particles exist because of they interfere with the behaviour and trajectory of other particles.

With all the resources that are being brought to bear on all this research, they will still not find out everything. The Scripture cannot be broken. (John10:35)

Can the origin of the Cosmos be proven mathematically?

The world's most advanced philosophers, thinkers, theoretical physicists and cosmologists have spent lifetimes seeking to understand the origin and nature of the universe and the purpose of life.

One such very famous and personable man, despite terrible health handicaps has explored the origin of life. The tool he has used further to develop his theories about 'Time' and the beginning of the universe is 'mathematics' at a very advanced level. He believes that it may be possible to find the 'simplest exquisite formula' which will encompass all his ideas concerning the origin of the universe and the process of time.

Despite being in his seventies, and suffering from a crippling disease, he is still pursuing and developing his concepts of time and space. His books have sold in the many millions.

The great tragedy of this man's decades of work is that the 'tool' of mathematics that he is using to find the answers he is looking for is 'lifeless'. He is searching for answers in the wrong place. Mathematics is an incredible 'tool' for many purposes and much research, but it is 'lifeless'.

The Cosmos was created by God, through the Word who is 'Life', and who is the only source of the energies which produced the expanding universe and sustain it.

God has written a Book in which He explains how He made the heavens and the earth and all that in them is. He explains that He converted His Spirit matter into physical matter which consists of His Power built into every atom in the Universe. This power is so large, there is no way any human can even begin to express it adequately.

Each atom contains an immense amount of power. The components of atoms, the orbiting of the particles cause them to have a 'shape', and the electrical charges give rise to the nature and properties of each of the many elements of the 'periodic table'.

The origin of the power of this seemingly physical movement inside the atom is not explained and cannot be. This is because that Power is part of the expression of God's Spiritual Power and cannot be totally understood by the minds of physical human beings.

Ancient knowledge of the Constellations and the expanding universe.

Recent developments in the power of telescopes, especially Hubble, the one located outside the Earth's atmosphere have enabled astronomers to conclude that our Universe is expanding. Modern knowledge yes, but the Author of the Bible written more than three centuries ago included references to that fact.

The book of Job is possibly the oldest book included in the books of the Bible. In Job there are many references which show how much was known about the constellations in his time. Back then Job even mentions the now relatively recently discovered fact by scientists that the universe is expanding!

Job 9:5 Who hath laid the measures thereof, if thou knowest? or who hath stretched the line upon it? 6 Whereupon are the foundations thereof fastened? or who laid the corner stone thereof; He **stretcheth out** (Strong's 5186) the north over the empty place, and hangeth the earth upon nothing.

Job 9:8 (God) Which alone spreadeth out the heavens, and treadeth upon the waves of the sea.

'Spreadeth out', this verb is present continuous: Strong's {5186} hf;n; — natah, *naw-taw'*; a primitive root; to stretch or spread out;

Can anyone really explain how it is that the earth and the planets, indeed all the heavenly bodies occupy the space they do? Or that they are either stationary or rotate in such an orderly manner, and exist in relationship to each other in such an incredibly accurate and timely way?

Some put it all down to the 'hero' of the 'Big Bang' which they state is 'gravity'. Gravity is not the 'hero' of the Big Bang, which undoubtedly occurred at the moment of Creation, but God is!! Gravity is another mysterious Power that cannot be completely explained by human minds because it is part of God's Spiritual Power.

One notion being considered is that our observations of the heavens are as if we are looking at a "hologram", this is not to say that the universes *are* a hologram, but our view of them may be. A hologram gives the appearance of something being three dimensional even though it is flat.

Psalm 8:3 When I consider thy heavens, the work of thy fingers, the moon and the stars, which thou hast ordained;

Job 9:9 (God) Which maketh Arcturus, Orion, and Pleiades, and the chambers of the south.

Humans cannot do these things but God can and does control everything.

Job 38:31 Canst thou bind the sweet influences of Pleiades, or loose the bands of Orion?

Amos 5:8 Seek him that maketh the seven **stars** and Orion, and turneth the shadow of death into the morning, and maketh the day dark with night:

God's Powers are infinite.

Psalm 147:4 He telleth the number of the **stars**; he calleth them all by their names.

Human beings cannot even count accurately the number of galaxies in the universe, or the number of stars in a galaxy. God knows them all by name, how awe inspiring is that?

He can also 'know' the number of hairs on the head of every one of seven billion humans!

God has done all these things and claims the credit for doing so in His Word the Holy Bible which cannot be broken.

AVOID 'theories', they are guesswork

We need help with all the confusing theoretical human 'scientific' guesswork. The Bible comes to our rescue. First of all, the human brain is absolutely not equipped to fathom all the Works of God from the beginning to the end.

Ecclesiastes 3:11 He hath made every thing beautiful in his time: also he hath set the world in their heart, so that no **man can find out the work** that God maketh from the beginning to the end.

In a later chapter God repeats Himself for emphasis, and further states that it is impossible completely to understand His Creation no matter how hard they try!

Ecclesiastes 8:17 Then I beheld all the **work** of God, that **a man cannot find out the work** that is done under the sun: because though a man labour to seek it out, yet he shall not find it; yea farther; though a wise man think to know it, yet shall he not be able to find it.

Do scientists really know all about light? Would it be a help for scientists to learn those two scriptures and use them as a backdrop for their research, while they also appreciate the Glory and Power of the Creator God, and ask for His help to understand more about what He has made.

Even so, they would do well to be aware of another important statement from God.

Deuteronomy 29:29 The *secret* things belong unto the Lord our God.

God is the Origin of natural laws, The Lawgiver

We live in a law-abiding universe, where the laws are absolute and unchanging. As "science" has progressed, these laws have been discovered and codified, but mankind's understanding of the laws of the universe is still incomplete, and according to God's Word in Scripture, it always will be. Ecclesiastes 8:17 KJV Then I beheld all the work of God, that a man cannot find out the work that is done under the sun: because though a man labour to seek it out, yet he shall not find it; yea further; though a wise man think to know it, yet shall he not be able to find it.

What are the secret things that belong to God? They are everything about Him that He chooses not to reveal to us. Like how God's energy has the Power to create matter out of His Spirit. How God's Power can uphold, sustain, and maintain everything that is, all things that exist through Christ.

God has placed restrictions on His human children so that His secrets stay with Him, and are past finding out.

Romans 11:33 O the depth of the riches both of the wisdom and knowledge of God! how unsearchable are his judgments, and his ways past finding out!

Firstly, it is because these secrets are beyond our capacity fully to comprehend; and secondly because it is not our time to know them.

God's Power which expresses itself in so many forms is incomprehensible to human beings. Gravity, centrifugal force, magnetism, are all forces which humans can experiment with, measure, see something of how they work, and know that they can be changed but not destroyed. That is because God cannot be destroyed. But no physical human can actually tell what these energies are, only that they are observed to exist. The reason for this is that they are Spiritual manifestations of God who is Spirit.

CHAPTER 4

THEN GOD REFORMED THE EARTH TO MAKE IT HABITABLE FOR HIS CHILDREN

Isaiah 45:18 KJV For thus saith the LORD that created the heavens; God himself that formed (reformed, designed, or re-created after a flood) the earth and made it; he hath established it, he created it not in vain, he (re)formed it to be inhabited: I am the LORD; and there is none else.

The miracle of Light

The very first thing God did through the Word was to create **light** and banish the darkness.

James 1:17 Every good gift and every perfect gift is from above, and cometh down from the Father of lights, with whom is no variableness, neither shadow of turning.

Genesis 1:2 And the earth was without form, and void; and darkness was upon the face of the deep. And the Spirit of God moved upon the face of the waters. 3 And God said, Let there be light: and there was light. 4 And God saw the light, that it was good: and God divided the light from the darkness. 5 And God called the light Day, and the darkness he called Night. And the evening and the morning were the first day.

God was making our earth his footstool and His eventual headquarters for 'olam' or forever. So because there is no darkness in God, He had to banish the 'thick darkness' from the earth.

What is Light?

So what is **light**? Is it a wave, a particle, photons, and more? Or is **light** all of those and more?

Light is a tiny window, the visible part of the entire electromagnetic spectrum which exists from the lowest frequencies of sound up to the highest frequencies, the shorter wavelengths of ultraviolet light, and above that of x-rays and gamma rays.

Without the **light** of the Sun, **life** on earth would be impossible. But part of the light of the Sun is lethal to life, and life on Earth has to be shielded from that part.

The Earth's magnetosphere, its magnetic field, protects us here on Earth from the effects of the plasma, the deadly ionised gas of the Sun's 'flares, and keeps it safely away from the surface of our planet.

The sun gives off a great deal of radiation that would destroy life on earth were it not for the ozone layer. The ozone layer is a special region of the atmosphere which acts as a filter that absorbs much of the shorter wavelength and highly hazardous ultraviolet radiation (UVR) from the sun. How amazing are God's Works!

The notion put forth by many 'scientific' communities that humans could establish a home on other planets in our Solar system that have environments totally hostile to life is completely ludicrous.

There is a lot of talk nowadays about 'terraforming' or making earth on Mars and transporting millions there from Earth. This is a nonsensical idea since the radiation levels on Mars, which is not protected like the Earth is, would 'fry' humans in an instant if they were not protected by their space suit.

However, they say that there are 'holes' in the surface of Mars, the pipes of extinct volcanoes where people could hide and make a home. Really? What sort of life would that be? Oh dear, they cannot be serious!! But it seems they are, they are already selling the one way tickets to Mars!!

We have everything we need to enjoy a wonderful life here on Earth, but clearly, we are failing miserably to do this even though we have, or did have perfect conditions, until the result of way we have misused the fauna, flora, and mineral wealth appears now to have damaged our environment beyond repair. Not content with that, we think how we can get to another planet and proceed to spoil that. Incredible lunacy!

Although protected from the lethal emissions of radiation from the Sun, human beings, with reckless disregard for God's Laws, have found a way to pollute the whole world with atomic and hydrogen bombs that give off radiation which could potentially erase all life from our earth. How insane is that? And knowing that is true, governments still pursue the development of nuclear weapons. The word 'insane' is inadequate to describe their dangerous thinking.

The Fauna and Flora reformation of the earth.

Genesis 1:31 And God saw every thing that he had made, and, behold, it was very good. And the evening and the morning were the sixth day.

The earth's land was reformed and repopulated with all the fauna and flora, and the seas were contained, the pure waters provided, and everything that would be needed to provide a perfect home for human beings was complete in six days.

This does not suggest for a moment that the earth is only six thousand years old! But it does reveal the Power of God in action in terms of time we understand

Life can only come from 'Life'

All life comes from God who is Spirit and Who is Life.

All life, everything that lives has a 'life spirit' that enlivens it and gives it the characteristics of that living thing. Humans have the only 'spirit' that is capable of communicating with God.

Nowadays a fundamental law of science is the law of 'biogenesis'. Despite how obvious biogenesis may seem now, it was only accepted by the scientific community at large about 150 years ago. It wasn't until Louis Pasteur experimentally proved that the notion of spontaneous generation was false, in the 1860s, that the scientific community fully accepted biogenesis as the only natural source of living things.

The term *biogenesis* refers to the production of life from already-living matter or organisms. This is in contrast to abiogenesis which refers to the production of life from non-living matter. Natural abiogenesis has never been observed, nor are there any generally accepted models for how it could occur.

But that has not stopped large numbers in the evilution brigade from stating categorically that it did occur in the primordial seas from 'primitive proteins'. There is no such thing as a 'primitive protein'. Proteins are formed from hundreds of amino-acids which in themselves could hardly be called 'primitive', since they are formed from many molecules themselves. How that occurred has never been explained.

Biogenesis is routinely observed at all levels of life. When a bacteria divides, a plant produces seeds, or a mammal gives birth, biogenesis is occurring.

Biogenesis is also different from creation 'Creation ex nihilo' which is a spurious human idea which refers to God's forming something supernaturally out of something that never existed in any form previously which He did not. God Created everything out of His Spirit matter of which He consists and over which He has complete Power.

In biogenesis, living creatures form more of their own kind, with possible slight variations, through a natural process.

Despite the insistence of Godless men and women, 'life' cannot come from inanimate material, as is suggested by the 'everything comes from nothing' brigade, or evolutionists who think that 'life' developed in inanimate proteins in the primordial seas.

They claim to be 'scientific' but even this 'science' is false.

1 Timothy 6:20 O Timothy, keep that which is committed to thy trust, avoiding profane and vain babblings, and **oppositions of science falsely so called:**

So when human beings attempt to make sense of everything that is, but leave God out of the picture, they lose themselves in the insanity and vanity of their own minds.

They become 'fools' when they embrace instead the godless notion of Evolution, and continue to insist that the miracle of life comes from inanimate objects. Unhappily their ridiculous untrue pronouncements are accepted as 'gospel' by the gullible masses who reject God.

Then the Word Created the Man and the Woman

Genesis 2:7 And the LORD God formed man *(Heb. Adam)* of the dust of the ground, and breathed into his nostrils the breath of life; and man became a living soul.

The Bible states that human beings are made in God's image, in His form and shape.

Male and Female human beings are temporal and are bound by time. They have a beginning and an end. Our minds are not built to be able to comprehend timelessness. God is timeless.

All humans have a human spirit.

Genesis 2:7 And the Lord God formed man **of** the dust **of** the ground, and **breathed** into his nostrils the **breath of life**; and man became a living soul.

Humans have a hu-man, a God-man 'spirit' breathed into them with 'the breath of life' at birth. This spirit was designed so that God's children would be able to relate to and communicate with God's via His Holy Spirit.

Job 32:8 But there is a **spirit in man**: and the **inspiration** of the Almighty giveth them understanding.

This type of inspiration regarding spiritual understanding is not available to carnal minded human beings.

Romans 8:7 Because the **carnal mind** is enmity against God: for it is not subject to the law of God, neither indeed can be.

When God created Adam, the Hebrew word used in all the instances in Genesis 2:7,15,16,19,20,22,23, for his name was 'Adam' Strong's 120 '**adam,** *aw-dawm*'*;* from 119; ruddy i.e. a human being (an individual or the species, mankind, etc.

Genesis 2:15 And the LORD God took the man, and put him into the Garden of Eden to dress it and to keep it.

So God gave Adam a job to do, to take good care of it, make it even more beautiful, and keep it in good condition. This work is extended to humans in the whole world who should have, and should be, 'dressing and keeping' the world in good condition throughout history.

Then God's gave His first commandment to Adam, spelling it out carefully.

Genesis 2:16 And the Lord God commanded the man, saying, Of every tree of the garden thou mayest freely eat: 17 But of the tree of the knowledge of good and evil, thou shalt not eat of it: for in the day that thou eatest thereof thou shalt surely die.

This instruction about the forbidden tree was given to Adam before Eve was formed.

Genesis 2:18 And the Lord God said, It is not good that the man should be alone; I will make him an help meet for him.

It is interesting that this verse comes here, as God had another job for Adam, for him to name all the animals and birds that He was about to create.

Genesis 2:19 And out of the ground the Lord God formed every beast of the field, and every fowl of the air; and brought them unto Adam to see what he would call them: and whatsoever Adam called every living creature, that was the name thereof. 20 And Adam gave names to all cattle, and to the fowl of the air, and to every beast of the field; but for Adam there was not found an help meet for him.

Having named all the creatures, God then prepared Adam so that He could make the help 'meet' or fitting for him.

Up to this time in the narrative, where 'Adam' occurs God uses the 'neutral' Hebrew Word *Adam* species, mankind.

Genesis 2:21 And the Lord God caused a deep sleep to fall upon Adam, and he slept: and he took one of his ribs, and closed up the flesh instead thereof; 22 And the rib, which the Lord God had taken from man, made he a woman, and brought her unto the man.

The word 'rib' in Hebrew is Strong's {6763} [l;xe — tsela`, *tsay-law'*; or (feminine) h[;l]x"tsalah, *tsal-aw'*; from 6760; a rib (as curved), literally (of the body)

Now a very interesting change is made in the Hebrew word for man, instead of 'Adam' God now uses the Hebrew word 'ish'. In the English language –ish is the suffix to denote peoples as in British, English, Scottish, Irish etc. And for Eve, God uses the word 'isha'.

Genesis 2:23-24 *(Adam)* said, "This is now bone of my bones, and flesh of my flesh; she shall be called Woman *(ishah)*, Because she was taken out of Man *(ish)*." For this reason, a man *(ish)* shall leave his father and his mother, and be joined to his wife *(ishah)*; and they shall become one flesh.

Interesting to note also that the word human contains 'man', and 'woman' also contains 'man'. Also that when 'joined' in marriage and especially during intercourse:

One man plus one woman make One flesh.

'Adam' as a male also contained the potential of producing a female, which God separated out of Adam, and made Eve. From then on, the male and the female contributed to make a whole 'One'.

God who is male and female is also One. And since God produced a Son, they are still One.

Christ said: 'My Father and I are One'.

So when a man and a woman become one, they are figuratively and one in the same way that God is One.

Then in accordance with God's Plan, Satan exposed Adam and Eve to the 'tree of the knowledge of good and evil' which God had created. It was God's intention that Adam and Eve His very first children should eat of that tree so that they would have the knowledge of good and evil.

Satan was selling deceptive knowledge, and offering Eve the chance to be like God. Eve did not know that the very reason for her being brought into existence was for her to become God. So Eve took of the fruit ate some, and gave some to Adam who also ate the fruit.

As a result of this rebellion, God expelled them from the Garden of Eden.

With the knowledge of evil, all human beings would be able to learn from their human experience that God's Laws and ways are the only way to life and happiness, and Satan's ways are the ways of death.

Deuteronomy 30:19 I call heaven and earth to record this day against you, that I have set before you **life** and death, blessing and cursing: therefore **choose life**, that both thou and thy seed may live:

What is a Human Being?

The word Hu-man is derived from an ancient word root where 'Hu' means God. So Humans are God-men.

John10:34 Jesus answered them, Is it not written in your law, I said, Ye are gods? 35 If he called them gods, unto whom the word of God came, and the scripture cannot be broken;

This is a key scripture in that Christ clearly says that human beings have 'God' status, and are potentially to become 'God' when raised to Eternal Life.

Secondly Christ who wrote the Bible by inspiring His prophets and disciples states categorically that the Scriptures cannot be broken, or proved wrong, because they are Truth.

Human beings are god-men (and women) in a continuous state being-ness or existing life until death.

In human terms, we produce children during the loving God-given sex act which should be deeply revered, honoured, and respected. Sadly sex is far too often dragged into degradation by God ignoring people.

During coitus cells may unite. Each ovum that is fertilised with a sperm becomes a separate individual, 'alive' because of the specific gift of life from God who is the only source of 'life'.

Job 33:4 The spirit of **God** hath made me, and the breath of the Almighty hath given me **life**.

The tiny embryo or foetus as it develops has no cognizance of being alive or conscious. In the womb it is not aware of its relationship with its mother who is extremely large by comparison to itself. Once born it relies on its parents for survival, but initially is not aware of this fact.

The embryo starts to grow in the mother's womb, and within a few weeks develops a heart and lungs to pump the blood of its mother through the umbilical cord upon which it relies for its life and development.

The 'life' of the foetus in the womb is totally dependent upon the 'life' of the mother until it is born, when the baby takes its first breath and becomes independently alive, and a new person.

The 'life' is in the blood. When most of the blood drains out of a living person or an animal, it dies. When anything 'dies', and is truly 'dead', life cannot be restored by any means.

Leviticus 17:11 For the life of the flesh is in the blood:

Unfortunately, almost all humans do not appreciate where their 'life' comes from nor do they understand or appreciate that they are the children of the Almighty God.

How many people on this Earth think about the miracle of 'life' they have? Are they aware that every heartbeat is a continuous Act of God? That every breath they take is also a continuous Act of God.

Strange as it might sound, there are now a number of companies which, for a large fee, offer a service to freeze a dead body at a very low temperature. This is done on their assumption that the branch of science called 'cryogenics' will one day find a way to restore life to the dead body of the person. Apparently in some cases, all the blood of the corpse is drained out and replaced with an embalming liquid. Since we know that 'life' can only come from Life, this would seem to be a pointless exercise.

This 'cryogenic' concept In physics is the study of the production and behaviour of materials at very low temperatures. This program also ignores the fact that all humans who die will one day be resurrected to human life by God. At that time their human spirit in which the entire lifetime experiences of the person are stored, and which has been preserved and retained by God at their death will be installed into a new physical body.

God has made all nations of one blood. God also originally determined the times of the nations, and the boundaries of their countries.

Acts 17:26 And hath made of one blood all nations of men for to dwell on all the face of the earth, and hath determined the times before appointed, and the bounds of their habitation;

So it is a fact that all men and women are of 'one blood' regardless of their race or nationality. A sobering thought to those who have destructive racist views.

Acts 17:27 That they should seek the Lord, if haply they might feel after him, and find him, though he be not far from every one of us:

Everyone on earth would do well to recognise that God is indeed close to us, watching over each and every one of His embryonic family, and that God is not at all far away as some suggest. Our very existence is actually **in** God.

Acts 17:28 For in him (**in God**) we live, and move, and have our being (our life, and our conscious existence); as certain also of your own poets have said, For we are also his offspring.

In a sense, the whole human race is in God's 'womb', the earthly home we have been born into. Seven billion people are not really even remotely aware that they are alive and exist consciously as a gift from God, that we are God's Offspring, or that a Father/child relationship exists between God, Christ and all humanity. How does that make God the Father feel, do you think?

However, God has allowed them to be blinded to it by Satan so that God does not hold them fully accountable for their ignorance or arrogant defiance.

2 Corinthians 4:4 In whom the god of this world hath **blinded** the minds of them which believe not, lest the light of the glorious gospel of Christ, who is the image of God, should shine unto them.

According to God's Plan, this is not the time for most people to be given the gift of seeing the relationship humans have with the Creator God. Most humans do not appreciate that they are indeed 'tiny', and so very miniscule compared with the Great God their Father.

This analogy of our being in God's 'womb' may just help some appreciate how loving our God is to tolerate the ignorance, rebellion and waywardness of his children.

We are 'in' God as much as He is 'in' us so again…

*Acts 17:27 That they should seek the Lord, if haply they might feel after him, and find him, though he be not far from every one of us: 28 For in him we live, and move, and have our **being**; as certain also of your own poets have said, For we are also his offspring.*

Our 'being-ness', our 'life' as offspring of God is entirely within God who Is Life.

There are a few exceptions to this universal blindness however, very few at this time, and they are those human beings who have been called by God into a more personal relationship with Him. We can pray for our eyes to be opened if we wish to believe and have a closer walk with God.

God's 'Sons' on Earth

It is important to appreciate that the 'Sons of God' were part of God's spirit being family. They are first mentioned in Deuteronomy 32:8-9 but due to the fact that the King James Version was translated from the Masoretic texts, the words concerning the sons of God do not appear in that version.

Deuteronomy 32:8 When the Most High divided to the nations their inheritance, when he separated the sons of Adam, he set the bounds of the people according to the number *of the children of Israel.* (This should have read of the Sons of God) {as opposed to the Lord's portion for Israel} 9 For the LORD's portion is his people; Jacob is the lot of his inheritance.

In the English Standard Version (ESV) translation, there the Septuagint version is used, direct from the Dead Sea Scrolls, verse 8-9 appear thus:

When the Most High gave to the nations their inheritance,
    when he divided mankind,
he fixed the borders[a] of the peoples
    according to the number of the sons of God.[b]
9But the LORD's portion is his people,
    Jacob his allotted heritage.

This happened when God gave the nations their inheritance and divided humankind at the time of the Tower of Babel.

What was the function of the 'sons of God', and how do they figure in God's Plan? They were those spirit beings, a part of God's Government who were lesser 'Elohim' who were appointed as spirit leaders over the nations of Genesis 10.

Up until the time of Babel, God had been working with humans, but this is now when God is 'giving up' on the nations, and giving them what they wanted which was god of their own. Similar to when Israel demanded that God gave them a human king, and God said OK, but that a human king will not take care of you like I have, but will take everything they can from you as is explained in 1 Samuel 8.

However, many of the sons of God 'defected' to Satan's perverted way of thinking, and this can be seen in Job chapters one and two. They became the pantheon of gods that ruled over the Gentile nations.

Psalm 82 tells of how these 'gods' betrayed their original remit, and did not rule justly, fairly,

Psalm 82:1 God standeth in the congregation of the mighty; he judgeth among the gods. 2 How long will ye judge unjustly, and accept the persons of the wicked? Selah.

What they should have been doing was what God would do, as the Psalm goes on to say.

Psalm 82:3 Defend the poor and fatherless: do justice to the afflicted and needy. 4 Deliver the poor and needy: rid them out of the hand of the wicked. 5 They know not, neither will they understand; they walk on in darkness: all the foundations of the earth are out of course.

So God passes judgement on the sons of God, and tells them because of their actions, they will die like men.

Psalm 82:6 I have said, Ye are gods; and all of you are children of the most High. 7 But ye shall die like men, and fall like one of the princes.

And of course they did die like men, and apparently could no longer manifest themselves in human form.

So God will have His sway, and He will arise and judge the nations, and will inherit them all when He becomes All in All.

Psalm 82:8 Arise, O God, judge the earth: for thou shalt inherit all nations.

The state of the Earth in the 21st century is witness to the fact that many world leaders are clearly under powerful ungodly influences to say the least.

In the early days, as human beings began to grow in numbers these spirit beings could manifest themselves in human form and have sexual relations with women.

Genesis 6:1 And it came to pass, when men began to multiply on the face of the earth, and daughters were born unto them, 2 That the sons of God saw the daughters of men that they were fair; and they took them wives of all which they chose.

Now were the 'sons of God' supposed to be consorting with women? From other contexts in the Scriptures it appears that in having children with women, the sons of God were 'exceeding their brief' so to speak and sinning against God. In fact in doing so, clearly they had departed from God's service and become associated with Satan in his work of leading the people away from God.

There are two places in the first chapter of Job, again repetition for emphasis that the sons of God were in conference with God in heaven on more than one occasion.

Job 1:6 Now there was a day when the sons of God came to present themselves before the Lord, and Satan came also among them 7 And the Lord said unto **Satan**, Whence comest thou? Then **Satan** answered the Lord, and said, From going to and fro in the earth, and from walking up and down in it.

Job 2:1 Again there was a day when the sons of God came to present themselves before the Lord, and Satan came also among them to present himself before the Lord. 2 And the Lord said unto Satan, From whence comest thou? And Satan answered the Lord, and said, From going to and fro in the earth, and from walking up and down in it.

Notice here, that Satan and the sons of God as spirit beings had the freedom to be in heaven, and also to walk up and down in the earth.

Genesis 6:4 There were giants in the earth in those days; and also after that, when the sons of God came in unto the daughters of men, and they bare children to them, the same became mighty men which were of old, men of renown.

Clearly the children of the sons of God had considerable powers, they were 'mighty men'.

Strong's {**1368**} rwOBGi — **gibbowr,** *ghib-bore';* or rBoGi (shortened) **gibbor,** *ghibbore';* intensive from the same as 1397; powerful; by implication, warrior, tyrant: — champion, chief, X excel, giant, man, mighty (man, one), strong (man), valiant man.

These 'mighty men' were 'renowned' for what? They were being powerful tyrants who oppressed the people, and lead their minds away from God.

One such 'mighty man' was Nimrod.

Genesis 10:8 And Cush begat Nimrod: he began to be a mighty one (Heb 1368 - a tyrant) in the earth. 9 He was a mighty hunter **before** the LORD: wherefore it is said, Even as Nimrod the mighty hunter **before** the LORD.

Notice the repetition for emphasis in this verse of 'Before' meaning 'against' God, impudently setting himself up as a god, having the people worship him in place of God,

Strong's 6440 {6440} μynip; — **paniym,** *paw-neem';* plural… the face (before, etc.): — + accept, a-(be-) fore(-time), against, anger, at, + battle, + because (of), + beseech, countenance, edge, + impudent, + in, it, look(-eth) (- s), X me, + meet, over against,

The sons of God had rebelled against God, and gone over to Satan's adversarial activities. Many of them were destroyed by God because of their rebellion, but others retained positions of authority under Satan to influence human beings against God.

It is likely that it was these sons of God that became the 'gods' worshipped by the nations through the centuries.

The gods of Egypt, Isis, Osiris, Horus, Ra; the Israelites and the Canaanites, Ashtoreth, Baal, Chemosh; the Philistines, Dagon the fish god, a symbol of Dagon continues to this day with the hats of the church hierarchy; and Greece, Zeus, Poseidon, Athena, Apollo; the Romans, Jupiter, Juno and Minerva; may well have been the actual 'sons of God' who could manifest themselves in human form, but also remain invisible as they held humans under their sway.

Were the magicians of Egypt sons of God, or men working under their influence? They were able to turn their staffs into snakes, produced a plague of frogs, and turned the river into blood. They clearly possessed superhuman or supernatural powers to be able to mimic the miracles performed by God through Moses.

Do the spirit 'sons of God' have positions of power in our present day world? It would seem that they do. It is reasonable to suppose that every leader in the governments of this world have their own 'principality and power' working with them, both from the angelic and the Satanic world.

Ephesians 6:12 For we wrestle not against flesh and blood, but against principalities, against powers, against the rulers of the darkness of this world, against spiritual wickedness in high places.

Can they manifest themselves as the 'Nimrods' of this present age? Are they the ones inspiring the tyrants of this evil world? Perhaps.

Remember that God called Nebuchadnezzar, who was the ruler of the whole world at that time, 'My servant'. Note that God also allowed him to commit heinous crimes against humanity. This is clearly happening in many of the world's countries right now.

Remember also the incident in Daniel where he had a vision of a powerful spirit being who had come to his aid when Daniel had cried out to God for help. But even this powerful angelic being had to fight with a powerful ruler of darkness who was preventing him from coming to Daniel for three weeks.

We really do not have any idea at all concerning the activities of the good and bad spirit entities that are involved with life on Earth. Here is the story, remember Christ wrote it and put it into the Bible for us today:

Daniel 10:2 In those days I Daniel was mourning three full weeks. 3 I ate no pleasant bread, neither came flesh nor wine in my mouth, neither did I anoint myself at all, till three whole weeks were fulfilled. 4 And in the four and twentieth day of the first month, as I was by the side of the great river, which is Hiddekel; 5 Then I lifted up mine eyes, and looked, and behold a certain man clothed in linen, whose loins were girded with fine gold of Uphaz: 6 His body also was like the beryl, and his face as the appearance of lightning, and his eyes as lamps of fire, and his arms and his feet like in colour to polished brass, and the voice of his words like the voice of a multitude.

This is some very powerful spirit being indeed, and he was doing his best to come to Daniel's aid, but had to fight an opponent for weeks first.

Daniel 10:7 And I Daniel alone saw the vision: for the men that were with me saw not the vision; but a great quaking fell upon them, so that they fled to hide themselves. 8 Therefore I was left alone, and saw this great vision, and there remained no strength in me: for my comeliness was turned in me into corruption, and I retained no strength. 9 Yet heard I the voice of his words: and when I heard the voice of his words, then was I in a deep sleep on my face, and my face toward the ground. 10 And, behold, an hand touched me, which set me upon my knees and upon the palms of my hands. 11 And he said unto me, O Daniel, a man greatly beloved, understand the words that I speak unto thee, and stand upright: for unto thee am I now sent. And when he had spoken this word unto me, I stood trembling. 12 Then said he unto me, Fear not, Daniel: for from the first day that thou didst set thine heart to understand, and to chasten thyself before thy God, thy words were heard, and I am come for thy words. 13 But the prince of the kingdom of Persia withstood me one and twenty days: but, lo, Michael, one of the chief princes, came to help me; and I remained there with the kings of Persia.

So the unseen spirit world has beings of different power and authority that war with each other.

Daniel 10:14 Now I am come to make thee understand what shall befall thy people in the latter days: for yet the vision is for many days.

We might well wonder when we who are in Christ will start to understand what is going to happen in the latter days which are ahead of us now.

The Flood

Adam and Eve had children, and their children had more children, and sadly they were all tarred with the same Satanic brush of giving in to their own human nature. Wickedness became epidemic, then pandemic, until God wearied of seeing the way His Children were behaving.

Genesis 6:3 And the LORD said, My spirit shall not always strive with man, for that he also is flesh: yet his days shall be an hundred and twenty years.

Verse 3 introduced the idea that God is not at all happy to strive with the human race and warns of the flood to come. to the point.

So the days of the peoples of the earth were numbered, in that in one hundred and twenty years, God would destroy all but eight of them in the flood.

God regrets having created man, and changes His mind and decides to destroy all humans, and the fauna and flora on the Earth with the flood.

Genesis 6:5 And God saw that the wickedness of man was great in the earth, and that every imagination of the thoughts of his heart was only evil continually. 6 And it repented the Lord that he had made man on the earth, and it grieved him at his heart.

When it says God 'repented', it means that He decided to change His mind and act in a different way.

Genesis 6:7 And the Lord said, I will destroy man whom I have created from the face of the earth; both man, and beast, and the creeping thing, and the fowls of the air; for it repenteth me that I have made them.

But thankfully, God and Christ still had their Plan to build their Family, even though they had come to this dramatic decision.

All nations on the Earth today have in their folklore the story of a devastating flood.

However, following their Plan, God showed mercy to Noah and His family. The eight people who survived the Flood have now grown to seven billion, and again like in Genesis 6:5 God is seeing that the wickedness of human beings is great in the earth, and that every imagination of the thoughts of his heart was only evil continually. Who knows when God will step in and get the attention of His children in a very dramatic manner?

Genesis 6:8 But Noah found grace in the eyes of the Lord. 9 These are the generations of Noah: Noah was a just man and perfect in his generations, and Noah walked with God. 10 And Noah begat three sons, Shem, Ham, and Japheth. 11 The earth also was corrupt before God, and the earth was filled with violence. 12 And God looked upon the earth, and, behold, it was corrupt; for all flesh had corrupted his way upon the earth. 13 And God said unto Noah, The end of all flesh is come before me; for the earth is filled with violence through them; and, behold, I will destroy them with the earth. 14 Make thee an ark of gopher wood; rooms shalt thou make in the ark, and shalt pitch it within and without with pitch.

Ignorant people mock the Biblical record of the Flood, but they would do better to heed the warning it gives to us today. God does nothing except He reveals it to His servants the prophets. (Amos 3:7)

1 Corinthians 10:11 Now all these things happened unto them for examples: and they are written for our admonition, upon whom the ends of the world are come. 12 Wherefore let him that thinketh he standeth take heed lest he fall.

So to whom is the story of the Flood directed? Why to us who are indeed approaching the ends of the world. All the chaos in the world, the renewed discussions about the possibility of nuclear war, certainly indicate that things are getting much worse and not better.

This is emphatically not 'doom and gloom' talk, it is pure realism. Christ warned that a time would come when if it were not for His intervention, no flesh would be saved alive. This is not 'religious' talk either, they are the words of the Creator of the Universe, so we had better give most earnest heed… or else!

Matthew 24:21 For then shall be great tribulation, such as was not since the beginning of the world to this time, no, nor ever shall be. 22 And except those days should be shortened, there should no flesh be saved: but for the elect's sake those days shall be shortened.

It has only been possible for humans to destroy all flesh since the invention of nuclear bombs and hydrogen weapons. It is said by those who know that enough of these awesome horrific weapons exist to destroy not only all flesh, but all life on Earth a hundred times over.

What can we do in the face of these awful facts? Well one thing would be to turn to God, and beg him to open our eyes to the truth.

CHAPTER 5

IS GOD WORKING IN THIS AGE THROUGH THOUSANDS OF DENOMINATIONS AND .ORGS?

God works with individuals not organisations

There are supposedly more than 2.4 billion people who claim to be Christian in this world, but they belong to many thousands of competing churches, groups, and 'denominations'. So if we think about that for a minute, how would Christ view these people? Would He have a different way to deal with 1.285 billion Catholics, than with 920 million members of the Church of England Lutherans, Methodists, Baptists and all the other Protestants? How about 270 million Eastern Orthodox, 86 million Oriental Orthodoxy, or 35 million Restorationism and Nontrinitarianism, and all the other 'isms' and .orgs?

Anyone who is thoroughly familiar with God's Word, the Holy Bible, will be aware that through the ages, God has worked mostly with individuals and families. In fact if one were to count all the people mentioned as having been close to God and a part of His 'ecclesia' of group, they would be surprised at the relatively small number that God has been directly involved with.

So are all those 2.4 billion part of Christ's ecclesia, His group? Are some of them? We are not talking about whether people are sincere, well-meaning, or ardent in their version of 'Churchianity', but simply to ask, are they really in touch with God and are they following His wishes concerning the way they live their lives? Sadly in the vast majority of cases the answer is no.

A careful study of what 'churches' believe will reveal that there is not one 'ism' or .org which does not differ widely in their teachings from what God requires in the Bible. All 'churches' wittingly or unwittingly engage every year in religious celebrations which God hates. They embrace pagan and heathen traditions and practices woven into their special days of worship.

Are you deceived? Here is a reality check:

1. Are you comfortable to observe the Crucifixion and Resurrection of Christ over Easter, an ancient Sun worshipping and sex festival involving bunny rabbits and eggs held during the Spring Equinox? Disgusting mixture of ideas is it not?

2. Is it appropriate to celebrate Christmas as Christ's birthday when He was actually born on September 11th, 3BC, which was the Day of Trumpets announcing Christ's Birth. Especially not when December 25th was observed as the 're-birth' of the Sun millennia before Christ. Or the charade of the 'Nativity' scene where Jesus is in the manger with the shepherds looking on, with three wise men present who did not actually meet Christ until two years later in a house?

3. How does God view All hallows e'en, Halloween with its Ghoulies, ghosties, Witches, and pumpkins with lights in to guide the spirits? Any activity which involves such things is a million years from Christianity and should be shunned.

4. Does it please God to see billions of people supposedly worshipping Him in churches full of images, statues, relics, all of which He forbids?

What have any of these practices to do with Christ? Are they Biblical? Absolutely not, they are all abominations in God's sight.

Certainly, you may have thought you were doing the right thing, but God thinks differently. He is extremely blunt in His language about the solemn feast days people used to worship Him thousands of years before Christ. But Christendom has perpetuated their celebrations to this day.

Malachi 2:3 Behold, I will corrupt your seed, and spread **dung** upon your faces, even the **dung** of your solemn feasts; and one shall take you away with it.

Like it or not, these are the Words of our Father God! As he says in Ezekiel, God does not like it when people worship in ways that in a sense they are putting their fingers to their noses at Him like rude children are known to do.

Christendom practices a fatal mixture of truth and error which God finds obnoxious. Even their buildings evidence many types of architecture which 'get up God's nose' like the phallic steeples, and the Sun worshipping stained glass windows. God says over and over again: Do not make likenesses, graven images, or any other thing connected with the wordship of Him. Yet churches and cathedrals are full of effigies and statues of 'saints' and other revered individuals.

Bye the bye, Christ says do not call anyone 'Rabbi', or 'Father' in a religious connection. Even the term 'Reverend' should not be used by clergy, as that is one of God's names. They are not to be revered, God is.

Psalm 119:9 He sent redemption unto his people: he hath commanded his covenant for ever: holy and reverend is his name.

No, God and Christ are not working with thousands of 'churches', how could They be?

The body of belief, the practices of each of these 'churches' conflict with each other, and so cannot all represent God's truth. There is only one version of the Truth. Only God's Word can be relied upon to be 'Truth'.

Is Christ divided? Is He working with countless Christian divisions of opinion?

Under the inspiration of Christ, Paul when addressing the Corinthians opens the subject of divisive groups.

1 Corinthians 1:10 Now I beseech you, brethren, by the name of our Lord Jesus Christ, that ye all speak the same thing, and that there be no divisions among you; but that ye be perfectly joined together in the same mind and in the same judgment.

So Christ Himself is saying to the Corinthians through Paul in the 1st century, and this message is even more pertinent in the 21st century. There were not 30,000+ different Christian differing 'churches' then like there are now. Scripture goes on to say:

1 Corinthians 1:11 For it hath been declared unto me of you, my brethren, by them which are of the house of Chloe, that there are contentions among you. 12 Now this I say, that every one of you saith, I am of Paul; and I of Apollos; and I of Cephas; and I of Christ.

Now here is the crunch statement. Is Christ divided?

1 Corinthians 1:13 Is Christ divided? was Paul crucified for you? or were ye baptized in the name of Paul? 14 I thank God

that I baptized none of you, but Crispus and Gaius; 15 Lest any should say that I had baptized in mine own name.

So the answer is No! Christ is NOT divided, and cannot be. Christ was accused by the Pharisees of working with Satan, so He explained the vital principle.

Matthew 12:25 And Jesus knew their thoughts, and said unto them, Every kingdom **divided against** itself is brought to desolation; and every city or house **divided against** itself shall not stand:

Mark 3:24 And if a kingdom be divided against itself, that kingdom cannot stand. 25 And if a house be divided against itself, that house cannot stand.

Christ is a King, the King of Kings, and He owns the Kingdom and rules it without division. It is Satan who divides people, not Christ.

Anyone who is deceived, does not know they are deceived.

Christ was speaking of the end of the age when He said to His disciples:

Matthew 24:4 And Jesus answered and said unto them, Take heed that no man deceive you. 5 For many shall come in my name, saying, I am Christ; and shall deceive many.

Luke 21:7 And they asked him, saying, Master, but when shall these things be? and what sign will there be when these things shall come to pass? 8 And he said, Take heed that ye be not deceived: for many shall come in my name, saying, I am Christ; and the time draweth near: go ye not therefore after them.

God and Christ use repetition for emphasis concerning deception all through the Bible. When God and Christ repeat themselves many times it is for even greater emphasis.

Since so many are deceived now in this 21st century, what will happen to 'believers' when the sparks begin to fly with frightening physical signs and wonders on Earth and appearing in the skies?

Matthew 24:11 And many false prophets shall rise, and shall deceive many. 12 And because iniquity shall abound, the love of many shall wax cold. 24 For there shall arise false Christs, and false prophets, and shall shew great signs and wonders; insomuch that, if it were possible, they shall deceive the very elect.

Even those who think they are 'in Christ' may be in for a shock!

Nobody can serve or worship with any human organisation with their conflicting ideas of what God requires of His children **and** have a personal relationship with God the Father and Christ Jesus. No man can serve two masters, Christ is not divided.

The 'Sermon on the Mount', in Matthew chapters 5, 6 and 7 contain many of the most important sayings of Christ about what is required of a Christian. One would imagine that all churchgoers would have read those three chapters so many times the principles would be burned into their brains, and practicing what Christ taught would be a daily challenge.

Matthew 7:22 Many will say to me in that day, Lord, Lord, have we not prophesied in thy name? and in thy name have cast out devils? and in thy name done many wonderful works?

People will say: I attended church every Sunday, I put money in the plate, I kept all the special days, I read my Bible every day, I prayed for the sick…

Matthew 7:23 And then will I profess unto them, I never knew you: depart from me, ye that work iniquity.

One day wailing and gnashing of teeth will certainly be heard in the land!

Matthew 7:24 Therefore whosoever heareth these sayings of mine, and doeth them, I will liken him unto a wise man, which built his house upon a rock: 25 And the rain descended, and the floods came, and the winds blew, and beat upon that house; and it fell not: for it was founded upon a rock.

Can you be sure that your spiritual 'house' is built on the true Rock which is Christ?

1 Corinthians 10:3 And did all eat the same spiritual meat; 4 And did all drink the same spiritual drink: for they drank of that spiritual Rock that followed them: and that Rock was Christ.

Is your connection with Him directly as your 'mediator'? Or do you accept the mediation of mere men in strange garb between yourself and your Creator?

Not all in Sinai were obedient to God's Laws and Commandments, with the result they were punished. If our efforts to please God are not in accordance with His wishes, we cannot please him.

1 Corinthians 10:6 But with many of them God was not well pleased: for they were overthrown in the wilderness.

Matthew 7:26 And every one that heareth these sayings of mine, and doeth them not, shall be likened unto a foolish man, which built his house upon the sand: 27 And the rain descended, and the floods came, and the winds blew, and beat upon that house; and it fell: and great was the fall of it. 28 And it came to pass, when Jesus had ended these sayings, the people were astonished at his doctrine:

One day in the future, all these 'houses' built on the sands of Churchianity will fall, and those who attended them will know about it.

Matthew 6:24 No man can serve two masters: for either he will hate the one, and love the other; or else he will hold to the one, and despise the other. Ye cannot serve God and mammon.

What does 'mammon' mean? Wealth, avarice, or worldly things. 'Churches' are worldly, manmade ideas about God. Most are very concerned about money, and make merchandise of their adherents.

There are so many warnings about deception from Christ the Master in many parts of the Bible, one wonders that people are not more careful about who they listen to. The author of this book was completely deceived for over sixteen years, and only came to realise it when the activities of the hierarchy were so obviously evil, but even then, it was a miracle from God that enabled him to see through the deception.

2 Peter 2:1 But there were false prophets also among the people, even as there shall be false teachers among you, who privily shall bring in damnable heresies, even denying the Lord that bought them, and bring upon themselves swift destruction. 2 And many shall follow their pernicious ways; by reason of whom the way of truth shall be evil spoken of. 3 And through covetousness shall they with feigned words make merchandise of you: whose judgment now of a long time lingereth not, and their damnation slumbereth not.

Yes, many Christian churches preach 'Christ crucified', but their mongrel teachings actually deny Christ and His sacrifice. Especially those denominations which teach adherence to the Mosaic law, which blinds those who attempt to keep it in their own strength, or think that God is helping them do so.

2 Corinthians 3:14 But their minds were blinded: for until this day remaineth the same vail untaken away in the reading of the old testament; which vail is done away in Christ. 15 But even unto this day, when Moses is read, the vail is upon

their heart. 16 Nevertheless when it (they) shall turn to the Lord, the vail shall be taken away.

It is only when law-keepers realise the folly of their feeble attempts to keep the law, that the blindness is removed.

So who is God dealing with individually and personally?

Each person who has ever lived on this Earth, and today all seven billion of them, are known intimately by God who has been aware of each of us and all about us personally long before the Universe was Created.

Ephesians 1:3 Blessed be the God and Father of our Lord Jesus Christ, who hath blessed us with all spiritual blessings in heavenly places in Christ: 4 According as he hath chosen us in him before the foundation of the world, that we should be holy and without blame before him in love:

Every human being who would ever live on this Earth was known to God individually long before the creation of Adam! Incredible, but true. Not only that, but God sees each one as an adopted person in His Family. Amazing? Yes! It is the ultimate destiny of all people.

Ephesians 1:5 Having predestinated us unto the adoption of children by Jesus Christ to himself, according to the good pleasure of his will,

Does that mean then that everyone is in this privileged position from the moment they are born? No it does not. Each person will come to this at the time when it is appropriate for them. God calls individuals to have a personal relationship with Him at His pleasure.

Ephesians 1:11 In whom also we have obtained an inheritance, being predestinated according to the purpose of him who worketh all things after the counsel of his own will:

Many, if not all, have to go through a life of deception and alienation from God, until the moment when God decides to work with them personally. That moment when God decides to work with each of those who are 'the called' according to His purpose at that particular time.

A fantastic calling, and is not always an easy path to tread.

2 Timothy 3:12 Yea, and all that will live godly in Christ Jesus shall suffer persecution.

And we need constantly to be vigilant, and strive to love God and our neighbour, and keep close to God.

1 Corinthians 10:12 Wherefore let him that thinketh he standeth take heed lest he fall.

However with that statement comes another promise.

1 Corinthians 10:13 There hath no temptation (or test) taken you but such as is common to man: but God is faithful, who will not suffer you to be tempted above that ye are able; but will with the temptation also make a way to escape, that ye may be able to bear it.

No matter how bad things might appear on this human plane, we can be assured that God is watching over out spiritual health.

God is calling individuals at this time in history

Christ said that many are called but few are chosen. God seems to be working with few indeed in this era. Those who avoid church organisations and rely on direct contact with God for their inspiration are few indeed.

John mentions aspects of false teaching and says:

1 John 2:26 These things have I written unto you concerning them that seduce you.

So there were seductive teachings in the 1st century, as there are now even more so. Those who are under the spell of seductive human ideas are blinded to God's Truth.

But the called 'few' now have the advantage of having direct contact with God and Christ by reason of God's powerful spirit working in their minds.

1 John 2:27 But the anointing which ye have received of him abideth in you, and ye need not that any man teach you: but as the same anointing teacheth you **of** all things, and is truth, and is no lie, and even as it hath taught you, ye shall abide in him.

Notice, Christ is telling us that we do not need any 'man' to teach us. God is working with each individual that He is calling and giving that only that measure of the Truth that is appropriate for that person at any given time.

Also notice that 'the same anointing teaches you **of**', the word of here means 'that which is concerning and pertaining to' all things, not teaches you all things!

Ephesians 4:6 One God and Father of all, who is above all, and through all, and in you all. 7 But unto every one of us is given grace according to the measure of the gift of Christ.

Each one of the 'called' receives their own measure of knowledge. Nobody can claim infallibility concerning all the truth, but the 'few' can be sure that whatever God's Spirit teaches and inspires them to believe is the specific Truth for them at any given time. As we abide in Christ, we all have to grow in Grace and Knowledge.

God knows each of the 'called' intimately, in every detail

Christ made it clear that God knows all about each of us, and if he chooses, even down to the number of hairs on our head!

Matthew 10:29 Are not two sparrows sold for a farthing? and one of them shall not fall on the ground without your Father. 30 But the very hairs of your head are all numbered. 31 Fear ye not therefore, ye are of more value than many sparrows.

Luke 12:7 But even the very hairs of your head are all numbered. Fear not therefore: ye are of more value than many sparrows.

These two verses may be literal, or they may be figurative, or both, take your choice, but either way, God knows us and cares about the most specific and individual aspects of our lives.

Consider this. Every single person's DNA is different, everyone's fingerprint is different. Not only that, but no two people on Earth are exactly alike in every way, or in every detail of their lives, but God knows each of us in the most minute detail. He is our Father, and a Father who is totally Loving and Omniscient. He sees each of us for who we are.

Consider this. Every single person's DNA is different, everyone's fingerprint is different. Not only that, but no two people on Earth are exactly alike in every way, or in every detail of their lives, but God knows each of us in the most minute detail. He is our Father, and a Father who is totally Loving and Omniscient. He sees each of us, His beloved children, for who and what we are, and how we live our lives.

Human beings are not just billions of faceless people to our Father. He has a specific purpose in His mind for each of us. Hard to imagine, and almost impossible to believe, but this is what His Word teaches us. We need to ask for the gifts of belief and the faith in order for this to become a reality in our minds.

Ultimately human beings will be raised to God status with Eternal Life as a Gift of God. Our role will be to live and reign with Christ, the King of Kings, in peace for the aeons to come. Reign over what? Over God's entire Kingdom the expansion of which has no end.

Isaiah 9:6 For unto us a child is born, unto us a son is given: and the government shall be upon his shoulder: and his name shall be called Wonderful, Counsellor, The mighty God, The everlasting Father, The Prince of Peace. 7 Of the increase of his government and peace there shall be no end, upon the throne of David, and upon his kingdom, to order it, and to establish it with judgment and with justice from henceforth even for ever. The zeal of the LORD of hosts will perform this.

Even with all the technical advances, humans cannot really fathom the extent of the Universe. The vastness of it as it expands, the countless billions of galaxies and stars are all there to glorify God. His children are destined to be heirs of all this, and to be a part of God's government. Astounding.

Romans 8:6 The Spirit itself beareth witness with our spirit, that we are the children of God: 17 And if children, then heirs; heirs of God, and joint-heirs with Christ; if so be that we suffer with him, that we may be also glorified together. 18 For I reckon that the sufferings of this present time are not worthy to be compared with the glory which shall be revealed in us.

Every human being will eventually be raised to God status and inherit the Will of God. A more than incredible and amazing future awaits us. Those in Christ at all times, have been changed in nature to become a chosen race of people for God's own purpose to form Christ's ecclesia,

1 Peter 2:9 But you are a chosen race, a royal priesthood, a holy nation, a people for his own possession, that you

may proclaim the excellencies of him who called you out of darkness into his marvelous light.

This information is not widely known among Christendom.

The Christianity of 'Churchianity' has lost its way because of 'Attitude'

ATTITUDE is the reason why 'CHURCHIANITY' is SO RESISTANT TO CHANGE?

For forty years of my life I have had the opportunity to give lectures and teach thousands of people. When meeting any group for the first time I would always pose a question to the audience.

"What do you think is the most important word in the English language?" The answers offered by the assembly of people always varied. Some said love, some said diligence, and others suggested acceptance, tolerance, patience, kindness, forgiveness, and other spiritual attributes.

My preference for the most important word and attribute is "ATTITUDE" This is because all other words suggested involve attributes which are determined by ATTITUDE.

We live in a very different world from Bible times. We have to retain in our minds what it might have been like then, and also move on in our perception of how to relate the 'then' to the 'now' in the 21st Century.

We pray daily, 'Thy Kingdom come.' And we have to have an attitude continually of 'watching' as Christ said.

Matthew 24:42 Watch therefore: for ye know not what hour your Lord doth come. 43 But know this, that if the goodman of the house had known in what watch the thief would come, he would have watched, and would not have suffered his house to be broken up.

Mark 13:33 Take ye heed, watch and pray: for ye know not when the time is. 34 For the Son of Man is as a man taking a far journey, who left his house, and gave authority to his servants, and to every man his work, and commanded the porter to watch. 35 Watch ye therefore: for ye know not when the master of the house cometh, at even, or at midnight, or at the cockcrowing, or in the morning:

Being set in our own concepts, ideas, and our ways is a fatal position, as is thinking we know it all.

As far as Theology, Religion, Politics, Economics, Health, and for that matter concerning every topic under the sun, people are very resistant to anything new, and have a great reluctance to change.

The greatest fear for us humans is the fear of the unknown. Change involves the 'unknown' to a degree, and this touches the deepest fear humans have. All human beings have a great resistance to change. We all have this resistance built into our minds. This is nothing new.

If we are to be mature people, serious Christians, and have a proper approach to life, we have constantly to be open to new information and be willing to make the necessary changes that are involved when we find it. We need to be in a continual attitude of willingness to change.

Things we have believed in the past ten or fifteen years, a couple of years ago, even last week, or this very day, may need considerable revision, and we have to be constantly in an attitude of being open mentally minded.

Religious people are known to say "What was good enough for Christ is good enough for me", but that is only an excuse for not being willing to change.

Resistance to change was very much in evidence in Christ's day. The Jews and Israelites wanted their own ideas to prevail, and had no intention of making any changes. Both the religious leaders and the attitudes of the populace were set like concrete in their 'tradition'. Over time, their traditions had slowly become more important to them than the Mosaic Laws of God.

Interestingly, the Laws of God were all in existence more than three thousand years before the Law of Moses was given to the twelve tribes of Israel. They were there in the Garden of Eden with Adam and Eve, and with Noah in the Ark 1656 years later. Interestingly the food advice of God was clear to Noah, as God instructed him to take seven pairs of clean (edible, good to eat) animals into the Ark, but only a pair of the animals that are not good to eat. Those quoted in Leviticus 11 and Deuteronomy 14 are not Israelite or 'Jewish' laws at all, but God's recommendations to humans for all time but not **binding** on Christians today.

Attention to the 'Torah', the 'Law of Moses', the first five books (or Pentateuch) of the Holy Scriptures which contained the 'Mosaic Law' given to the Jews and Israelites by God Himself through his angel gradually gave way to the 'Oral Law' of 'Traditions' invented by the religious leaders of the Jewish nation who observe them to this day

These 'Oral Laws' were commentaries on the Torah expanding on and giving more detail than is present in the Old Testament. For instance, Exodus 20 says nobody should work in the Sabbath day, but it does not define exactly what is meant by 'work'. The oral traditions would comment on this, and provide many examples of what they considered to be 'work'. For instance people were allowed to eat on the Sabbath, so it was alright to carry half a fig, but not a whole one as that would be considered a 'burden' which was work.

The religious leaders were far more interested laying down the law to people about the 'jot and tittle' of obedience to physical matters than the far more important matters of judgment, mercy, faith and so on. Yes the Torah was all about physical laws for a physical people, but nevertheless, there were all the many spiritual implications as well.

Matthew 15:8 This people draweth nigh unto me with their mouth, and honoureth me with their lips; but their heart is far from me. 9 But in vain they do worship me, teaching for doctrines the commandments of men.

Between the period when the Old Testament Bible was canonised in the 5th century B.C., and the birth of Christ, Jewish religious leaders very gradually put less and less emphasis on the manuscripts of the Torah in God's Word, and more on their 'traditions' which became 'commandments of men'.

As their reliance on the inspired Word of God diminished, so their reliance on, indeed insistence on obedience to their 'traditions' that were contained in the Torah or 'Oral Law' which was a commentary of their own devising on the Increased. The enforcement of the principles outlined by the 'traditions' began to take preference.

Matthew 23:1 Then spake Jesus to the multitude, and to his disciples, 2 Saying The scribes and the Pharisees sit in Moses' seat:

Christ was saying that the religious leaders 'sit in Moses' seat which meant that they were those who in the time of Christ were responsible for explaining and maintaining God's Law, but they had changed their attitude to God's Law in favour of their traditions.

Matthew 23:3 All therefore whatsoever they bid you observe, that observe and do; but do not ye after their works: for they say, and do not. 4 For they bind heavy burdens and grievous to be borne, and lay them on men's shoulders; but they themselves will not move them with one of their fingers.

Since the 'traditions' were not the Word of God, the traditions were far from perfect, they were onerous, tedious and invariably imposed emphases that were never intended. The Pharisees had a rebellious attitude to God which indeed was opposite to the Love of God and His Law. They were proud exhibitionists, no meekness in sight.

Matthew 23:5 But all their works they do for to be seen of men: they make broad their phylacteries, and enlarge the borders of their garments, 6 And love the uppermost rooms at feasts, and the chief seats in the synagogues,

They wore phylacteries, leather thongs attached to their skirts with parts of the Law embroidered on them for all to see, as some do in Israel to this day, but their hearts were not right.

Matthew 23:7 And greetings in the markets, and to be called of men, Rabbi, Rabbi. 8 But be not ye called Rabbi: for one is your Master, even Christ; and all ye are brethren. 9 And call no man your father upon the earth: for one is your Father, which is in heaven.

Jewish religious leaders of today who study and teach Jewish law are called 'Rabbi', and the largest religious denomination in the world calls all their priests 'Father'. Whatever God says 'do not do', people 'do', and whatever God says 'do', they 'do not do'. This reveals the attitude and state of mind of those who claim to be people of God, that they are in rebellion against God.

The Jewish leaders of Christ's day were totally resistant to change, unless it involved changes they wanted to make in the application of God's Law, their 'traditions' were sacrosanct to them, and far more important in their eyes.

It would appear that this attitude towards 'traditions' is just as rife today among the Jewish communities of the world, especially in the country of Israel where many of the Jewish men wear the 'Kippah', and still display phylacteries and 'payot', long ringlets of hair at the side of their heads that they feel are their interpretation of Leviticus 19:27.

Matthew 23:10 Neither be ye called masters: for one is your Master, even Christ. 11 But he that is greatest among you shall be your servant. 12 And whosoever shall exalt himself shall be abased; and he that shall humble himself shall be exalted.

Pride of this sort, expecting others to use titles when speaking to ministers, priests and so on, is not a Godly trait, but reveals in them an attitude of self-aggrandisement, the opposite of humility.

Then in Matthew 23 follows a series of **'woe'** statements made to the Jewish leaders. Woe is a very strong word, and it behoves us as Christians to check our own thoughts and behaviours to make sure we are not in any way being Pharisaical ourselves.

Matthew 23:13 But **woe** unto you, scribes and Pharisees, hypocrites! for ye shut up the kingdom of heaven against men: for ye neither go in yourselves, neither suffer ye them that are entering to go in.

The religions of 'churchianity' do not understand the real nature of the 'Kingdom of Heaven', and by insisting on adherence to their false gospel, they prevent their flocks from understanding either.

Matthew 23:14 **Woe** unto you, scribes and Pharisees, hypocrites! for ye devour widows' houses, and for a pretence make long prayer: therefore ye shall receive the greater damnation.

We can see pictures today of the 'Wailing Wall' in Israel where the Jewish men clothed in black pray for hours, bobbing up and down for all to see.

Matthew 6:6 But thou, when thou prayest, enter into thy **closet**, and when thou hast shut thy door, pray to thy Father which is in secret; and thy Father which seeth in secret shall reward thee openly.

Christ said that those who followed Him should pray in private, and we should follow that principle today.

Matthew 23:15 **Woe** unto you, scribes and Pharisees, hypocrites! for ye compass sea and land to make one proselyte, and when he is made, ye make him twofold more the child of hell than yourselves.

People who follow the dictates of 'Christian' religions of men have no idea that their beliefs, practices and behaviour are a million miles from the true Gospel of God. It is well to remember the truism:

A person who is deceived does not know that they are deceived.

Matthew 23:16 **Woe** unto you, ye blind guides, which say, Whosoever shall swear by the temple, it is nothing; but whosoever shall swear by the gold of the temple, he is a debtor! 17 Ye fools and blind: for whether is greater, the gold, or the temple that sanctifieth the gold?

Matthew 23:23 **Woe** unto you, scribes and Pharisees, hypocrites! for ye pay tithe of mint and anise and cumin, and have omitted the weightier matters of the law, judgment, mercy, and faith: these ought ye to have done, and not to leave the other undone.

The spiritual qualities of love, mercy, and faith were furthest from their minds, they were only interested in enforcing the minutiae of physical things on their hapless people.

Matthew 23:24 Ye blind guides, which strain at a gnat, and swallow a camel.

The devil of the Pharisaic traditions was in the detail! They 'choked' on little peccadilloes or 'sins', yet failed to see the huge important issues.

Matthew 23:25 **Woe** unto you, scribes and Pharisees, hypocrites! for ye make clean the outside of the cup and of the platter, but within they are full of extortion and excess. 26 Thou blind Pharisee, cleanse first that which is within the cup and platter, that the outside of them may be clean also.

Again, this is all about making a 'vain show', looking good with outside appearances, but within full of evil.

Matthew 23:27 **Woe** unto you, scribes and Pharisees, hypocrites! for ye are like unto whited sepulchres, which indeed appear beautiful outward, but are within full of dead men's bones, and of all uncleanness. 28 Even so ye also outwardly appear righteous unto men, but within ye are full of hypocrisy and iniquity.

The same could be said today of the ministers of religion whose widespread practice of paedophilia and child abuse as well as homosexual immorality among their ranks which has become news all around the world. The ministers of the high churches adorned in beautiful robes and skirts, or those with their collars on backwards may look fine outwardly, but inwardly many are morally and spiritually bankrupt.

Matthew 23:29 **Woe** unto you, scribes and Pharisees, hypocrites! because ye build the tombs of the prophets, and garnish the sepulchres of the righteous, 30 And say, If we had been in the days of our fathers, we would not have been partakers with them in the blood of the prophets. 31 Wherefore ye be witnesses unto yourselves, that ye are the children of them which killed the prophets. 32 Fill ye up then the measure of your fathers. 33 Ye serpents, ye generation of vipers, how can ye escape the damnation of hell?

Self-righteous to the core, saying that they would never have persecuted the prophets in the 'olden days', but of course they would have, and they proved their foul attitudes by having Christ killed in the most horrendous way possible.

Luke 11:42 But woe unto you, Pharisees! for ye tithe mint and rue and all manner of herbs, and pass over judgment and the love of God: these ought ye to have done, and not to leave the other undone.

These religious hypocrites, like those in our era, have never understood the Love of God, but are inwardly filled with uncleanness, cruelty to children, and all forms of excess.

Repentance means to change one's mind and behaviour.

It is essential for anyone claiming to be a Christian to be in a constant state of willingness to change, and a willingness to repent and change their minds and their ways, as God reveals new truth to them as they grow in Grace and Knowledge.

Repentance is an old word. Since 1300 A.D., to repent has meant to feel such regret for sins or crimes mental or physical that it produces the desire to make changes in the way we live.

Repentance goes beyond feeling sorrow or regret. It involves the express and distinct intention to turn from sin to righteousness. The words in the Bible most often translated 'repentance' means a change of mental and spiritual attitude toward sin. A change of heart. We have to ask for that gift at least daily.

Psalm 51:10 Create in me a clean heart, O God; and renew a right spirit within me. 11 Cast me not away from thy presence; and take not thy holy spirit from me.

Our *minds*, the way our brains think and reason, are our most precious possession. God holds us all responsible for the way we use our minds. We are exhorted to learn how to think like Christ thinks.

Philippians 2:2 Fulfil ye my joy, that ye be like-minded, having the same love, being of one accord, of one mind. 3 Let nothing be done through strife or vainglory; but in lowliness of mind let each esteem other better than themselves. 4 Look not every man on his own things, but every man also on the things of others. 5 Let this *mind* be in you, which was also in Christ Jesus:

We do not have to strive for Christ's mind, which is to keep our minds on God and the needs of others. It is ours as a gift for the asking.

1 Corinthians 2:16 For who hath known the **mind** of the Lord, that he may instruct him? but we have the **mind** of Christ.

But as we have already seen, it is inherent in our nature to be resistant to change. Paul knew all about this, and explains that while we might be 'in love' with God and His Gospel, we do have a fight on our hands.

Romans 7:22 For I delight in the law of God after the inward man: 23 But I see another law in my members, warring against the law of my mind, and bringing me into captivity to the law of sin which is in my members.

Our human nature has components that are enmity to God. We need help moment by moment to stay in the Godly frame of mind. One help is to put on the whole armour of God.

Ephesians 6:10 Finally, my brethren, be strong in the Lord, and in the power of his might. 11 Put on the whole armour of God, that ye may be able to stand against the wiles of the devil. 12 For we wrestle not against flesh and blood, but against principalities, against powers, against the rulers of the darkness of this world, against spiritual wickedness in high places. 13 Wherefore take unto you the whole armour of God, that ye may be able to withstand in the evil day, and having done all, to stand.

We pray daily, 'Deliver us from evil' or the 'evil ones'. There is one part of the armour of God that protects the mind in our battle with our nature and the 'evil ones', the helmet.

Ephesians 6:17 And take the helmet of salvation, and the sword of the Spirit, which is the word of God:

The 'helmet' protects the mind, as we study and apply what we learn from the sword of the Spirit, God's Holy Bible. Like all spiritual gifts from God, we have to pray to the Father and Christ ask and for that gift on a daily, and even moment by moment basis.

Mark 12:30 And thou shalt love the Lord thy God with all thy heart, and with all thy soul, and with all thy **mind**, and with all thy strength: this is the first commandment.

Love God wholeheartedly, but the Golden Rule also includes loving everyone.

Luke 10:27 And he (Christ) answering said, Thou shalt love the Lord thy God with all thy heart, and with all thy soul, and with all thy strength, and with all thy **mind**; and thy neighbour as thyself.

Loving God is not to be something that we take lightly. As we grow, we find that we love God more and more than we have ever done before, and He and Christ become more real when we are living (present continuous) 'in Him' at the right hand of God the Father.

Ephesians 4:22 That ye put off concerning the former conversation (*Gk. conduct*) the old man, which is corrupt according to the deceitful lusts; 23 **And be renewed in the spirit of your mind;** 24 And that ye put on the new man, which after God is created in righteousness and true holiness.

We have to take an active part in this renewal change, this repentant attitude, and work at it, always remembering that it is God who actually does the work. Here repeated for emphasis.

Philippians 2:12 Wherefore, my beloved, as ye have always obeyed, not as in my presence only, but now much more in my absence, work out your own salvation with fear and trembling.

So often quoted out of context, we do have to 'work' on ourselves, but it is Christ Jesus and God who actually do all the work!!

Philippians 2:13 *For it is God which worketh in you* both to will and to do of his good pleasure.

And gives us the Spiritual gifts we need earnestly to follow Him.

Romans 2:4 Or despisest thou the riches of his goodness and forbearance and longsuffering; not knowing that (it is) the goodness of God (that) leadeth thee to *repentance*?

Colossians 1:21 And you, that were sometime alienated and enemies in your **mind** by wicked works, yet now hath he (Christ) reconciled.

Thank God!

Colossians 3:12 Put on therefore, as the elect of God, holy and beloved, bowels of mercies, kindness, humbleness of **mind**, meekness, longsuffering;

These words: Mercies, kindness, humbleness, meekness (teachableness) longsuffering, patience, are burned into the consciousness of the fervent Christian affecting everything we think and do.

2 Timothy 1:7 For God hath not given us the spirit of fear; but of power, and of love, and of a sound **mind**.

We can rely on that wonderful gift of sound mindedness which we as Christians possess! Carnal people are not of a sound mind, just look at the state of the world today. People say that the world has gone mad, and they are right. The state of the world now is nothing like it was five, ten years, or a lifetime ago, it has so quickly slid down further into a morass of the worst types of sin.

When John the Baptist began to preach, the very first word he used was "Repent".

Matthew 3:1 In those days came John the Baptist, preaching in the wilderness of Judea, 2 And saying, ***Repent*** ye (change your minds!): for the kingdom of heaven is at hand. 3 For this is he that was spoken of by the prophet Esaias, saying, The voice of one crying in the wilderness, Prepare ye the way of the Lord, make his paths straight.

Matthew 3:7 But when he (John) saw many of the Pharisees and Sadducees come to his baptism, he said unto them, O generation of vipers, who hath warned you to flee from the wrath to come? 8 Bring forth therefore fruits (the fruits of changes in mind and behaviour) meet for repentance: 9 And think not to say within yourselves, We have Abraham to our father: for I say unto you, that God is able of these stones to raise up children unto Abraham.

We should not smugly rely on the fact that we are on a Christian path, and relax, we need to be continually on our guard to be in a state of change.

We see the dictionary meaning of *'repent'* involves *a change of mind, a change of attitude*. Repenting also means to possess the willingness to change continually in order to 'grow in grace and knowledge.

The first word Christ used as He began His Ministry was **'repent'**.

Matthew 4:17 From that time Jesus began to preach, and to say, **Repent**: for the kingdom of heaven is at hand.

Certainly it is difficult even to address the need to change. Everything we do is habitual, it is hard to change any details. Breakfast, lunch, dinner, TV, are all routine events and we do not like them disturbed. Our journey to work usually takes the same route with no exceptions unless they are forced on us.

When Christ first began to teach, He got quite a warm reception from the Jewish Hierarchy and the public. As they witnessed the many healings, the miracles, some Pharisees and other religious leaders began to wonder if Christ was indeed the One to come. They thought He might even be the Messiah. At around this time so many were looking for that 'coming' of the King they were desperately hoping would sweep away the Roman rule.

Seeing all the miracles, many were moved, and realised that this Man was perhaps the Messiah, and wanted to make Him the King that would save them from the oppressive Roman rulers.

John 6:14 Then those men, when they had seen the miracle that Jesus did, said, This is of a truth that prophet that should come into the world. 15 When Jesus therefore perceived that they would come and take him by force, to make him a king, he departed again into a mountain himself alone.

But Christ was on a Mission from the Father to witness to all men. We can only imagine how the Priests, Pharisees, Jews must have reacted when Christ drove out of the Temple those who were trading in cattle and money changing.

John 2:13 And the Jews' passover was at hand, and Jesus went up to Jerusalem. 14 And found in the temple those that sold oxen and sheep and doves, and the changers of money sitting: 15 And when he had made a scourge of small cords, he drove them all out of the temple, and the sheep, and the oxen; and poured out the changers' money, and overthrew the tables; 16 And said unto them that sold doves, Take these things hence; make not my Father's house an house of merchandise. 17 And his disciples remembered that it was written, The zeal of thine house hath eaten me up.

This would have upset the whole pattern of the accepted life in the Temple, and of course because there was a lot of money involved, this would have made those affected by Christ's actions very angry indeed.

But then the Jews posed another question to Christ.

John 2:18 Then answered the Jews and said unto him, What sign shewest thou unto us, seeing that thou doest these things? 19 Jesus answered and said unto them, Destroy this temple, and in three days I will raise it up. 20 Then said the Jews, Forty and six years was this temple in building, and wilt thou rear it up in three days? 21 But he spake of the temple of his body. 22 When therefore he was risen from the dead, his disciples remembered that he had said this unto them; and they believed the scripture, and the word which Jesus had said.

But the Priests and the Pharisees did not understand what Christ was talking about, their minds were only on the physical. But again the Jews asked Jesus for a sign!

Matthew 12:38 Then certain of the scribes and of the Pharisees answered, saying, Master, we would see a sign from thee. 39 But he answered and said unto them, An evil and adulterous generation seeketh after a sign; and there shall no sign be given to it, but the sign of the prophet Jonas: 40

For as Jonas was three days and three nights in the whale's fishes' belly; so shall the Son of man be three days and three nights in the heart of the earth. 41 The men of Nineveh shall rise in judgment with this generation, and shall condemn it: because they repented at the preaching of Jonas; and, behold, a greater than Jonas is here.

This sign they asked for was shortly to be demonstrated to them all. Christ's resurrection was not 'done in a corner', it shook the world, and thousands saw Him after His three days in the grave. The event is a historical fact.

1 Corinthians 15:6 After that, he was seen of above five hundred brethren at once; of whom the greater part remain unto this present, but some are fallen asleep

So everyone began to get more out of step with Christ when He started to address the error of their own form of the Law, and show where they were wrong. If Christ would have gone along with the teachings, everything would have been fine, but He did not. They wanted 'Moses' and the 'Law' not to be changed.

Matthew 12:24 But when the Pharisees heard it, they said, This fellow doth not cast out devils, but by Beelzebub the prince of the devils. 25 And Jesus knew their thoughts, and said unto them, Every kingdom divided against itself is brought to desolation; and every city or house divided against itself shall not stand: 26 And if Satan cast out Satan, he is divided against himself; how shall then his kingdom stand? 27 And if I by Beelzebub cast out devils, by whom do your children cast them out? therefore they shall be your judges. 28 But if I cast out devils by the Spirit of God, then the kingdom of God is come unto you.

They got more incensed until they stirred up the Jews, the crowd and the Romans to get Christ killed, and He of course

He was killed, stone dead from both the crucifixion imposed by the Romans, and the stoning from the Jews.

The religious leaders of Christ's day were virtually committing the 'unpardonable sin', that of blasphemy against the Holy Spirit, as it seems are so many on Earth, perhaps two or three billion people involved with 'churchianity' today.

Matthew 12:30 He that is not with me is against me; and he that gathereth not with me scattereth abroad. 31 Wherefore I say unto you, All manner of sin and blasphemy shall be forgiven unto men: but the blasphemy against the Holy Ghost (God's Power) shall not be forgiven unto men. 32 And whosoever speaketh a word against the Son of man, it shall be forgiven him: but whosoever speaketh against the Holy Ghost, it shall not be forgiven him, neither in this world, neither in the world to come. 33 Either make the tree good, and his fruit good; or else make the tree corrupt, and his fruit corrupt: for the tree is known by his fruit. 34 O generation of vipers, how can ye, being evil, speak good things? for out of the abundance of the heart the mouth speaketh. 35 A good man out of the good treasure of the heart bringeth forth good things: and an evil man out of the evil treasure bringeth forth evil things. 36 But I say unto you, That every idle word that men shall speak, they shall give account thereof in the day of judgment. 37 For by thy words thou shalt be justified, and by thy words thou shalt be condemned.

What a serious warning to us all to be very careful what we say in an 'idle moment'. Christ tells us in the Sermon on the Mount.

Matthew 5:37 But let your communication be, Yea, yea; Nay, nay: for whatsoever is more than these cometh of evil.

In Peter's first sermon recorded in Acts 2 Peter nailed those present by telling them that they had crucified the Son of God, they were smitten in their hearts, and Peter said: "Repent ye..."

Acts 2:38 Then Peter said unto them, Repent, and be baptised every one of you in the name of Jesus Christ for the remission of sins, and ye shall receive the gift of the Holy Ghost. 39 For the promise is unto you, and to your children, and to all that are afar off, even as many as the LORD our God shall call.

When you change from one belief to another, if that religion is part of the ruling state, and Christianity was at one time, the Roman Empire considered it to be treason. The Jewish leaders considered it to be blasphemous. So everyone rose up against Christ and chose to have Him beaten and slaughtered.

As Christians we need to want to be in a constant attitude of change, and it is always difficult to do so. It was difficult for Paul who was Saul, who was one of the top men in his society, being so zealous in what he considered to be the truth.

Galatians 1:13 For ye have heard of my conversation conduct in time past in the Jews' religion, how that beyond measure I persecuted the church ekklesia of God, and wasted it: 14 And profited in the Jews' religion above many my equals in mine own nation, being more exceedingly zealous of the traditions of my fathers.

Saul had a good heart, he thought he was doing God's work by persecuting those who he considered were trying to change the traditions of the religion he was a top person. Many people have been members of organisations which taught that they were doing 'God's Work', when in fact they were doing the opposite!

Saul had the orders to haul into prison and worse anyone who believed in these 'Christian' changes. But as soon as

Christ talked to Paul on the road to Damascus, Saul changed, became Paul and then he himself began to be persecuted by others who were still stuck in their fallacious beliefs and would not change.

The Jews in Jerusalem were also stuck in old belief patterns. Paul and Peter had come to realise that Gentiles did not need to be circumcised.

Acts 15:1 And certain men which came down from Judea taught the brethren, and said, Except ye be circumcised after the manner of Moses, ye cannot be saved. 2 When therefore Paul and Barnabas had no small dissension and disputation with them, they determined that Paul and Barnabas, and certain other of them, should go up to Jerusalem unto the apostles and elders about this question.

In Jerusalem in 49 A.D., there were great arguments about the whole issue, and many problems, finally came to realise that God was in it, and they changed their minds. But that was extremely difficult for them.

Acts 15:4 And when they were come to Jerusalem, they were received of the church, and of the apostles and elders, and they declared all things that God had done with them. 5 But there rose up certain of the sect of the Pharisees which believed, saying, That it was needful to circumcise them, and to command them to keep the law of Moses. 6 And the apostles and elders came together for to consider of this matter. 7 And when there had been much disputing, Peter rose up, and said unto them, Men and brethren, ye know how that a good while ago God made choice among us, that the Gentiles by my mouth should hear the word of the gospel, and believe. 8 And God, which knoweth the hearts, bare them witness, giving them the Holy Ghost, even as he did unto us; 9 And put no difference between us (Jews and

Israelites) and them (the Gentiles), purifying their hearts by faith. 10 Now therefore why tempt ye God, to put a yoke upon the neck of the disciples, which neither our fathers nor we were able to bear? 11 But we believe that through the grace of the LORD Jesus Christ we (Jews) shall be saved, even as they (the Gentiles).

As always, there are differences of opinion among those who earnestly seek God.

Acts 15:13 And after they had held their peace, James (the head of the ekklesia in Jerusalem) answered, saying, Men and brethren, hearken unto me:...18 Known unto God are all his works from the beginning of the world. 19 Wherefore my sentence is, that we trouble not them, which from among the Gentiles are turned to God: 20 But that we write unto them, that they abstain from pollutions of idols, and from fornication, and from things strangled, and from blood.

So the Council of Jerusalem had moved forward in their understanding, so the determined to spread the good news to the Gentiles.

Acts 15:23 And they wrote letters by them after this manner; The apostles and elders and brethren send greeting unto the brethren which are of the Gentiles in Antioch and Syria and Cilicia. 24 Forasmuch as we have heard, that certain which went out from us have troubled you with words, subverting your souls, saying, Ye must be circumcised, and keep the law: to whom we gave no such commandment: 25 It seemed good unto us, being assembled with one accord, to send chosen men unto you with our beloved Barnabas and Paul, 26 Men that have hazarded their lives for the name of our Lord Jesus Christ. 27 We have sent therefore Judas and Silas, who shall also tell you the same things by mouth. 28 For it seemed good to the Holy Ghost (the Comforter!), and to us, to lay upon you no greater burden than these necessary things; 29 That ye abstain from meats offered to idols, and from blood, and from things strangled, and from fornication: from which if ye keep yourselves, ye shall do well. Fare ye well. 30 So when they were dismissed, they came to Antioch: and when they had gathered the multitude together, they delivered the epistle: 31 Which when they had read, they rejoiced for the consolation.

What a wonderful relief it must have been to learn that physical circumcision was a thing of the past!

However, even after six or seven years later under Christ's inspiration, Paul had come to a different understanding concerning meats offered to idols. All those who lived in Corinth would have had to become vegetarians, as it was not possible to find meat in the market that had not been offered to idols. So Paul writes to the Corinthians to give them the new information.

Chapter 8 in first Corinthians is all about food offered to idols, and the avoidance of giving offence to others. Paul continues this theme in chapter 10.

1 Corinthians 10:27 If any of them that believe not bid you to a feast, and ye be disposed to go; whatsoever is set before you, eat, asking no question for conscience sake. 28 But if any man say unto you, this is offered in sacrifice unto idols, eat not for his sake that shewed it, and for conscience sake: for the earth is the Lord's, and the fulness thereof: 29 Conscience, I say, not thine own, but of the other: for why is my liberty judged of another man's conscience?

Paul is advising, (under inspiration) that it was perfectly all right to buy and eat meat that others had offered to idols, as the idol was nothing, and only what God thinks matters. This was all about not giving offence to other brothers. If you go to a feast, and there is meat offered to idols, just eat it, says Paul, unless your host makes an issue of it, and expects you to go along with that. In that case, refuse it politely, but if at all possible avoid the issue if you can. This was a completely new truth revealed by Christ to Paul as part of His 'Progressive Revelation' of Truth. Paul had to change his mind about so many different things, and so do we all in our progress, and as we grow in Grace and Knowledge.

Many of the Jews and throughout Judea began to wonder about all these changes, even those who had converted to Christianity, were very resistant to change. We have to be in order to grow.

There were yet more continuing differences of opinion in the Jerusalem camp. Fourteen years later Paul writes in Galatians.

Galatians 2:1 Then fourteen years after I went up again to Jerusalem with Barnabas, and took Titus with me also. 2 And I went up by revelation, and communicated unto them that gospel which I preach among the Gentiles, but privately to them which were of reputation, lest by any means I should run, or had run, in vain. 4 And that because of false brethren unawares brought in, who came in privily to spy out our liberty which we have in Christ Jesus, that they might bring us into bondage: 5 To whom we gave place by subjection, no, not for an hour; that the truth of the gospel might continue with you. 6 But of these who seemed to be somewhat, (whatsoever they were, it maketh no matter to me: God accepteth no man's person:) for they who seemed to be somewhat in conference added nothing to me: 7 But contrariwise, when they saw that the gospel of the uncircumcision was committed unto me, as the gospel of the circumcision was unto Peter; 8 (For he that wrought effectually in Peter to the apostleship of the circumcision, the same was mighty in me toward the Gentiles:)

Even among the disciples and Apostles, adapting to the new Truths which Christ was revealing to Paul was a more than difficult challenge to them. There was the great issue of the 'Law' which those dyed in the wool of Judaism were not willing to let go easily.

Galatians 2:9 And when James, Cephas, and John, who seemed to be pillars, perceived the grace that was given unto me, they gave to me and Barnabas the right hands of fellowship; that we should go unto the heathen, and they unto the circumcision. 10 Only they would that we should remember the poor; the same which I also was forward to do. 11 But when Peter was come to Antioch, I withstood him to the face, because he was to be blamed. 12 For before that certain came from James, he did eat with the Gentiles: but when they were come, he withdrew and separated himself, fearing them which were of the circumcision. 13 And the other Jews dissembled likewise with him; insomuch that Barnabas also was carried away with their dissimulation.

Very big arguments and trouble among the top people! God does not pull punches when He reveals the attitudes of their human side.

Galatians 2:14 But when I saw that they walked not uprightly according to the truth of the gospel, I said unto Peter before them all, If thou, being a Jew, livest after the manner of Gentiles, and not as do the Jews, why compellest thou the Gentiles to live as do the Jews?

Peter was still hanging on to his old concepts and ideas, and not changing with the appearance of new Truth as the New Gospel was being revealed to Paul by Christ.

Galatians 2:15 We who are Jews by nature, and not sinners of the Gentiles, 16 Knowing that a man is not justified by the works of the law, but by the faith of Jesus Christ, even we have believed in Jesus Christ, that we might be justified by the faith of Christ, and not by the works of the law: for by the works of the law shall no flesh be justified.

Christ through Paul was again making the point very strongly that the old attitudes to the Law had passed into history with the advent of New Truth.

Acts 21:17 And when we were come to Jerusalem, the brethren received us gladly. 18 And the day following Paul went in with us unto James; and all the elders were present. 19 And when he had saluted them, he declared particularly what things God had wrought among the Gentiles by his ministry. 20 And when they heard it, they glorified the Lord, and said unto him, Thou seest, brother, how many thousands of Jews there are which believe; and they are all zealous of the law: 21 And they are informed of thee, that thou teachest all the Jews which are among the Gentiles to forsake Moses, saying that they ought not to circumcise their children, neither to walk after the customs. 22 What is it therefore? the multitude must needs come together: for they will hear that thou art come.

James, who was not privy to all Christ was teaching Paul about the New Gospel, and a completely new approach to the Law, says in effect "Paul you are teaching that Jews do not have to keep the laws of Moses" which was a shock to him. He like us all found it difficult to adjust.

It is tragic that two thousand years later, some people think that they are superior Christians because they still attempt, (and fail miserably!) to keep aspects of the Law like the Sabbath and 'Clean and Unclean Meats', tithing and so on.

They do not realise that by attempting to keep the Law (which is totally impossible), they are actually denying the life, teaching and sacrifice of the Lord who bought them!!

The whole purpose of Christ coming to Earth was to free everyone up from bondage to the old law, and usher in His New Covenant of the Law of the Heart, and finally to reveal the 'mystery' to Paul in 63 A.D. It is impossible to keep one foot in the Old, and almost not even a toe in the New, and be a Christian, but blinded, they cannot see it.

Then when Paul learned about the 'mystery', what he learned about being able to be in heaven with Christ infuriated the Christians who still had the background of the Temple Laws.

The 'mystery' teaching was so radical, it meant they had to make more changes to the way they were used to thinking. Some even said that Paul had gone off his head, and was crazy. 2 Timothy written when Paul's life was near his end, everyone had deserted him.

2 Timothy 1:15 This thou knowest, that all they which are in Asia be turned away from me; of whom are Phygellus and Hermogenes.

Most around Paul had rejected the new truth that Christ had revealed to him.

2 Timothy 4:10 For Demas hath forsaken me, having loved this present world, and is departed unto Thessalonica; Crescens to Galatia, Titus unto Dalmatia. 11 Only Luke is with me.

Everyone had abandoned Paul, only Luke with him, all others had deserted him, Demas, and even Titus, … Paul was left to die a lonely man. It is no wonder God allows us who are in the ekklesia now to feel we are all alone in this world apart from our close connection with Christ Jesus.

Some older people feel they cannot change. Abraham was seventy-five years old before God asked him to cross the river, and he obeyed. When he was ninety-nine, God gave him the ritual of circumcision, and Abraham had to make a HUGE change and follow God, which of course he did. An example of willingness to change at any age!

The result of these changes means that our relationship with God changes, and we begin to learn more about Him and the way He thinks, and find we are able to love Him more than ever.

When we look at First and Second Peter, they are so very different that scholars question whether they were written by the same person, but of course they were.

When we read John's Gospel, it is so completely different from the three earlier Gospels, and this was because God had been revealing more truth to those who were close to God even at that time in the end of the first century A.D.

We have to be willing to change in this 21st century, or how can we grow in grace and knowledge. We all have to have the attitude of continual repentance, and it is beautiful and wonderful to embrace the changes that God sends to us in the expansion of His Government.

Attitude is everything! Willingness to change and continual repentance are the only safe way forward for those who are now 'in Christ'

Isaiah 9:6 For unto us a child is born, unto us a son is given: and the government shall be upon his shoulder: and his name shall be called Wonderful, Counsellor, The mighty God, The everlasting Father, The Prince of Peace. 7 Of the increase of his government and peace there shall be no end, upon the throne of David, and upon his kingdom, to order it, and to establish it with judgment and with justice from henceforth even for ever. The zeal of the LORD of hosts will perform this.

CHAPTER 6

THE NATURE AND HEART OF HUMAN BEINGS

Jeremiah 17:9 The heart is deceitful above all things, and desperately wicked: who can know it?

So humans start off at a considerable disadvantage when it comes to emulating the Love of God. However, God deals with each one of us individually He knows all our frailties and our strengths.

Jeremiah 17:10 I the LORD search the heart, I try the reins, even to give every man (person) according to his ways, and according to the fruit of his doings.

The heart 'attitude' in the Bible

Our first responsible in the realm of love is to love God with all our heart mind and being. We need to realise that being saved is a gift, and know and appreciate that regardless of anything we are or do, we are 'saved', and will one day be glorified and become part of the family of God. No works on our part are needed, Christ did all the work that was needed for this to happen.

Although being 'saved' and given Eternal Life is a Gift from God for all, it is important to understand that there are still works for a Christian to do if we want to be granted a position in the Kingdom of God and reign with Christ a thousand years. If we neglect Christian works, we may miss out on the initial Kingdom Phase and have to sleep in death until the second resurrection when all will be given the opportunity to become part of God's Family.

Deuteronomy 10:12 And now, Israel, (Christians are the Israel of God) what doth the LORD thy God require of thee, but to fear the LORD thy God, to walk in all his ways, and to love him, and to serve the LORD thy God with all thy heart and with all thy soul,

Deuteronomy 11:13 And it shall come to pass, if ye shall hearken diligently unto my commandments which I command you this day, to love the Lord your God, and to serve him with all your heart and with all your soul

Matthew 22:37 Jesus said unto him, Thou shalt love the Lord thy God with all thy heart, and with all thy soul, and with all thy mind.

The Human spirit, mind, heart, and attitude make up who we really are. While the human body is temporary, the spirit of a person is potentially eternal. This is why we are exhorted to have an attitude of constantly growing and developing our spirit in Grace and Knowledge to become more like our Father and Christ.

When Christ says through Paul in Philippians:

Philippians 2:5 Let this mind (heart, attitude) be in you, which was also in Christ Jesus:

But what exactly is the mind of Christ. It is explained in the previous verse.

Philippians 2:4 Look not every man on his own things, but every man also on the things of others.

While taking proper care of ourselves, our focus to the maximum of our ability is to be emulating the Love of God.

God's love could be expressed as 'outgoing concern for others' as evidenced by His Love for us.

John 13:34 A new commandment I give unto you, That ye love one another; as I have loved you, that ye also love one another.

James 2:8 If ye fulfil the royal law according to the scripture, Thou shalt love thy neighbour as thyself, ye do well:

This is of course only one aspect of His love, but this should be our constant attitude of mind and heart every day.

Jesus Christ said to His disciples and to us today:

Matthew 6:19 Lay not up for yourselves treasures upon earth, where moth and rust doth corrupt, and where thieves break through and steal:

Why not? Because everything physical about us is temporary, and will pass away when we turn to dust in death, or are resurrected into the Kingdom.

Matthew 6:20 But lay up for yourselves treasures in heaven, where neither moth nor rust doth corrupt, and where thieves do not break through nor steal:

Christ is telling us WHY we are to grow in Grace and Knowledge. It is because the attitude of learning, development, and training our spirit and mind in the Word and Thoughts of God results in ***permanent changes in our beingness.***

The treasures that each of us lays up for ourselves in heaven will become a permanent part of us in our new life as fully fledged children of God. The more we use our talents to develop Godliness, the greater will be our reward in the Kingdom of Heaven.

Two parables emphasise that in this life we are to be making the best use of our talents, hearts and minds. This will be part of our 'treasures in heaven'.

The Parable of the Talents or pounds in Luke

Luke 19:13 And he (Christ) called his ten servants, and delivered them ten pounds, and said unto them, Occupy till I come… 15 And it came to pass, that when he was returned (at the second coming), having received the kingdom, then he commanded these servants to be called unto him (in the Kingdom!), to whom he had given the money, that he might know how much every man had gained by trading. 16 Then came the first, saying, Lord, thy pound hath gained ten pounds. 17 And he (Christ) said unto him, Well, thou good servant: because thou hast been faithful in a very little, have thou authority over ten cities. 18 And the second came, saying, Lord, thy pound hath gained five pounds. 19 And he (Christ) said likewise to him, Be thou also over five cities.

The Parable of the Talents in Matthew

Matthew 25:14 For the kingdom of heaven is as a man travelling into a far country, who called his own servants, and delivered unto them his goods. 15 And unto one he gave five talents, to another two, and to another one; to every man according to his several ability; and straightway took his journey. 16 Then he that had received the five talents went and traded with the same, and made them other five talents. 17 And likewise he that had received two, he also gained other two… 19 After a long time the lord of those servants cometh, and reckoneth with them. 20 And so he that had received five talents came and brought other five talents, saying, Lord, thou deliveredst unto me five talents: behold, I have gained beside them five talents more. 21 His lord said unto him, Well done, thou good and faithful servant: thou hast been faithful over a few things, I will make thee ruler over many things: enter thou into the joy of thy lord. 22 He also that had received two talents came and said, Lord, thou deliveredst unto me two talents: behold, I have gained two other talents beside them. 23 His lord said unto him, Well done, good and faithful servant; thou hast been faithful over a few things, I will make thee ruler over many things: enter thou into the joy of thy lord.

Both these stories tell of a person who did nothing with the pound or the talent he had been given, so it was taken from them and given to those who had made the most of the talents they had been given. There is a lesson there for everyone to heed.

Isaiah 40:10 Behold, the Lord God (Christ) will come with strong hand, and his arm shall rule for him: behold, his **reward** is with him, and his work before him.

Christ will bring His reward with Him when He returns.

Isaiah 62:11 Behold, the Lord hath proclaimed unto the end of the world, Say ye to the daughter of Zion, Behold, thy salvation cometh; behold, his **reward** is with him, and his work before him.

1 Corinthians 3:8 Now he that planteth and he that watereth are one: and every man shall receive his own **reward** according to his own labour… 3:14 If any man's work abide which he hath built thereupon, he shall receive a **reward**.

Revelation 22:12 And, behold, I come quickly; and my **reward** is with me, to give every man according as his work shall be.

The word Heart includes our Attitudes of Mind

The old English word heorte, now spelled 'heart' since circa 1500, *literally* means the hollow muscular organ that circulates blood.

Figuratively the word heart does embrace and include the attitude of mind, spirit, will, intellect, soul (dust+spirit+breath = the whole person);

Most of the modern figurative senses were present in Old English from 1500 A.D. onwards, including "memory" from the notion of the heart as the seat of all mental faculties, learn 'by heart'.

The ***heart*** is the 'seat' of inmost feelings; the will; seat of emotions, especially love and affection; seat of courage. It also means the 'inner part of anything' like a cabbage, which goes back to the earlier 14th Century.

'Heart' in the Bible reveals many things about human thought and attitudes. In the Old Testament Hebrew: Strong's Hebrew 3820 *ble — leb, labe; a form of 3824; the heart; also used (figuratively) very widely for the feelings, the will and even the intellect; likewise for the centre of anything: — + care for, comfortably, consent, X considered, courag(-eous), friend(-ly), ((broken-), (hard-), (merry-), (stiff-), (stout-), double) heart((-ed)),X heed, X I, kindly, midst, mind(-ed), X regard((-ed)), X themselves, X unawares, understanding, X well, willingly, wisdom.*

The first time the 3820 word 'heart' appears in the Bible is in Genesis 6:5

Genesis 6:5 And God saw that the wickedness of man was great in the earth, and that every imagination of the thoughts of his ***heart*** was only evil continually.

The Bible interprets itself, and here the 'heart' figuratively (and literally!) embraces and includes 'every imagination' and 'the thoughts' of human beings. So the 'heart' is clearly an extension of the brain and the mind.

In fact, there is a concept in physical health care that the heart is the 'second brain' of the body. Examination of its activities clearly reveals that to an extent it acts independently of the brain in the regulation of its pumping activities. An amazing truth!

Heart Strong's 3824 *bb;le — lebab, lay-bawb'; from 3823; the heart (as the most interior organ); used also like 3820: — + bethink themselves, breast, comfortably, courage, ((faint), (tender-) heart((-ed)), midst, 348 mind, X unawares, understanding.*

Strong's 3824 first appears in Genesis 20:5-6 in relation to 'integrity' which is an attitude of mind.

Genesis 20:5 Said he not unto me, She is my sister? and she, even she herself said, He is my brother: in *the integrity of my heart* and innocency of my hands have I done this. 6 And God said unto him in a dream, Yea, I know that thou didst this in *the integrity of thy heart*; for I also withheld thee from sinning against me: therefore suffered I thee not to touch her.

Heart Strong's 4578 *h[,me — me`ah, may-aw'; from an unused root probably meaning to be soft; used only in plural the intestines, or (collectively) the abdomen, figuratively, sympathy; by implication, a vest; by extension the stomach, the uterus (or of men, the seat of generation), the heart (figuratively): — belly, bowels, X heart, womb.*

Strong's 4578 first appears in Psalm 40:8

Psalm 40:8 I delight to do thy will, O my God: yea, thy law is within my heart.

This Hebrew word for heart includes the meanings of 'soft' and 'sympathy'. In Acts, David was described as a man after God's own heart.

Acts 13:22 And when he (God) had removed him, he (God) raised up unto them David to be their king; to whom also he gave their testimony, and said, I have found David the son of Jesse, *a man after mine own heart (Strong's Gr. 2588, kardi>a, — kar-dee'-ah; the heart, i.e. (figurative) the thoughts or feelings (mind);) which shall fulfil all my will. 23 Of this man's seed hath God according to his promise raised unto Israel a Saviour, Jesus:*

Heart Strong's 5315, — *nephesh, neh'-fesh; from 5314; properly, a breathing creature, i.e. animal of (abstractly) vitality; used very widely in a literal, accommodated or figurative sense (bodily or mental): — any, appetite, beast, body, breath, creature, desire, (dis-) contented, greedy, lust, man, me, mind, mortally, one, own, person, pleasure, (her-, him-, my-, thy-) self,*

Strong's 5315 first appears in Exodus 23:9

Exodus 23:9 Also thou shalt not oppress a stranger: for ye know the heart of a stranger, seeing ye were strangers in the land of Egypt.

In other words, you know what it feels like to be a stranger in a foreign land.

'Heart' in the Bible reveals many things about human thought and attitudes. In the New Testament Greek

Strong's Greek 2588 *kardi>a, — kar-dee'-ah; prolonged from a primary ka>r (Latin cor, "heart"); the heart, i.e. (figurative) the thoughts or feelings (mind); also (by analogy) the middle: — (+ broken-) heart (-ed).*

In English we have Cardiac from the Greek kardia relating to the physical heart. There are many figurative meanings of 'heart' in English. E.G. take heart, kind hearted, broken hearted, and so on.

2588 kardia is first used in Matthew 5:8

Matthew 5:8 Blessed are the pure in **heart**: *for they shall see God.*

Hardness of heart: Strong's **4641** *sklhrokardi>a, — sklay-rok-ar-dee'-ah; feminine; hardheartedness, i.e. (special) destitution of (spiritual) perception: — hardness of heart.*

Mark 10:5 And Jesus answered and said unto them, For the hardness of your **heart** he wrote you this precept.

5590 *yuch>, — psoo-khay'; from (5594) (yu>cw); breath, i.e. (by implication) spirit, abstract or concrete (the animal sentient principle only; thus distinguished on the one hand from (4151) (pneu~ma), which is the rational and immortal(!) soul; and on the other from (2222) (zwh>), which is mere vitality, even of plants: these terms thus exactly correspond respectively to the Hebrew Hebrew {5315} (nephesh), Hebrew {7307} (ruwach) and Hebrew {2416} (chay)): — heart (+ -ily), life, mind, soul, + us, + you.*

Ephesians 6:6 Not with eyeservice, as menpleasers; but as the servants of Christ, doing the will of God from the **heart**;

Attitudes of heart and mind.

Adulterous heart Matthew 5:28 But I say unto you, That whosoever looketh on a woman to lust after her hath committed adultery with her already in his **heart**.

Answering heart 1 Peter 3:15 But sanctify the Lord God in your **heart**s: and be ready always to give an answer to every man that asketh you a reason of the hope that is in you with meekness and fear:

Astonishment, madness and blindness of heart

Deuteronomy 28:28 The Lord shall smite thee with madness, and blindness, and astonishment of **heart**:

When it says 'astonishment' it is in the sense of consternation, not a good feeling.

Bible study heart Hebrews 4:12 For the word of God is quick, and powerful, and sharper than any two-edged sword, piercing even to the dividing asunder of soul and spirit, and of the joints and marrow, and is a discerner of the thoughts and intents of the **heart**.

Blame-free loving heart 1 Thessalonians 3:12 And the Lord make you to increase and abound in love one toward another, and toward all men, even as we do toward you: 13 To the end he may stablish your **heart**s unblameable in holiness before God, even our Father, at the coming of our Lord Jesus Christ with all his saints.

Blinded to self heart Isaiah 10:7 Howbeit he meaneth not so, neither doth his **heart** think so; but it is in his **heart** to destroy and cut off nations not a few.

Broken heart Psalm 34:18 The Lord is nigh unto them that are of a broken **heart**; and saveth such as be of a contrite spirit.

Cautious thinking heart Proverbs 15:28 The **heart** of the righteous studieth to answer: but the mouth of the wicked poureth out evil things.

Cheerful giving heart 2 Corinthians 9:7 Every man according as he purposeth in his **heart**, so let him give; not grudgingly, or of necessity: for God loveth a cheerful giver.

Clean heart with a right spirit Psalm 51:10 Create in me a clean **heart**, O God; and renew a right spirit within me.

Contrite heart, broken spirit Psalm 51:17 The sacrifices of God are a broken spirit: a broken and a contrite **heart**, O God, thou wilt not despise.

Circumcised heart Deuteronomy 30:6 And the Lord thy God will circumcise thine **heart**, and the **heart** of thy seed, to love the Lord thy God with all thine **heart**, and with all thy soul, that thou mayest live.

Conscience smitten heart 1 Samuel 24:5 And it came to pass afterward, that David's **heart** smote him, because he had cut off Saul's skirt.

Consult and consider your heart Deuteronomy 7:17 If thou shalt say in thine **heart**, These nations are more than I; how can I dispossess them? ... 8:5 Thou shalt also consider in thine **heart**, that, as a man chasteneth his son, so the Lord thy God chasteneth thee.

Covetous 'religious' heart Ezekiel 33:31 And they come unto thee as the people cometh, and they sit before thee as my people, and they hear thy words, but they will not do them: for with their mouth they shew much love, but their **heart** goeth after their covetousness.

Cursed heart Jeremiah 17:5 Thus saith the Lord; Cursed be the man that trusteth in man, and maketh flesh his arm, and whose **heart** departeth from the Lord.

Deaf and dumb heart of people not called Isaiah 6:10 Make the **heart** of this people fat, and make their ears heavy, and shut their eyes; lest they see with their eyes, and hear with their ears, and understand with their **heart**, and convert, and be healed. Isaiah 44:18 They have not known nor understood: for he hath shut their eyes, that they cannot see; and their **heart**s, that they cannot understand.

Deceived heart Deuteronomy 11:16 Take heed to yourselves, that your **heart** be not deceived, and ye turn aside, and serve other gods, and worship them;

Deceitful heart Jeremiah 9:8 Their tongue is as an arrow shot out; it speaketh deceit: one speaketh peaceably to his neighbour with his mouth, but in **heart** he layeth his wait.

Jeremiah 17:9 The **heart** is deceitful above all things, and desperately wicked: who can know it?

Delayed hope makes a sick heart Proverbs 13:12 Hope deferred maketh the **heart** sick: but when the desire cometh, it is a tree of life.

Despising heart 2 Samuel 6:16 And as the ark of the LORD came into the city of David, Michal Saul's daughter looked through a window, and saw king David leaping and dancing before the LORD; and she despised him in her heart.

Diligent heart Proverbs 4:23 Keep thy **heart** with all diligence; for out of it are the issues of life.

Discouragement of heart Numbers 32:7 And wherefore discourage ye the **heart** of the children of Israel from going over into the land which the Lord hath given them?

Double hearted, double minded Psalm 12:2 They speak vanity every one with his neighbour: with flattering lips and with a double **heart** do they speak.

James 1:8 A **double minded** man is unstable in all his ways. James 4:8 Draw nigh to God, and he will draw nigh to you. Cleanse your hands, ye sinners; and purify your hearts, ye **double minded**.

Drunken homosexual heart Judges 19:22 Now as they were making their **heart**s merry, behold, the men of the city, certain sons of Belial, ...*Bring forth the man that came into thine house, that we may know (have a carnal relationship with) him. (sexually)*

Ego heart Deuteronomy 8:17 And thou say in thine **heart**, My power and the might of mine hand hath gotten me this wealth.

Evil imagining heart Zechariah 8:17 And let none of you imagine evil in your **heart**s against his neighbour; and love no false oath: for all these are things that I hate, saith the Lord.

Evil thoughts and words defile a person's heart
Matthew 15:18 But those things which proceed out of the mouth come forth from the **heart**; and they defile the man. 19 For out of the **heart** proceed evil thoughts, murders, adulteries, fornications, thefts, false witness, blasphemies:

Envying heart Proverbs 23:17: Let not thine **heart** envy sinners: but be thou in the fear of the Lord all the day long.

False prophet's heart Jeremiah 23:16 Thus saith the Lord of hosts, Hearken not unto the words of the prophets that prophesy unto you: they make you vain: they speak a vision of their own **heart**, and not out of the mouth of the Lord. 23:26 How long shall this be in the **heart** of the prophets that prophesy lies? yea, they are prophets of the deceit of their own **heart**;

Family caring heart Malachi 4:6 And he shall turn the **heart** of the fathers to the children, and the **heart** of the children to their fathers, lest I come and smite the earth with a curse.

Failure, fearfulness of heart Genesis 42:28 And he said unto his brethren, My money is restored; and, lo, it is even in my sack: and their **heart** failed them, and they were afraid, saying one to another, What is this that God hath done unto us?

Fainthearted, fearful, trembling, terrified Deuteronomy 20:3 let not your **heart**s faint, fear not, and do not tremble, neither be ye terrified because of them; Leviticus 26:36 And upon them that are left alive of you I (God) will send a faintness into their **heart**s in the lands of their enemies;

Fasting heart Joel 2:12 Therefore also now, saith the Lord, turn ye even to me with all your **heart**, and with fasting, and with weeping, and with mourning:

Fixed, stable, perfect, established heart Psalm 57:7 My heart is fixed, O God, **my heart is fixed:** I will sing and give praise. Psalm 108:1 O God, my **heart is fixed**; I will sing and give praise, even with my glory. Psalm 112:7 He shall not be afraid of evil tidings: **his heart is fixed,** trusting in the LORD.

Strong's 3559 Fixed — kuwn, koon; a primitive root; properly, to be erect, to set up, render sure, proper or prosperous, certainty, confirm, direct, faithfulness, fashion, fasten, firm, be stable be fitted, be fixed, be meet (fitting), perfect, prepared, established, stand.

Fearful heart Isaiah 35:4 Say to them that are of a fearful **heart**, Be strong, fear not: behold, your God will come with vengeance, even God with a recompence; he will come and save you.

Fool's heart Psalm 14:1 The fool hath said in his **heart**, There is no God. They are corrupt, they have done abominable works, there is none that doeth good.

Psalm 53:1 The fool hath said in his **heart**, There is no God. Corrupt are they, and have done abominable iniquity: there is none that doeth good.

Forgiving heart Matthew 18:35 So likewise shall my heavenly Father do also unto you, if ye from your **heart**s forgive not every one his brother their trespasses.

Froward, rebellious heart Psalm 101:4 A froward **heart** shall depart from me: I will not know a wicked person.

Gladness of heart Exodus 4:14 And the anger of the Lord was kindled against Moses, and he said, Is not Aaron the Levite thy brother? I know that he can speak well. And also, behold, he cometh forth to meet thee: and when he seeth thee, he will be glad in his **heart**.

God-given heart 1 Samuel 10:9 And it was so, that when he had turned his back to go from Samuel, God gave him another **heart**: and all those signs came to pass that day. Jeremiah 24:7 And I will give them an **heart** to know me, that I am the Lord: and they shall be my people, and I will be their God: for they shall return unto me with their whole **heart**. 29:13 And ye shall seek me, and find me, when ye shall search for me with all your **heart**. 32:39 And I will give them one **heart**, and one way, that they may fear me for ever, for the good of them, and of their children after them: Ezekiel 36:26 A new **heart** also will I give you, and a new spirit will I put within you: and I will take away the stony **heart** out of your flesh, and I will give you an **heart** of flesh.

Godless heart Deuteronomy 8:14 Then thine **heart** be lifted up, and thou forget the Lord thy God, which brought thee forth out of the land of Egypt, from the house of bondage;

God-touched hearts 1 Samuel 10:26 And Saul also went home to Gibeah; and there went with him a band of men, whose **heart**s God had touched.

Good servant's heart Colossians 3:22 Servants, obey in all things your masters according to the flesh; not with eyeservice, as menpleasers; but in singleness of heart, fearing God; 23 And whatsoever ye do, do it heartily, as to the Lord, and not unto men; 24 Knowing that of the Lord ye shall receive the reward of the inheritance: for ye serve the Lord Christ.

Grieving heart Psalm 73:21 Thus my **heart** was grieved, and I was pricked in my reins.

Happy or sad heart Proverbs 15:13 A merry **heart** maketh a cheerful countenance: but by sorrow of the **heart** the spirit is broken.

Hardness of heart Exodus 4:21 see that thou do all those wonders before Pharaoh, which I have put in thine hand: but I will harden his **heart**, that he shall not let the people go.

Heart of good treasure and attitude, or evil

Matthew 12:5 A good man out of the good treasure of the **heart** bringeth forth good things: and an evil man out of the evil treasure bringeth forth evil things.

Luke 6:45 A good man out of the good treasure of his **heart** bringeth forth that which is good; and an evil man out of the evil treasure of his **heart** bringeth forth that which is evil: for of the abundance of the **heart** his mouth speaketh.

Heart exalted by riches is punished Ezekiel 28:5 By thy great wisdom and by thy traffick hast thou increased thy riches, and thine **heart** is lifted up because of thy riches: 6 Therefore thus saith the Lord God; Because thou hast set thine heart as the heart of God; 7 Behold, therefore I will bring strangers upon thee, the terrible of the nations: and they shall draw their swords against the beauty of thy wisdom, and they shall defile thy brightness.

Heart – poor law enforcement - the key to more evil Ecclesiastes 8:11 Because sentence against an evil work is not executed speedily, therefore the **heart** of the sons of men is fully set in them to do evil.

Heart speaks through the mouth Matthew 12:34 O generation **of** vipers, how can ye, being evil, speak good things? for out **of the abundance of the heart the** mouth speaketh.

Heart stirs up spirit Exodus 35:21 And they came, every one whose **heart** stirred him up, and every one whom his spirit made willing,

Heart that plans and invents wicked imaginations
Proverbs 6:18 An **heart** that deviseth wicked imaginations, feet that be swift in running to mischief,

Heart that rejects instruction and reproof

Proverbs 5:12 And say, How have I hated instruction, and my **heart** despised reproof;

Heart which turns away from God Deuteronomy 29:18 Lest there should be among you man, or woman, or family, or tribe, whose **heart** turneth away this day from the Lord our God

Human Limited heart Ecclesiastes 3:11 He (God) hath made every thing beautiful in his time: also he hath set the world in their **heart**, so that no man can find out the work that God maketh from the beginning to the end. Ecclesiastes 8:17 Then I beheld all the work of God, that a man (**a man's mind or his heart**) cannot find out the work that is done under the sun: because though a man labour to seek it out, yet he shall not find it; yea farther; though a wise man think to know it, yet shall he not be able to find it.

Hasty heart Ecclesiastes 5:2 Be not rash with thy mouth, and let not thine **heart** be hasty to utter any thing before God: for God is in heaven, and thou upon earth: therefore let thy words be few.

Hateful attitude of heart Leviticus 19:17 Thou shalt not hate thy brother in thine **heart**: thou shalt in any wise rebuke thy neighbour, and not suffer sin upon him.

Haughty hearts lead to destruction Proverbs 18:12 Before destruction the **heart** of man is haughty, and before honour is humility.

Investing in heaven heart Matthew 6:21 For where your treasure is, there will your heart be also.

Knowledge seeking heart Proverbs 15:14 The **heart** of him that hath understanding seeketh knowledge: but the mouth of fools feedeth on foolishness.

Love in deed and truth heart 1 John 3:18 My little children, let us not love in word, neither in tongue; but in deed and in truth. 19 And hereby we know that we are of the truth, and shall assure our hearts before him. 20 For if our heart condemn us, God is greater than our heart, and knoweth all things.21 Beloved, if our **heart** condemn us not, then have we confidence toward God.

Lusting heart Proverbs 6:25 Lust not after her beauty in thine **heart**; neither let her take thee with her eyelids.

Meditating heart Psalm 19:14 Let the words of my mouth, and the meditation of my **heart**, be acceptable in thy sight, O Lord, my strength, and my redeemer.

Merry hearts are healthy Proverbs 17:22 A merry **heart** doeth good like a medicine: but a broken spirit drieth the bones.

Murderous heart *Genesis 27:41* And Esau hated Jacob because of the blessing wherewith his father blessed him: and Esau said in his **heart**, The days of mourning for my father are at hand; then will I slay my brother Jacob.

Obstinate heart Deuteronomy 2:30 But Sihon king of Heshbon would not let us pass by him: for the Lord thy God hardened his spirit, and made his **heart** obstinate,

Perfect heart a gift of God 1 Chronicles 29:19 And give unto Solomon my son a perfect **heart**, to keep thy commandments, thy testimonies, and thy statutes, and to do all these things, and to build the palace, for the which I have made provision.

Oppress nobody heart Zechariah 7:10 And oppress not the widow, nor the fatherless, the stranger, nor the poor;

and let none of you imagine evil against his brother in your **heart**.

Patient heart 2 Thessalonians 3:5 And the Lord direct your **heart**s into the love of God, and into the patient waiting for Christ.

Perverse heart sows discord Proverbs 6:14 Frowardness is in his **heart**, he deviseth mischief continually; he soweth discord.

Proverbs 6:19 A false witness that speaketh lies, and he that soweth **discord** among brethren.

Proud heart Deuteronomy 17:20 That his **heart** be not lifted up above his brethren, and that he turn not aside from the commandment, to the right hand, or to the left: Psalm 101:5 Whoso privily slandereth his neighbour, him will I cut off: him that hath an high look and a proud **heart** will not I suffer.

Proud heart is abomination to the Lord Proverbs 16:5 Every one that is proud in **heart** is an abomination to the Lord: though hand join in hand, he shall not be unpunished.

Prudent, sagacious, circumspect hearts Proverbs 18:15 The **heart** of the prudent getteth knowledge; and the ear of the wise seeketh knowledge.

Pure heart Psalm 24:14 He that hath clean hands, and a pure **heart**; who hath not lifted up his soul unto vanity, nor sworn deceitfully. Matthew 5:8 Blessed are the **pure in heart**: for they shall see God.

Pure unfeigned heart 1 Timothy 1:5 Now the end of the commandment is charity (love) out of a pure **heart**, and of a good conscience, and of faith unfeigned:

Purposeful, self-disciplined heart Daniel 1:8 But Daniel purposed in his **heart** that he would not defile himself with the portion of the king's meat, nor with the wine which he drank: therefore he requested of the prince of the eunuchs that he might not defile himself.

Rebellious, revolting heart that does not fear God

Jeremiah 5:23 But this people hath a revolting and a rebellious heart; they are revolted and gone. 24 Neither say they in their heart, Let us now fear the LORD our God, that giveth rain, both the former and the latter, in his season: he reserveth unto us the appointed weeks of the harvest.

Rejoicing heart Psalm 19:8 The statutes of the Lord are right, rejoicing the **heart**: the commandment of the Lord is pure, enlightening the eyes.

Religious, 'Churchianity' heart Isaiah 29:13 Wherefore the Lord said, Forasmuch as this people draw near me with their mouth, and with their lips do honour me, but have removed their **heart** far from me, and their fear toward me is taught by the precept of men: Matthew 15:8 This people draweth nigh unto me with their mouth, and honoureth me with their **lips**; but their **heart** is far from me.

Secretive heart Psalm 44:21 Shall not God search this out? for he knoweth the secrets of the **heart**.

Self-deceived heart Deuteronomy 29:19 And it come to pass, when he heareth the words of this curse, that he bless himself in his **heart**, saying, I shall have peace, though I walk in the imagination of mine **heart**, to add drunkenness to thirst:

Self directed heart Proverbs 16:9 A man's **heart** deviseth his way: but the Lord directeth his steps.

Sorrowness of heart Leviticus 26:16 I also will do this unto you; I will even appoint over you terror, consumption, and the burning ague, that shall consume the eyes, and cause sorrow of **heart**:

Seeking heart loving God with heart and soul Deuteronomy 4:29 But if from thence thou shalt seek the Lord thy God, thou shalt find him, if thou seek him with all thy **heart** and with all thy soul.

Self-righteous hearts Proverbs 21:2 Every way of a man is right in his own eyes: but the Lord pondereth the **heart**s.

Sober, serious heart Ecclesiastes 7:4 The **heart** of the wise is in the house of mourning; but the **heart** of fools is in the house of mirth.

Spirit sealed heart 2 Corinthians 1:22 Who hath also sealed us, and given the earnest of the Spirit in our **heart**s. Galatians 4:6 And because ye are sons, God hath sent forth the Spirit of his Son into your **heart**s, crying, Abba, Father.

Stiffnecked heart Deuteronomy 6:16 Circumcise therefore the foreskin of your **heart**, and be no more stiffnecked.

Stony heart Zechariah 7:12 Yea, they made their **heart**s as an adamant stone, lest they should hear the law, and the words which the Lord of hosts hath sent in his spirit by the former prophets: therefore came a great wrath from the Lord of hosts.

Subtle whorish heart Proverbs 7:10 And, behold, there met him a woman with the attire of an harlot, and subtil of **heart**.

Talk with your heart – know its attitude Ecclesiastes 1:16 I communed with mine own **heart**, saying, Lo, I am come to great estate, and have gotten more wisdom than all they that have been before me in Jerusalem: yea, my **heart** had great experience of wisdom and knowledge. Ecclesiastes 2:15 Then said I in my **heart**, As it happeneth to the fool, so it happeneth even to me; and why was I then more wise? Then I said in my **heart**, that this also is vanity.

Tenderhearted, humble 2 Kings 22:9 Because thine **heart** was tender, and thou hast humbled thyself before the Lord,

Trust God, not your own heart Proverbs 3:5 Trust in the Lord with all thine **heart**; and lean not unto thine own understanding.

Tongue controlled deceived heart James 1:26 If any man among you seem to be religious, and bridleth not his tongue, but deceiveth his own **heart**, this man's religion is vain.

Unbelieving heart Hebrews 3:12 Take heed, brethren, lest there be in any of you an evil **heart** of unbelief, in departing from the living God.

Uncircumcised heart Leviticus 26:42 And that I (God) also have walked contrary unto them, and have brought them into the land of their enemies; if then their uncircumcised **heart**s be humbled, and they then accept of the punishment of their iniquity:

Unperceptive, blind and deaf heart Deuteronomy 29:4 Yet the Lord hath not given you an **heart** to perceive, and eyes to see, and ears to hear, unto this day.

Untroubled heart John 14:1 Let not your **heart** be troubled: ye believe in God, believe also in me. 14:27 Peace I leave with you, my peace I give unto you: not as the world giveth, give I unto you. Let not your **heart** be troubled, neither let it be afraid.

Upright in heart Psalm 32:11 Be glad in the Lord, and rejoice, ye righteous: and shout for joy, all ye that are upright in heart.

Vain and foolish heart Romans 1:21 Because that, when they knew God, they glorified him not as God, neither were thankful; but became vain in their imaginations, and their foolish **heart** was darkened.... 24 Wherefore God also gave them up to uncleanness through the lusts of their own **heart**s, to dishonour their own bodies between themselves:

Whoring heart Numbers 15:39 and that ye seek not after your own **heart** and your own eyes, after which ye use to go a whoring:

Wicked thinking heart Deuteronomy 15:9 Beware that there be not a thought in thy wicked **heart**,

Willingness of heart Exodus 25:2 Speak unto the children of Israel, that they bring me an offering: of every man that giveth it willingly with his **heart** ye shall take my offering.

Wisdom of heart in skilled work Exodus 35:35 Them hath he filled with wisdom of heart, to work all manner of work, of the engraver, and of the cunning workman, and of the embroiderer, in blue, and in purple, in scarlet, and in fine linen, and of the weaver, even of them that do any work, and of those that devise cunning work.

Wisdom seeking heart Ecclesiastes 7:25 I applied mine **heart** to know, and to search, and to seek out wisdom, and the reason of things, and to know the wickedness of folly, even of foolishness and madness:

Wise hearted Exodus 28:3 And thou shalt speak unto all that are wise **heart**ed, whom I have filled with the spirit of wisdom,

Wholehearted Psalm 119:10 With my whole **heart** have I sought thee: O let me not wander from thy commandments.

Wisdom and knowledge in the heart Proverbs 2:10 When wisdom entereth into thine **heart**, and knowledge is pleasant unto thy soul;

CHAPTER 7

THE DEVELOPMENT OF TRUE SPIRITUALITY

How does God go about promoting genuine spirituality, love of God and our fellow human beings?

Most people think that God uses His Supernatural Powers in many ways to accomplish this. Yes God does teach people how to love Him and our neighbour which is everyone in the world. God can do this by both external and internal means.

In the Bible there is a good deal of evidence showing that God has applied many physical pressures on His children to further His purposes. But have those pressures He used in an external way resulted in permanent change in the attitude of His people, and enabled them to develop proper spirituality?

This use of external means to develop humans can be, and have been, beneficial in a temporary way historically, but very rarely if ever had a permanent or satisfying result.

What sort of external pressures has God used and will use in the future? They can be very profound. He can show an abundance of miracles to people to demonstrate Who He Is. Like the miracles of the plagues of Egypt, parting of the Red Sea in the Exodus; or the daily provision of manna in the desert for forty years every day except the Sabbath which was miracle in itself! The fact that their shoes did not wear out as they tramped those forty years in the desert!

But did any of these miracles result in a change of heart in those Israelites, the people of God? No it did not, and so apart from just two people, for their many rebellions against God, all those around two million Israelites died in Sinai, and only their children were allowed to enter the Promised Land. One can read of an almost endless number of miracles where God has dealt with people in a physical manner.

Christ worked a huge number of miracles in the course of His ministry. They were evidence that Christ was a Special Person, and they affected many thousands of people some even believed He was the Son of God. Christ turned huge containers of water into wine, performed miraculous healings galore, fed thousands from a few loaves and fishes, and even raised the dead, these and many other miracles were known to the religious Pharisees and secular leaders. But the question is did they result in any significant change in the people of that time? No, the entire population forgot all about the miracles He had performed and chose a robber to be set free, and crucified Christ. The effect of these awesome miracles did not last long, did they?

And over the centuries since that time, has the knowledge of these miraculous events resulted in any permanent change in the spiritual attitude of humanity towards their heavenly Father? A quick view of history, and an objective look at the state of our present evil world, tells us that none of God's outpouring of miracles to show His Power and Love for has changed the hearts and behaviour of humanity. Nor has it led them to become truly 'spiritual' according to God's wishes and intentions.

Miracles are one form of influence, but God has used many other means including external judgements and punishment for disobedience, even a religious system to control them, and these run as a thread throughout the Bible. But have these punishments been effective or result in a permanent change of heart or inculcate spirituality in humanity?

What about God putting in force a religious system where people were forced to live in a certain way, and practice righteousness under threat of punishment, and were governed from dawn to dusk every day of their lives. Has that ever happened in history? It did under the Mosaic Law. Did it work to change people's minds and hearts in a permanent way?

Religious practices which people involve themselves in are all external, although they may also have an internal effect, this does not always bring about any of the real form of true spirituality that God wants us to experience. Neither did all the punishments result in any permanent change, nor did the miracles.

The Bible shows very clearly that none of these three major pressures that God has used changed people even externally, some have perhaps had some internal effect. It is true that there have sometimes been some slight temporary benefits, but have not resulted in a permanent change in the way people behave or how they use their passions in sinful ways.

Most people think of these three things, miracles, punishment, and religion as the means whereby God creates spirituality, but clearly they have failed to bring about any long lasting development of proper spirituality. They have not had the effect of transforming the heart of humanity to behave in ways that are more like God's heart and character, with His Love, His Wisdom, His understanding. Time without number history shows that none of these things God has used have resulted in the development of more Godlike behaviour in humanity.

Paul explains in the book of Corinthians that that group of people were earnestly seeking gifts, but they were all physical gifts. However they were also committing every type of physical misdeed, and Paul makes this plain. He eventually explains in forceful terms that they should have been seeking the Spiritual gifts.

God wants us to seek his gifts, but the important ones are the spiritual gifts of love, compassion, belief, repentance, joy and so on.

Miracles galore are coming in the near future. A man calling himself God and his associate the Beast will perform more and greater miracles than seen in the whole of history. What will the result be?

God will send two witnesses so that the Gospel is preached throughout the world, but the 'world' kills them, and then send presents to each other to celebrate.

God then showers the Earth with miraculous horrendous devastating plagues, but this still does not cause the people to repent.

Revelation 9:20 And the rest of the men which were not killed by these plagues yet repented not of the works of their hands, that they should not worship devils, and idols of gold, and silver, and brass, and stone, and of wood: which neither can see, nor hear, nor walk:

The rebellion of the population of the whole world will be the result and they will turn to fight Christ at His coming.

Even at the end of time and the world as we know it, incredibly there will still be those who 'work abominations who will be forbidden from entering the Jerusalem the great city.

Revelation 21:10 And he carried me away in the spirit to a great and high mountain, and shewed me that great city, the holy Jerusalem, descending out of heaven from God,

11 Having the glory of God: and her light was like unto a stone most precious, even like a jasper stone, clear as crystal;

People do not learn from miracles.

There is only one thing that is going to bring in true spirituality, and that is LOVE. Love for God, Love for neighbour, and for all humanity and for everything that is in the universe, and that is very difficult for us to do. The first thing we need is to realise that even to start on this pathway to spirituality, we have to ask God for the gift of Holy Spirit, and the attendant gifts of belief, faith, and repentance.

God wants to Love us, and He shows this to us in so many ways. If sometime trials, and even what might seem like punishments come our way, provided we take them as God loving us, then we will have developed, with His help, a degree of true spirituality.

Love is the Key to everything. To love God with all your heart mind and soul, and your neighbour as yourself is the answer to all the problems of being human. Love never fails!

Luke 10:27 And he answering said, Thou shalt love the Lord thy God with all thy heart, and with all thy soul, and with all thy strength, and with all thy mind; and thy neighbour as thyself.

We also have to love and respect ourselves, as we can only love and respect others to the extent that we love ourselves.

Matthew 19:19 Honour thy father and thy mother: and, Thou shalt love thy neighbour as thyself.

That is the Golden Rule, and I will ask God to treat me the way you want to be treated.

Christ gave up his position with the Father, to being a man, who bore the sicknesses of the world, and was in total degradation. This is what they did to Christ, to come down from being next to the Father, and this shows that God was willing not only to become a human to suffer but this is how God showed His love to us.

John 3:1616 For God so loved the world, that he gave his only begotten Son, that whosoever believeth in him should not perish, but have everlasting life. 17 For God sent not his Son into the world to condemn the world; but that the world through him might be saved.

Despite all Christ did for us, does that really help us to bear the sufferings of this life? He completely understands what it is like to be human. It should and does help us through this life, and it does when we are diligent in our contact with Him.

But what leads us to the best form of spirituality. Here is the only thing that is going to work. That is when God Almighty shows you literally that he loves YOU, yes you reading this.

The disciples began to argue about who should hold which position. So Christ began to serve the meal and then the disciple's feet, the Creator of all things He showed how He loves us, by our serving Him and one another. That is true Spirituality!

The Glorious future of Human Beings

Isaiah 9:7 KJV Of the increase of his government and peace there shall be no end, upon the throne of David, and upon his kingdom, to order it, and to establish it with judgment and with justice from henceforth even for ever. The zeal of the LORD of hosts will perform this.

One day, when God's human children are introduced to the reality of Christ and His Power when the Kingdom of God is established on this earth, they will have a huge awakening to the reality of God and His Plan for us which is quite beyond our ability to comprehend at this time.

1 Corinthians 2:9 But as it is written, Eye hath not seen, nor ear heard, neither have entered into the heart of man, the things which **God** hath prepared for them that **love** him

The Word was appointed to be heir of all things, and as His children, human beings will also become heirs of all things in the Family of God.

Romans 8:16 The Spirit itself beareth witness with our spirit, that we are the children of God: 17 And if children, then heirs; heirs of God, and joint-heirs with Christ; if so be that we suffer with him, that we may be also glorified together.

Satan has deceived the whole world.

When God says that Satan has deceived the whole world, He means just that. Of the seven billion people on earth, how many of them are deceived? Nobody can say, but clearly most of them!

However, just look at the world in an objective way, and see how ghastly everything is. Christ said how it would be in Matthew 24, and that chapter reads like a modern day newscast.

Wars, famines, natural disasters, corrupt governments, disease epidemics due to poor hygiene or bad diets are pandemic, universal.

The majority of people in the world worship idols and false gods. Even those involved in Churchianity and its deadly mix of truth and error who think they are worshipping the true God are definitely not, very far from it.

Even the desire to 'find' God, and want to obey Him is a gift from God. Nobody can decide they want to be a Christian! No man can 'call' anyone, or 'convert' or 'save' anyone, that is entirely God's prerogative.

Christ said 'few' there be that find it, and it seems that fewer indeed are having their eyes and ears opened at this time.

When Christ said that He would build His ecclesia, his group, His body, he meant just that! He did not mean that He would allow any human organisation of any kind to be involved.

Anyone who is a true Christian knows only too well how lonely a pathway the Christian life can be. It is very difficult to find another Spirit lead Christian to associate with. But those who are led by God's Holy Spirit in their minds know that God's Spirit does indeed witness with our human spirit.

Romans 8:16 The Spirit itself beareth witness with our spirit, that we are the children of God:

When a person is given the gift of God's Holy Spirit in their minds God inspires them, breathes into that person, knowledge and understanding of His truths. They also receive other Spiritual gifts of belief, repentance, and the earnest desire to live up to the letter and the Spirit of the New Law that Christ brought.

Proverbs 20:27 The spirit of man is the candle of the Lord, searching all the inward parts of the belly.

When a person has God's Spirit, it illuminates the mind and heart of that person via the spirit in man given to them with their first breath. It gives each person the gift of the ability to 'see' themselves, and their need to change.

Our Salvation - planned before the world began.

Ephesians 1:4 According as he hath chosen us in him **before the foundation** of **the** world, that we should be holy and without blame **before** him in love:

The 'called' who are now 'in' Christ were known to God and His Son before the Creation of all things.

Colossians 2:9 For in him (Christ) dwelleth all the fulness of the Godhead bodily. 10 And ye are complete in him, which is the head of all principality and power:

The 'called' are now in a very special relationship with God and Christ.

Romans 8:17 And if children, then **heirs**; **heirs** of God, and joint-**heirs** with Christ; if so be that we suffer with him, that we may be also glorified together.

1 Peter 2:9 But ye are a chosen generation, a royal priesthood, an holy nation, a peculiar people; that ye should shew forth the praises of him who hath **called you out of darkness** into his marvellous *light*;

And in a figurative sense, those who are 'in Christ' are with Christ in Heaven sitting at the Right Hand of God!

Colossians 3:3 If ye then be risen with Christ, seek those things which are above, where Christ sitteth on the right hand of God.

1 John 1:5 This then is the message which we have heard of him, and declare unto you, that God is **light**, and in him is **no darkness at all**.

Christ as God's Son as a human had His Father's characteristic of being a **'light'**.

John 8:12 **Then spake Jesus again unto them,** saying, I am **the light of the world**: he that followeth me shall not walk in darkness, but shall have **the light of** life.

Who are the 'Called'?

Matthew 22:14 For many are called, but few are chosen.

The chosen few are rarely people of great position or stature in this life, but those who God wishes to work with who have a contrite heart, and are willing to have a deep respect for His Word.

1 Corinthians 1:26 For ye see your calling, brethren, how that not many wise men after the flesh, not many mighty, not many noble, are called: 27 But God hath chosen the foolish things of the world to confound the wise; and God hath chosen the weak things of the world to confound the things which are mighty;

Notice not many 'wise after the flesh' are called, who in truth make themselves fools by denying their Creator. The word 'meek' means teachable, and it is usually those who have that character trait that God calls and uses to build his ecclesia.

Isaiah 66:2 For all those things hath mine hand made, and all those things have been, saith the Lord: but to this man will I look, even to him that is poor and of a contrite spirit, and trembleth at my word.

Expanded version of 66:2: "These are the people ·I am pleased with [^{L} upon whom I look]: those who are ·not proud or stubborn [humble and contrite in spirit] and who ·fear [tremble at] my word.

The seemingly very 'few' that are the 'called' have access to God's Holy Spirit flowing through their hearts and minds in feelings, thoughts, inspirations, concepts, and ideas.

Romans 5:5 And hope maketh not ashamed; because the **love** of **God** is shed abroad in our hearts by the Holy Ghost which is given unto us.

The 'called' have a very special relationship with God and His Son Christ Jesus. For in the same was as we humans are 'in' God, when 'called' we are also 'in' Christ.

Colossians 2:6 ye have therefore received Christ Jesus the Lord, so walk ye **in** him: 7 Rooted and built up **in** him, and stablished in the faith, as ye have been taught, abounding therein with thanksgiving.

Beware of false Ministers, religions, churches

We have to be on our guard continually, as the subtleties of Satan guided people can appear to have attractive ideas and philosophies.

Colossians 2:8 Beware lest any man spoil you through philosophy and vain deceit, after the tradition of men, after the rudiments of the world, and not after Christ.

Such seemingly religious people will often mention Christ, quote the Bible, and what they say may seem very attractive, but only those who are alert to the machinations of the Devil, and have the clear mindedness to recognise them for who they are can be safe. They may dress, look and sound in such a manner as to appear to be Godly, but inwardly they are as dangerous as rabid wolves. Christ warned about them.

Matthew 7:15 Beware of false prophets, which come to you in sheep's clothing, but inwardly they are ravening wolves. 16 Ye shall know them by their fruits. Do men gather grapes of thorns, or figs of thistles?

And what are their 'fruits'? Oh, on the surface they may have all the appearance of 'holiness', but take careful note of the number of reports being produced daily about priests, clergy, and ministers being discovered to be involved in paedophilia, child abuse in all its forms, and other horrific immoral practices within their ranks. These reports and court cases are now a common occurrence as their victims finally come forward with the ghastly detailed evidence of their crimes, and the personal behaviour of clerics is revealed.

2 Corinthians 11:13 For such are false apostles, deceitful workers, transforming themselves into the apostles of Christ. 14 And no marvel; for Satan himself is transformed into an angel of light.

We need to avoid such people, and ask God to protect our minds from any such influences with the 'armour of God'.

Ephesians 6:13 Wherefore take unto you the whole armour of God, that ye may be able to withstand in the evil day, and having done all, to stand. 14 Stand therefore, having your loins girt about with truth, and having on the breastplate of righteousness; 15 And your feet shod with the preparation of the gospel of peace; 16 Above all, taking the shield of faith, wherewith ye shall be able to quench all the fiery darts of the wicked. 17 And take the helmet of salvation, and the sword of the Spirit, which is the word of God:

The way 'to put on' this armour, is to be in touch with God and Christ daily through the daily practice of asking for Guidance, and spending time in the earnest study of God's Word the Holy Bible. It is imperative to avoid at all costs the religious ideas of deceptive men. Everything that happens to 'called' Christians is ultimately for their benefit.

Romans 8:28 And we know that all things work together for good to them that **love God**, to them who are the called according to his purpose.

The Joys of the Called, their freedom in Christ

But the called have an absolute assurance that nothing can separate them from God's Love.

Romans 8:38 For I am persuaded, that neither death, nor life, nor angels, nor principalities, nor powers, nor things present, nor things to come, 39 Nor height, nor depth, nor any other creature, shall be able to separate us from the love of God, which is in Christ Jesus our Lord.

Christians who follow Christ are called to come out of the 'darkness' of this world, and into the 'light' of Christ.

1 Peter 2:9 But ye are a chosen generation, a royal priesthood, an holy nation, a peculiar people; that ye should shew forth the praises **of** him who hath called you **out of darkness** into his marvellous **light**;

Christ said to His disciples in private, and to all those who are Christian disciples today:

Matthew 5:14 Ye are the **light** of the world. A city that is set on an hill cannot be hid. 15 Neither do men light a candle, and put it under a bushel, but on a candlestick; and it giveth **light** unto all that are in the house. 16 Let your **light** so shine before men, that they may see your good works, and glorify your Father which is in heaven.

Those who are the 'called', who are led by Christ with His Spirit, have the light of life, a special form of **'light'** that enables them to see clearly the 'darkness' of this evil world

John 8:12 Then spake Jesus again unto them, saying, I am the **light** of the world: he that followeth me shall not walk in darkness, but shall have the **light** of life.

Many have observed that 'lights' do not make a sound, unless they are malfunctioning. We are saved by Grace as a Gift through Christ's works; and our 'light' is to be our 'good works' which we are commanded to perform, but even those 'works' we perform as Christians are the work of God in us and not from our own strength.

Ephesians 2:8 For by grace are ye saved through faith; and that not of yourselves: it is the gift of God: 9 Not of works, lest any man should boast. 10 For we are his workmanship, created in Christ Jesus unto good works, which God hath before ordained that we should walk in them.

1 John 1:5 This then is the message which we have heard of him, and declare unto you, that God is **light**, and in him is **no darkness at all**.

Christ as God's Son as a human had His Father's characteristic of being **'light'**.

John 8:12 **Then spake Jesus again unto them,** saying, I am **the light of the world**: he that followeth me shall not walk in darkness, but shall have **the light of** life.

Christ said to His disciples in private, and to all those who are Christian disciples today:

Matthew 5:14 Ye are the **light** of the world. A city that is set on an hill cannot be hid. 15 Neither do men light a candle, and put it under a bushel, but on a candlestick; and it giveth **light** unto all that are in the house. 16 Let your **light** so shine before men, that they may see your good works, and glorify your Father which is in heaven.

Those who are the 'called', who are led by Christ with His Spirit, have the light of life, a special form of **'light'** that enables them to see clearly the 'darkness' of this evil world.

Christians who follow Christ are called to come out of the 'darkness' of this world, and into the 'light' of Christ.

1 Peter 2:9 But ye are a chosen generation, a royal priesthood, an holy nation, a peculiar people; that ye should shew forth the praises **of** him who hath called you **out of darkness** into his marvellous **light**;

The Revelation of the Future

Then we come to the last book that Christ wrote and gave to John via an Angel nearly 100 A.D. In it we learn of the end of the world as we know it.

Revelation 20:1 And I saw an angel come down from heaven, having the key of the bottomless pit and a great chain in his hand. 2 And he laid hold on the dragon, that old serpent, which is the Devil, and Satan, and bound him a thousand years, 3 And cast him into the bottomless pit, and shut him up, and set a seal upon him, that he should deceive the nations no more, till the thousand years should be fulfilled: and after that he must be loosed a little season. 4 And I saw thrones, and they sat upon them, and judgment was given unto them: and I saw the souls of them that were beheaded for the witness of Jesus, and for the word of God, and which had not worshipped the beast, neither his image, neither had received his mark upon their foreheads, or in their hands; and they lived and reigned with Christ a thousand years. 5 But the rest of the dead lived not again until the thousand years were finished. This is the first resurrection. 6 Blessed and holy is he that hath part in the first resurrection: on such the second death hath no power, but they shall be priests of God and of Christ, and shall reign with him a thousand years. 7 And when the thousand years are expired, Satan shall be loosed out of his prison, 8 And shall go out to deceive the nations which are in the four quarters of the earth, Gog, and Magog, to gather them together to battle: the number of whom is as the sand of the sea. 9 And they went up on the breadth of the earth, and compassed the camp of the saints about, and the beloved city: and fire came down from God out of heaven, and devoured them. 10 And the devil that deceived them was cast into the lake of fire and brimstone, where the beast and the false prophet are, and shall be tormented day and night for ever and ever. 11 And I saw a great white throne, and him that sat on it, from whose face the earth and the heaven fled away; and there was found no place for them. 12 And I saw the dead, small and great, stand before God; and the books were opened: and another book was opened, which is the book of life: and the dead were judged out of those things which were written in the books, according to their works. 13 And the sea gave up the dead which were in it; and death and hell delivered up the dead which were in them: and they were judged every man according to their works. 14 And death and hell were cast into the lake of fire. This is the second death. 15 And whosoever was not found written in the book of life was cast into the lake of fire.

Then Christ tells us about the New Heavens and the New Earth which we can look forward to with great joyful anticipation.

Revelation 21:1 And I saw a new heaven and a new earth: for the first heaven and the first earth were passed away; and there was no more sea. 2 And I John saw the holy city, new Jerusalem, coming down from God out of heaven, prepared as a bride adorned for her husband. 3 And I heard a great voice out of heaven saying, Behold, the tabernacle of God is with men, and he will dwell with them, and they shall be his people, and God himself shall be with them, and be their God. 4 And God shall wipe away all tears from their eyes; and there shall be no more death, neither sorrow, nor crying, neither shall there be any more pain: for the former things are passed away. 5 And he that sat upon the throne said,

Behold, I make all things new. And he said unto me, Write: for these words are true and faithful. 6 And he said unto me, It is done. I am Alpha and Omega, the beginning and the end. I will give unto him that is athirst of the fountain of the water of life freely. 7 He that overcometh shall inherit all things; and I will be his God, and he shall be my son. 8 But the fearful, and unbelieving, and the abominable, and murderers, and whoremongers, and sorcerers, and idolaters, and all liars, shall have their part in the lake which burneth with fire and brimstone: which is the second death. 9 And there came unto me one of the seven angels which had the seven vials full of the seven last plagues, and talked with me, saying, Come hither, I will shew thee the bride, the Lamb's wife. 10 And he carried me away in the spirit to a great and high mountain, and shewed me that great city, the holy Jerusalem, descending out of heaven from God, 11 Having the glory of God: and her light was like unto a stone most precious, even like a jasper stone, clear as crystal; 12 And had a wall great and high, and had twelve gates, and at the gates twelve angels, and names written thereon, which are the names of the twelve tribes of the children of Israel: 13 On the east three gates; on the north three gates; on the south three gates; and on the west three gates. 14 And the wall of the city had twelve foundations, and in them the names of the twelve apostles of the Lamb. 15 And he that talked with me had a golden reed to measure the city, and the gates thereof, and the wall thereof. 16 And the city lieth foursquare, and the length is as large as the breadth: and he measured the city with the reed, twelve thousand furlongs. The length and the breadth and the height of it are equal. 17 And he measured the wall thereof, an hundred and forty and four cubits, according to the measure of a man, that is, of the angel. 18 And the building of the wall of it was of jasper: and the city was pure gold, like unto clear glass. 19 And the foundations of the wall of the city were garnished with all manner of precious stones. The first foundation was jasper; the second, sapphire; the third, a chalcedony; the fourth, an emerald; 20 The fifth, sardonyx; the sixth, sardius; the seventh, chrysolyte; the eighth, beryl; the ninth, a topaz; the tenth, a chrysoprasus; the eleventh, a jacinth; the twelfth, an amethyst. 21 And the twelve gates were twelve pearls: every several gate was of one pearl: and the street of the city was pure gold, as it were transparent glass. 22 And I saw no temple therein: for the Lord God Almighty and the Lamb are the temple of it. 23 And the city had no need of the sun, neither of the moon, to shine in it: for the glory of God did lighten it, and the Lamb is the light thereof. 24 And the nations of them which are saved shall walk in the light of it: and the kings of the earth do bring their glory and honour into it. 25 And the gates of it shall not be shut at all by day: for there shall be no night there. 26 And they shall bring the glory and honour of the nations into it. 27 And there shall in no wise enter into it any thing that defileth, neither whatsoever worketh abomination, or maketh a lie: but they which are written in the Lamb's book of life.

What an amazingly wonderful glorious future we have in prospect!! Hallelujah. What a privilege to be one of the called in this life at this time.

God speed Christ's coming and the Establishment of the Kingdom of Heaven, Thy Will be done in Earth as it is in Heaven. Amen.

APPENDIX

ASPECTS OF GOD'S CHARACTER OF "LOVE"

TO MEDITATE ON & TO LIVE BY

Psalm 19:14 Let the words of my mouth, and the meditation of my heart, be acceptable in thy sight, O Lord, my strength, and my redeemer.

ACCEPTANCE

Accepting, accession, acknowledgment, acquiescence, adoption, affirmation, agreement, approbation, approval, assent, belief, compliance, concession, concurrence, consent, cooperation, recognition, deference, standing, submission, yielding.

Accepting ourselves as we are, and being accepting of others as they are without criticism or judgement, is a powerful aspect of love. Self-denigration and lack of self-esteem is probably the world's number one sickness. We are taught from birth that it is vain to think well of ourselves, which of course is true if that leads to boasting, big-headedness, and lording it over others.

On the other hand, the main commandment is that we should love our neighbours AS we love ourselves. In fact, it is a well-known fact that people with poor self-love seem to be aggressively minded against the world. It is a truism that our ability to love others is conditional on, and in proportion to how much we love and accept ourselves as being worthy individuals.

Antonym: Rejection in any form, disapproval of or negating anything anyone thinks, says, or does, leads to a reduction in the flow of love.

ADDICTION Compulsion is that which leads one away from reality of the love and fruit of the spirit Gal 5:22, 23; and in to the works of the flesh Gal 5:19-21. The works of the flesh are also summed up these words: Self-seeking, selfishness, dishonesty, resentment and fear.

ADORE, ADORATION

To pay divine honours to, to adore, worship, praise, speak to formally, beseech, admiration, esteem, estimation, exaltation, glorification, honour, love, reverence, veneration, worship, worshipping.

God a Spirit: and they that worship him must worship him in spirit and in truth. John 4:24 KJV Give unto the LORD the glory due unto his name; worship the LORD in the beauty of holiness. Psalm 29:2 KJV

Ant: loathe, idolatry, idolization of worldly things

ALTRUISM

Altruism is unselfish concern for other people's happiness and welfare.

Philippians 2:4 Look not every man on his own things, but every man also on the things of others. 5 Let this mind be in you, which was also in Christ Jesus: 1 Corinthians 10:24 KJV Let no man seek his own, but every man another's wealth. (or welfare) In balance of course.

Ant: self-absorption, self-centredness, self-interest, selfishness, self-seeking,

AMBITION

Aim, aspiration, desire, dream, drive, eagerness, end, enterprise, goal, hope, intent, longing, objective, purpose, striving, yearning, wish, zeal.

There are right ambitions which will lead to personal development, and then there are wrong ambitions where people strive endlessly to be rich, and to have material possessions at the expense of their spiritual well-being.

Matthew 6:19 KJV Lay not up for yourselves treasures upon earth, where moth and rust doth corrupt, and where thieves break through and steal. 20. But lay up for yourselves treasures in heaven, where neither moth nor rust doth corrupt, and where thieves do not break through nor steal:

Mark 10:44 KJV And whosoever of you will be the chiefest, shall be servant of all.

Not all types of worldly ambition are appropriate for the Godly to pursue. We need to examine our ambitions and desires and check them against where our heart should be focused.

John 17:14 KJV I have given them thy word; and the world hath hated them, because they are not of the world, even as I am not of the world.

Romans 12:2 KJV And be not conformed to this world: but be ye transformed by the renewing of your mind, that ye may prove what is that good, and acceptable, and perfect, will of God.

1 Corinthians 3:19 KJV For the wisdom of this world is foolishness with God. For it is written, He taketh the wise in their own craftiness.

2 Corinthians 4:4 KJV In whom the god of this world hath blinded the minds of them which believe not, lest the light

of the glorious gospel of Christ, who is the image of God, should shine unto them.

1 John 2:15 KJV Love not the world, neither the things that are in the world. If any man love the world, the love of the Father is not in him.

Ant: apathy, aversion, dislike, idleness, inactivity, indifference, lethargy, disinterest

ANGER

Displeasure, enmity, exasperation, fury, gall, hatred, huff, ill humour, ill temper, impatience, indignation, infuriation, irascibility, ire, irritability, irritation, mad, miffed, outrage, passion, peevishness, petulance, pique, rage, rankling, resentment, stew, storm, tantrum, temper, tiff, umbrage, vexation, violence

Anger is a very difficult emotion to manage in a positive spiritual manner. God is angry with the wicked(ness) every day. We should experience righteous anger at the evils in this world, but never directed towards persons or individuals. The key is to hate the evil but not the evildoer.

It is a wonderful principle to clear the mind and the day of anger before going to sleep. Ephesians 4:26 KJV Be ye angry, and sin not: let not the sun go down upon your wrath:

Ant: Agreeability, calmness, contentment, enjoyment, good nature, happiness, joy, peace, pleasantness.

ASSURANCE

assertiveness, assuredness, boldness, certainty, confidence, conviction, coolness, courage, faith, firmness, nerve, poise, positiveness, security, self-confidence, self-reliance, sureness

Assurance is produced by faith: Heb 10:22 Let us draw near with a true heart in full assurance of faith, having our hearts sprinkled from an evil conscience, and our bodies washed with pure water. Hebrews 6:11 And we desire that every one of you do shew the same diligence to the full assurance of hope unto the end: 19 Which hope we have as an anchor of the soul, both sure and stedfast, and which entereth into that within the veil; Ephesians 3:11 According to the eternal purpose which he purposed in Christ Jesus our Lord: 12 In whom we have boldness and access with confidence by the faith of him.

Ant: apprehension, diffidence, distrust, doubt, self-doubt, self-effacement, shyness, timidity, uncertainty

ATTITUDE – the most important fundamental aspect of humans.

Approach, disposition, frame of mind, mood, opinion, outlook, perspective, point of view, position, posture, stance, standing, view, air, aspect, bearing, carriage, condition, demeanour, manner, mien (literary) pose, position, posture, stance

Deuteronomy 5:29 KJV O that there were such an heart (attitude) in them, that they would fear me, and keep all my commandments always, that it might be well with them, and with their children for ever!

Attitude is possibly the most important aspect of love, as everything we think, say, and do depends on our attitude at the time. If our attitude is "good" then our approach to whatever we are currently involved in will be positive, and likely to have a good outcome.

How can we be aware of how "good" or "bad" our attitude is? Simply make an analysis of what our attitude is? At any moment, take an objective assessment of our demeanour and intention in respect of the positive aspects of love, such as patience, kindness, gentleness, friendliness, etc., etc. Is what we are we thinking, saying and doing in harmony with those character traits and the many others which help to define Love in all its facets, or not?

Ant: Bad attitude. The definition of a "bad" attitude is anything that is anything less than our best attempt at feeling, expressing and acting out a spiritual aspect of love. Impatience, unkindness, harshness, resentment, unfriendliness, etc.

BACKSLIDING

When we allow full rein to the lower aspects of our human nature, we slowly but surely sink into a morass of negative spiritual behaviour. It takes a strong fish to swim upstream, against the current. We are surrounded by currents which would tend to sweep us away into bad reactions and worse habits.

Galatians 6:9 KJV And let us not be weary in well doing: for in due season we shall reap, if we faint not.

Ant: Zeal

BELIEF

Think something is so, credence, credo, creed, doctrine, dogma, faith, ideology, principles, tenet.

Mere belief in anything is not enough. Belief is no substitute for knowledge. Indeed belief is based in knowledge, and the greater the knowledge, the more understanding we have increases belief, and leads to faith. You can believe your home is on fire but what are you willing to act on that belief?

People can and do believe the most unbelievable things, and are convinced they are right!

Millions believe in the Theory of Evolution, the ridiculous notion that everything came from nothing, and without a cause. Yet scientists know the absolute law that for every effect there must be a cause, but they put that idea into suspension while they claim there is no Designer!

They start their evolutionary process with "nothing" except having in place all the immutable laws of gravity, magnetism, and physics, to say nothing of space and matter like hydrogen gas, and then claim that an explosion "created" everything! That is hard to grasp that for the ordinary person who only knows of the destructive force of explosions.

Oh, and ultimately "life" began when lightning struck complex protein molecules which just happened to have formed from substances that were not there! Lightning seems to destroy life nowadays, but back in the aeons of time it produced life? What mental agility those who deny God have to have!

Belief without knowledge to back it up is empty. Belief plus the right sort of knowledge gives confidence, which leads to conviction which leads to faith.

Ant: disbelief, distrust, doubt, dubiety, incredulity, mistrust, skepticism,

BENEVOLENCE

Altruism, charity, compassion, fellow feeling, generosity, goodness, goodwill, humanity, kind-heartedness, kindness, sympathy

Ant: Ill will, malevolence, selfishness, stinginess, unkindness.

BENEVOLENT

Charitable, kind, all heart, altruistic, beneficent, benign, big, big-hearted, bounteous, bountiful, caring, chivalrous, compassionate, considerate, generous, helpful, humane, humanitarian, kindhearted, liberal, magnanimous, philanthropic, tenderhearted, warmhearted, well-disposed.

Ant: greedy, malevolent, mean, selfish, spiteful, unkind

BENIGN

kind, kindly, merciful, gracious, amiable, beneficent, benevolent, benignant, complaisant, congenial, favorable, friendly, generous, genial, gentle, good, goodhearted, gracious, liberal, merciful, mild, obliging, sympathetic

And be ye kind one to another, tenderhearted, forgiving one another, even as God for Christ's sake hath forgiven you. Ephesians 4:32 KJV

Ant: Malignant, bad, disobliging, harsh, hateful, inhumane, malicious, malign, severe, stern, unfavourable, unkind, unpleasant, unsympathetic

BLASPHEMY

Thou shalt not take the name of the LORD thy God in vain; for the LORD will not hold him guiltless that taketh his name in vain. Exodus 20:7 KJV

Taking the Name of God in vain is a form of blasphemy, and goes directly against the third commandment. Almost universally all over the English speaking world, in every day 'normal' conversation people use the word 'Jesus', 'Christ', 'Jesus Christ', 'OMG' (Oh! My God), "Gor Blimey" (God blind me), even exclamations like 'jeepers creepers' is actually another version of Jesus Christ. So commonplace is this practice that it is difficult to tune it out, or God forbid, that we find ourselves involved in doing it too. See: Swearing

In fact, there was no such letter as a 'J' in 1611 when King James ordered the translation of the Bible we all treasure.

So the words like Jew, Jesus, etc., were used or inserted in 1875 by later translators. The name of our Saviour, as closely as we can ascertain should be 'Yashua'. But that is not important in the big scheme of things. God knows our heart, so long as we honour His 'name'.

Ant: Praise, honour, respect

BLESS, BLESSING.

Sanctify, set apart for a Holy purpose, hold in highest esteem, absolve, anoint, bless, cleanse, consecrate, dedicate, glorify, hallow, purify, worship, absolve, anoint, baptize, beatify, canonize, commend, confirm, consecrate, dedicate, exalt, extol, give thanks to, hallow, honor, invoke benefits, invoke happiness, laud, magnify, make holy, offer, offer benediction, ordain, panegyrize, praise, pray for, pronounce holy, sacrifice, sign, thank

We, the Israel of God, are blessed by God specifically and particularly. Although all humans will come to know God, we who are Christians have been singled out to receive specific blessings.

Numbers 6:22 And the LORD spake unto Moses, saying, 23 Speak unto Aaron and unto his sons, saying, On this wise ye shall bless the children of Israel, saying unto them, 24 The LORD bless thee, and keep thee: 25 The LORD make his face shine upon thee, and be gracious unto thee: 26 The LORD lift up his countenance upon thee, and give thee peace. 27 And they shall put my name upon the children of Israel; and I will bless them.

Leviticus 26:12 And I will walk among you, and will be your God, and ye shall be my people. 13 I am the LORD your God, which brought you forth out of the land of Egypt, that ye should not be their bondmen; and I have broken the bands of your yoke, and made you go upright.

1 Peter 3:9 KJV Not rendering evil for evil, or railing for railing: but contrariwise blessing; knowing that ye are thereunto called, that ye should inherit a blessing.

Psalm 67:1 KJV God be merciful unto us, and bless us; and cause his face to shine upon us; Selah.

BLINDNESS – MENTAL AND SPIRITUAL

Human beings are responsible for "closing their eyes" to the reality of God and the messages He has for us in His Word.

Jesus said, For this people's heart is waxed gross, and their ears are dull of hearing, and their eyes they have closed; lest at any time they should see with their eyes, and hear with their ears, and should understand with their heart, and should be converted, and I should heal them. Matthew 13:15 KJV

Having the understanding darkened, being alienated from the life of God through the ignorance that is in them, because of the blindness of their heart: Ephesians 4:18 KJV

BOLDNESS

Someone who is bold is not afraid to do the 'right thing' or do things which involve personal popularity, risk or even some danger.

Ephesians 3:11 According to the eternal purpose which he purposed in Christ Jesus our Lord: 12 In whom we have boldness and access with confidence by the faith of him.

Ant: Overly cautious, nervous, fearful.

BRAVERY

Someone who is brave is willing to do things which are dangerous, and does not show fear in difficult or dangerous situations.

Ant: Cowardly easily frightened and avoids dangerous or difficult situations.

BUSY-BODIES

Eavesdropper, gossip, intriguer, intruder, meddler, nosy parker, pry, scandalmonger, snoop, snooper, stirrer, troublemaker.

None of these are the behaviour of Godly people.

Proverbs 20:3 It is an honour for a man to cease from strife: but every fool will be meddling.

1 Timothy 5:13 And withal they learn to be idle, wandering about from house to house; and not only idle, but tattlers also and busybodies, speaking things which they ought not.

1 Peter 4:15 But let none of you suffer as a murderer, or as a thief, or as an evildoer, or as a busybody in other men's matters.

CALLED of God.

Appointed, chosen, named, selected

Romans 8:28 KJV And we know that all things work together for good to them that love God, to them who are the called according to his purpose.

2 Timothy 1:9 KJV Who hath saved us, and called us with an holy calling, not according to our works, but according to his own purpose and grace, which was given us in Christ Jesus before the world began.

God had a plan for each of us as individuals BEFORE even the world was created. He looked down the stream of time, and fore-ordained that we should be His children. Quite incredible.

CAPITALISM

Economic system of private ownership commercialism, competition, democracy, free enterprise, free market, industrialism, laissez faire economics, mercantilism, private enterprise

Genesis 39:3 KJV And his master saw that the LORD was with him, and that the LORD made all that he did to prosper in his hand.

God owns everything. We are part of His world, and are set to inherit eternal life, and all that means, including wealth that transcends the physical world.

Thieves also prosper in this world! Psalm 73:12 KJV Behold, these are the ungodly, who prosper in the world; they increase in riches. Their time of judgment will certainly come.

See PROSPERITY

Ant: Communism

CARES

Personal interest, concerns, affliction, aggravation, alarm, anguish, annoyance, anxiety, apprehension, bother, burden, chagrin, charge, consternation, discomposure, dismay, disquiet, distress, disturbance, encumbrance, exasperation, fear, foreboding, fretfulness, handicap, hardship, hindrance, impediment, incubus, load, misgiving, nuisance, onus, oppression, perplexity, pressure, responsibility, solicitude, sorrow, stew, strain, stress, sweat, tribulation, trouble, uneasiness, unhappiness, vexation, woe, worry

The cares of life in this world tend to choke out our intentions to seek God and His ways.

Matthew 13:22 He also that received seed among the thorns is he that heareth the word; and the cares of this world, and the deceitfulness of riches, choke the word, and he becometh unfruitful.

Ant: Trust in God, optimism.

CHARACTER

Attributes, bent, calibre, complexion, constitution, disposition, individuality, make-up, marked traits, nature, personality, quality, reputation, temperament.

The development of Godly character is the lifelong task we have been given. In every moment of life, we are confronted with having the opportunity to choose between acting in ways that develop good character, or to act in ways which develop bad character, or reactions that destroy good character.

I call heaven and earth to record this day against you, that I have set before you life and death, blessing and cursing: therefore choose life, that both thou and thy seed may live: Deuteronomy 30:19 KJV

Our human nature has a bias towards vanity, deceitfulness, self-interest, law breaking, and lacking love to God and our fellow man which breaks the Royal Law. People do not like to hear it, but... Jeremiah 17:9 The (human, natural, nature) heart is deceitful above all things, and desperately wicked: who can know it?

God wants us to fight those bad characteristics, and develop Godly character. This we cannot do very well at all without God's help. So He wants us to CHOOSE to ask Him for help moment by moment to overcome the evil side of our nature and build righteous, law abiding habits. Meditating on these aspects of love is a way to increase our consciousness of the need to daily strive to develop Godly character.

In essence character is knowing the true values, choosing the right values and performing them when no one takes notice

CHARACTER OF SAINTS

The saints are members of God's congregation, the ekklesia or called out ones. The word in the Bible does not refer to those people promoted to 'sainthood' by the religions of this world.

This book presents many of the attributes to be practiced or sought after by those who want to follow God, and be truly 'spiritual'. Examples are being:

Blameless and harmless: Philipians 2:15 That ye may be blameless and harmless, the sons of God, without rebuke, in the midst of a crooked and perverse nation, among whom ye shine as lights in the world;

Bold: Proverbs 28:1 1 The wicked flee when no man pursueth: but the righteous are bold as a lion.

Contrite and Humble Isaiah 57:15 For thus saith the high and lofty One that inhabiteth eternity, whose name is Holy; I dwell in the high and holy place, with him also that is of a contrite and humble spirit, to revive the spirit of the humble, and to revive the heart of the contrite ones.

Colossians 3:12 Put on therefore, as the elect of God, holy and beloved, bowels of mercies, kindness, humbleness of mind, meekness, longsuffering;

Pure in heart: Blessed are the pure in heart: for they shall see God. Matthew 5:8

Spirit led: Romans 8:14 For as many as are led by the Spirit of God, they are the sons of God.

CHARACTERISTICS OF WICKED

The Bible uses many words to describe the characteristics of the wicked. A study of any of the words with a concordance gives insight into the mind of the wicked.

Abominable, alienated from God, blasphemous, blinded, boastful, covetous, deceitful, destructive, disobedient, envious, fearful, fierce, foolish, fraudulent, hard-hearted, high minded, haughty, hostile to God, ignorant of God, impudent, liars, mischievous, murderous, persecuting, perverse, proud, reprobate, selfish, uncircumcised in heart, unjust, unmerciful, ungodly, unthankful, unwise.

CHARITY – OLD ENGLISH FOR LOVE

Affection, Agape, altruism, benevolence, benignity, bountifulness, bounty, compassion, fellow feeling, generosity, goodness, goodwill, humanity, indulgence, love, pity, tenderheartedness.

1 Corinthians 13:1 Though I speak with the tongues of men and of angels, and have not charity, I am become as sounding brass, or a tinkling cymbal. 2 And though I have the gift of prophecy, and understand all mysteries, and all knowledge; and though I have all faith, so that I could remove mountains, and have not charity, I am nothing. 3 And though I bestow all my goods to feed the poor, and though I give my body to be burned, and have not charity, it profiteth me nothing. 4 Charity suffereth long, and is kind; charity envieth not; charity vaunteth not itself, is not puffed up, 5 Doth not behave itself unseemly, seeketh not her own, is not easily provoked, thinketh no evil; 6 Rejoiceth not in iniquity, but rejoiceth in the truth; 7 Beareth all things, believeth all things, hopeth all things, endureth all things…. 13 And now abideth faith, hope, charity, these three; but the greatest of these is charity.

Money given to charities does not always reach the people intended, at least until a large proportion has been filtered off in 'expenses' or administration. Many charities perpetuate the situations they claim to address.

So the other definition of 'charity', alms-giving, assistance, benefaction, contributions, donations, endowment, fund, gift, hand-out, largesse, philanthropy, relief might sound laudable, but careful thought on the part of the giver is indicated. And on the other hand...

James 2:15 If a brother or sister be naked, and destitute of daily food, 16 And one of you say unto them, Depart in peace, be ye warmed and filled; notwithstanding ye give them not those things which are needful to the body; what doth it profit? 17 Even so faith, if it hath not works, is dead, being alone.

Matthew 25:40 KJV And the King shall answer and say unto them, Verily I say unto you, Inasmuch as ye have done it unto one of the least of these my brethren, ye have done it unto me.

Note: This is saying give to someone who has fallen on hard times, or is striving to be a Christian, not a drug addict or drunken tramp who will take your money and make their situation worse.

Colossians 3:10 And have put on the new man, which is renewed in knowledge after the image of him that created him: 11 Where there is neither Greek nor Jew, circumcision nor uncircumcision, Barbarian, Scythian, bond nor free: but Christ is all, and in all. 12 Put on therefore, as the elect of God, holy and beloved, bowels of mercies, kindness, humbleness of mind, meekness, longsuffering; 13 Forbearing one another, and forgiving one another, if any man have a quarrel against any: even as Christ forgave you, so also do ye. 14 And above all these things put on charity, which is the bond of perfectness. 15 And let the peace of God rule in your hearts, to the which also ye are called in one body; and be ye thankful.

Ant: Uncharitable.

CHASTITY

Chastity is the state of not having sex with anyone, avoiding fornication, (sex before marriage), or of only having sex with your husband or wife.

Exodus 20:14. Thou shalt not commit adultery. Adultery is now an almost universal sin.

Chastity is a word and concept that has all but disappeared from vocabulary in the Western world. Chastity has been replaced with barefaced displays of provocatively dressed or even nude 'models'.

Sex before marriage, fornication, is now a given. So is living and sleeping with a "partner". Homosexuality from being a capital offence in law only seventy years ago, is now socially "accepted". "Gay rights" movements are active everywhere. The Bible says that these activities will keep those who are involved with them out of the Kingdom of God. According to God's Word, you cannot be a Christian and do these things with impunity. People get angry when they feel their 'freedoms' are being imposed on, and attack those who explain what the Word of God says in these matters. They should not get angry at the people, but at God's Word!

1 Corinthians 6:9 KJV Know ye not that the unrighteous shall not inherit the kingdom of God? Be not deceived: neither fornicators, nor idolaters, nor adulterers, nor effeminate, nor abusers of themselves with mankind,

1 Corinthians 6:18 Flee fornication. Every sin that a man doeth is without the body; but he that committeth fornication sinneth against his own body.

1 Thessalonians 4:3 For this is the will of God, even your sanctification, that ye should abstain from fornication

Galatians 5:19 KJV Now the works of the flesh are manifest, which are these; Adultery, fornication, uncleanness, lasciviousness,

Colossians 3:5 Mortify therefore your members which are upon the earth; fornication, uncleanness, inordinate affection, evil concupiscence, and covetousness, which is idolatry:

1 Timothy 2:9 KJV In like manner also, that women adorn themselves in modest apparel, with shamefacedness and sobriety; not with broided hair, or gold, or pearls, or costly array. 1 Peter 3:3 Whose adorning let it not be that outward adorning of plaiting the hair, and of wearing of gold, or of putting on of apparel;

None of these passages are intended to suggest that we should not beautify ourselves and present ourselves appropriately and becomingly dressed. People can and should be dressed attractively, and beautifully, without drawing attention to themselves in such a way as to provoke notions of a sexual nature.

Ant: Unchaste, immoral, loose, See: Sex

CHILDLIKE

Matthew 18:1 At the same time came the disciples unto Jesus, saying, Who is the greatest in the kingdom of heaven? 2 And Jesus called a little child unto him, and set him in the midst of them, 3 And said, Verily I say unto you, Except ye be converted, and become as little children, ye shall not enter into the kingdom of heaven. 4 Whosoever therefore shall humble himself as this little child, the same is greatest in the kingdom of (which is from) heaven.

Psalm 131:1 LORD, my heart is not haughty, nor mine eyes lofty: neither do I exercise myself in great matters, or in things too high for me. 2 Surely I have behaved and quieted myself, as a child that is weaned of his mother: my soul is even as a weaned child.

CHOICE

Alternative, discrimination, election, option, pick, preference, say, selection, variety.

People say, "I have no choice". And in a way, this is correct. As human beings, although God has given us "free will", He does not give us a choice about choice! We HAVE to choose. Every day, our lives are a continual series of choices, and we have no choice but to make choices!

God tells us what He would like us to choose:

Deuteronomy 30:19 I call heaven and earth to record this day against you, that I have set before you life and death, blessing and cursing: therefore choose life, that both thou and thy seed may live: 20 That thou mayest love the LORD thy God, and that thou mayest obey his voice, and that thou mayest cleave unto him: for he is thy life, and the length of thy days: that thou mayest dwell in the land which the LORD sware unto thy fathers, to Abraham, to Isaac, and to Jacob, to give them.

Joshua 24:15 And if it seem evil unto you to serve the LORD, choose you this day whom ye will serve; whether the gods which your fathers served that were on the other side of the flood, or the gods of the Amorites, in whose land ye dwell: but as for me and my house, we will serve the LORD.

See: Free Will

CIRCUMCISION – NOW OF THE HEART!

Given by God to physical people under the old covenant as a sign that they were God's people, but they did not have the mentality to obey God.

Deuteronomy 5:29 KJV O that there were such an heart in them, that they would fear me, and keep all my commandments always, that it might be well with them, and with their children for ever!

In the New Covenant brought in by Jesus Christ, "circumcision" is now of the heart.

Romans 2:29 KJV But he is a Judean, (or a Christian) which is one inwardly; and circumcision is that of the heart, in the spirit, and not in the letter; whose praise is not of men, but of God.

CLEANLINESS

Freshness, immaculateness, neatness, purity, sanitation, spotlessness, spruceness, tidiness, trimness.

There is an old proverb which says that "Cleanliness is next to Godliness" which is probably taking it a bit too far. But in this era, personal cleanliness might be the norm, but mental and verbal cleanliness is almost extinct among the "worldly" people. Television and the movies have now have no word they will not use.

Ephesians 4:29 NLT Don't use foul or abusive language. Let everything you say be good and helpful, so that your words will be an encouragement to those who hear them.

Matthew 23:25 KJV Woe unto you, scribes and Pharisees, hypocrites! for ye make clean the outside of the cup and of the platter, but within they are full of extortion and excess.

Matthew 23:25 NLT How terrible it will be for you teachers of religious law and you Pharisees. Hypocrites! You are so careful to clean the outside of the cup and the dish, but inside you are filthy -- full of greed and self-indulgence!

The immorality and uncleanness of so many priests and ministers has appalled the public, but it continues.

Philippians 2:15 NLT So that no one can speak a word of blame against you. You are to live clean, innocent lives as children of God in a dark world full of crooked and perverse people. Let your lives shine brightly before them.

Ant: Unclean

COMFORT

Good feeling; ease, abundance, alleviation, amenity, assuagement, cheer, cheerfulness, contentment, convenience, coziness, creature comforts, enjoyment, exhilaration, facility, gratification, happiness, luxury, opulence, peacefulness, pleasure, plenty, poise, quiet, relaxation, relief, repose, rest, restfulness, satisfaction, snugness, succour, sufficiency, warmth, well-being.

All these words describe how God really wants us to enjoy our lives as we live in accordance with all the detailed instructions He gives us in His Word.

Tribulations and difficulties will come of course, in the process of our developing Godly character, but God is always there to comfort. 2 Corinthians 1:4 KJV Who comforteth us in all our tribulation, that we may be able to comfort them which are in any trouble, by the comfort wherewith we ourselves are comforted of God.

So it is a life of joy and positive hope that God wants us to experience.

Isaiah 40:1 KJV Comfort ye, comfort ye my people, saith your God.

Romans 15:4 KJV For whatsoever things were written aforetime were written for our learning, that we through patience and comfort of the scriptures might have hope.

2 Corinthians 1:3 KJV Blessed be God, even the Father of our Lord Jesus Christ, the Father of mercies, and the God of all comfort; 4 Who comforteth us in all our tribulation, that we may be able to comfort them which are in any trouble, by the comfort wherewith we ourselves are comforted of God

Ant: aggravation, annoyance, bother, botheration, discomfort, distress, exasperation, irritation, torment, torture, unease.

COMFORTER

Consoler, friend, pacifier, sympathizer. One who understands, and gives comfort.

Since the death of Christ, and His sending the Holy Spirit fifty days afterwards to those He chose then, and chooses to call at this time, we now have the possibility of a Spiritual relationship with God. This is the essence of the New Covenant. We have the comforting knowledge that we are not alone in our search for God, but that we have the continual help of God's Spirit available to us when we seek it, and even when we don't.

Most so-called Christian religions do not emphasise the role of the Comforter in the lives of their followers. They encourage a sense of fear, guilt, and sinfulness in order to control their adherents. But this is not what God or Christ intended, so very far from it.

2 Timothy 1:7 KJV For God hath not given us the spirit of fear; but of power, and of love, and of a sound mind.

Mankind under the Old Covenant had a type of relationship with God, but it was tenuous, and in most cases virtually non-existent, apart from a few individuals like Noah, Abraham, Isaac and Jacob, Moses, David and the prophets who had a measure of assistance from God's Spirit. Human nature had really no chance to even want to follow God and His laws, so they went there own unlawful way, usually seeking comfort in other gods, and practices which took them further from their Creator.

The vast majority of the population of this present evil world still does not have this comforting influence available to them. They are cut off in blindness, enmeshed in the worldiness of wars, poverty, famines, diseases, oppressive governments, all of which have afflicted human beings throughout history and will continue to do so until Christ returns and sets up His Kingdom.

Ecclesiastes 4:1 KJV So I returned, and considered all the oppressions that are done under the sun: and behold the tears of such as were oppressed, and they had no comforter; and on the side of their oppressors there was power; but they had no comforter.

Power is always on the side of the aggressor.

Why is the world like this? Because people cannot see or understand the benefits of living their lives according to the very laws which would bring them peace, abundance, health and happiness, and all they need for a wonderful life. Satan actively stirs up people to indulge their anti-God human nature of lusting after all the things that are bad for them.

War is a system that humans have used throughout history. James 4:1 KJV From whence come wars and fightings among you? Come they not hence, even of your lusts that war in your members?

John 14:26 KJV But the Comforter, which is the Holy Ghost, whom the Father will send in my name, he shall teach you all things, and bring all things to your remembrance, whatsoever I have said unto you.

John 14:16 KJV And I will pray the Father, and he shall give you another Comforter, that he may abide with you for ever;

John 15:26 KJV But when the Comforter is come, whom I will send unto you from the Father, even the Spirit of truth, which proceedeth from the Father, he shall testify of me:

John 16:7 KJV Nevertheless I tell you the truth; It is expedient for you that I go away: for if I go not away, the Comforter will not come unto you; but if I depart, I will send him unto you.

Ant: "Jobs comforters!"

COMMUNICATION

Giving, exchanging information, ideas, advice, advisement, announcing, articulation, assertion, communion, connection, contact, conversation, converse, correspondence, corresponding, declaration, delivery, disclosing, dissemination, elucidation, expression, intelligence, interchange, intercommunication, intercourse, link, making known, mention, notifying, publication, reading, reception, revelation, talk, talking, telling, transfer, translating, transmission, utterance, writing.

In all aspects of communication, godliness demands honesty and purity.

Ephesians 4:29 Let no corrupt communication proceed out of your mouth, but that which is good to the use of edifying, that it may minister grace unto the hearers.

Or as the New Living Translation renders it:

Ephesians 4:29 Don't use foul or abusive language. Let everything you say be good and helpful, so that your words will be an encouragement to those who hear them.

Controlling the tongue is one of the great challenges life offers. James 3:1 My brethren, be not many masters, (or teachers) knowing that we shall receive the greater condemnation. 2 For in many things we offend all. If any man offend not in word, the same is a perfect man, and able also to bridle the whole body. 3 Behold, we put bits in the horses' mouths, that they may obey us; and we turn about their whole body. 4 Behold also the ships, which though they be so great, and are driven of fierce winds, yet are they turned about with a very small helm, whithersoever the governor listeth. 5 Even so the tongue is a little member, and boasteth great things. Behold, how great a matter a little fire kindleth! 6 And the tongue is a fire, a world of iniquity: so is the tongue among our members, that it defileth the whole body, and setteth on fire the course of nature; and it is set on fire of hell. 7 For every kind of beasts, and of birds, and of serpents, and of things in the sea, is tamed, and hath been tamed of mankind: 8 But the tongue can no man tame; it is an unruly evil, full of deadly poison. 9 Therewith bless we God, even the Father; and therewith curse we men, which are made after the similitude of God. 10 Out of the same mouth proceedeth blessing and cursing. My brethren, these things ought not so to be. 11 Doth a fountain send forth at the same place sweet water and bitter? 12 Can the fig tree, my brethren, bear olive berries? either a vine, figs? so can no fountain both yield salt water and fresh.

Ant: Foul mouthed, rude, insulting.

COMMUNION

affinity, agreement accord, association, close relationship, closeness, communing, concord, contact, converse, fellowship, harmony, intercommunication, intercourse, intimacy, participation, rapport, sympathy, togetherness, unity

1 Corinthians 10:16 KJV The cup of blessing which we bless, is it not the communion of the blood of Christ? The bread which we break, is it not the communion of the body of Christ?

2 Corinthians 6:14 KJV Be ye not unequally yoked together with unbelievers: for what fellowship hath righteousness with unrighteousness? and what communion hath light with darkness?

2 Corinthians 13:14 KJV The grace of the Lord Jesus Christ, and the love of God, and the communion of the Holy Ghost, be with you all. Amen

Ant: antagonism, contention, disagreement, discord, disunity, division, hostility, variance

COMPASSIONATE

Show charity, clemency, commiseration, compunction, condolence, fellow feeling, heart, humanity, kindness, mercy, pity, soft-heartedness, sorrow, sympathy, tender-heartedness, tenderness.

Compassionate people feel or show pity, sympathy, empathy and understanding for others who are suffering, or who are in states or conditions which are less conducive to happiness than they would like.

Romans 12:15 Rejoice with them that do rejoice, and weep with them that weep.

Ant: Apathy, cold-heartedness, indifference, mercilessness, unconcern

CONDUCT

Attitude, bearing, behaviour, demeanour, involving manners, the nature of actions, the manner in which a person behaves.

When we are following a Christian path in life, we are seeking to conduct ourselves according to the all embracing simplification of the Royal Law spelled out by Christ:

Luke 10:27 KJV And he answering said, Thou shalt love the Lord thy God with all thy heart, and with all thy soul, and with all thy strength, and with all thy mind; and thy neighbour as thyself. To understand the law of conduct fully, it is necessary to be familiar with the Law in detail.

As we conduct ourselves through life, we are looking forward to immortality in the Kingdom of God. Romans 2:7 KJV To them who by patient continuance in well doing seek for glory and honour and immortality, eternal life. This chapter gives us some clear guidelines for conduct in many aspects of our daily life.

Colossians 3:1 If ye then (potentially) be risen with Christ, seek those things which are above, where Christ sitteth on the right hand of God. 2 Set your affection on things above, not on things on the earth. 3 For ye are dead, and your life is hid with Christ in God. 4 When Christ, who is our life, shall appear, then shall ye also appear with him in glory. 5 Mortify therefore your members which are upon the earth; fornication, uncleanness, inordinate affection, evil concupiscence, and covetousness, which is idolatry: 6 For which things' sake the wrath of God cometh on the children of disobedience: 7 In the which ye also walked some time, when ye lived in them. 8 But now ye also put off all these; anger, wrath, malice, blasphemy, filthy communication out of your mouth. 9 Lie not one to another, seeing that ye have put off the old man with his deeds; 10 And have put on the new man, which is renewed in knowledge after the image of him that created him: 11 Where there is neither Greek nor Jew, circumcision nor uncircumcision, Barbarian, Scythian, bond nor free: but Christ is all, and in all. 12 Put on therefore, as the elect of God, holy and beloved, bowels of mercies, kindness, humbleness of mind, meekness, longsuffering; 13 Forbearing one another, and forgiving one another, if any man have a quarrel against any: even as Christ forgave you, so also do ye. 14 And above all these things put on charity, which is the bond of perfectness. 15 And let the peace of God rule in your hearts, to the which also ye are called in one body; and be ye thankful. 16 Let the word of Christ dwell in you richly in all wisdom; teaching and admonishing one another in psalms and hymns and spiritual songs, singing with grace in your hearts to the Lord. 17 And whatsoever ye do in word or deed, do all in the name of the Lord Jesus, giving thanks to God and the Father by him. 18 Wives, submit yourselves unto your own husbands, as it is fit in the Lord. 19 Husbands, love your wives, and be not bitter against them. 20 Children, obey your parents in all things: for this is well pleasing unto the Lord. 21 Fathers, provoke not your children to anger, lest they be discouraged. 22 Servants, obey in all things your masters according to the flesh; not with eyeservice, as menpleasers; but in singleness of heart, fearing God: 23 And whatsoever ye do, do it heartily, as to the Lord, and not unto men; 24 Knowing that of the Lord ye shall receive the reward of the inheritance: for ye serve the Lord Christ. 25 But he that doeth wrong shall receive for the wrong which he hath done: and there is no respect of persons.

2 Peter 1:5 And beside this, giving all diligence, add to your faith virtue; and to virtue knowledge; 6 And to knowledge temperance; and to temperance patience; and to patience godliness; 7 And to godliness brotherly kindness; and to brotherly kindness charity.

CONFIDENCE

Belief, credence, dependence, faith, reliance, trust, assurance, boldness, courage, firmness, nerve, self-possession, self-reliance

Psalm 118:8 KJV It is better to trust in the LORD than to put confidence in man.

Micah 7:5 KJV Trust ye not in a friend, put ye not confidence in a guide: keep the doors of thy mouth from they that lieth in thy bosom.

Hebrews 3:6 KJV But Christ as a son over his own house; whose house are we, if we hold fast the confidence and the rejoicing of the hope firm unto the end.

CONTENTMENT

Contentedness, ease, equanimity, fulfillment, gladness, gratification, peace, pleasure, repletion, satisfaction, serenity.

There is a challenge for us to learn to be content with whatever our state or condition is, and that is not easy. If we truly believe that God knows our lives in great detail from moment to moment, and that what is happening to us is according to His will, we will not live in a continuum of discontent. This does not mean we should not strive to improve our lot in life, but praying always "Thy Will be done" not only "in earth" but also in my life. Paul said he had achieved that state: Philippians 4:11 KJV Not that I speak in respect of want: for I have learned, in whatsoever state I am, therewith to be content. Or as the complete Jewish Bible puts it: Philippians 4:11 CJB Not that I am saying this to call attention to any need of mine; since, as far as I am concerned, I have learned to be content regardless of circumstances.

Not an easy task. 1 Timothy 6:6 KJV But godliness with contentment is great gain.

Ant: discomfort, discontent, displeasure, dissatisfaction, misery, sadness, unhappiness

CONVERSION

Change, metamorphosis, transfiguration, transformation, change of heart, rebirth, reformation, regeneration

Matthew 18:3 KJV And said, Verily I say unto you, Except ye be converted, and become as little children, ye shall not enter into the kingdom of heaven.

A child-like attitude is a pre-requisite to conversion. That means a willingness and eagerness to learn. Not childish, however, which is a trait that lacks the depth to understand the serious meaning of conversion.

Acts 3:19 KJV Repent ye therefore, and be converted, that your sins may be blotted out, when the times of refreshing shall come from the presence of the Lord;

The word 'repent' means: *late 13c., "to feel regret for sins or crimes," from O.Fr. repentir (11c.), from re-, intensive prefix, + V.L. *penitire "to regret," from L. poenitire "make sorry," from poena (see penal). The distinction between regret (q.v.) and repent is made in many modern languages, but the differentiation is not present in older periods.*

Re-pent means to feel regret again, like re-vise means to look again. So repentance is actually a continuous state of mind of feeling sorrow for past, and present daily errors, for "falling short", or "missing the mark". That does not mean we hang our heads all day long!

These momentary feelings of sorrow are overtaken by the ongoing continuous joy of knowing that our misdeeds and shortcomings are instantly and forever absolved and forgiven. The 'slate' is wiped clean as we live our lives in the assurance that we are 'under grace' which is unmerited pardon.

Acts 2:36 Therefore let all the house of Israel know assuredly, that God hath made that same Jesus, whom ye have crucified, both Lord and Christ. 37 Now when they heard this, they were pricked in their heart, and said unto Peter and to the rest of the apostles, Men and brethren, what shall we do? 38 Then Peter said unto them, Repent, and be baptized every one of you in the name of Jesus Christ for the remission of sins, and ye shall receive the gift of the Holy Ghost. 39 For the promise is unto you, and to your children, and to all that are afar off, even as many as the Lord our God shall call.

Ant: Unrepentant

CONVICTION

Assurance, certainty, certitude, confidence, earnestness, fervour, firmness, reliance, belief, creed, faith, persuasion, principle, tenet, view

Conviction, unlike simple 'belief', comes from having belief that is backed by detailed knowledge, and that conviction leads to faith.

Ant: Unbelief, doubt

COURAGE

Courage is the quality shown by someone who decides to do something difficult or dangerous, even though they may be afraid. (=bravery) If you have the courage of your convictions, you have the confidence to do what you believe is right, even though other people may not agree or approve.

Psalm 27:14 KJV Wait on the LORD: be of good courage, and he shall strengthen thine heart: wait, I say, on the LORD.

Ant: Fearful. If you are fearful of something, you are afraid of it.

1 John 4:18 KJV There is no fear in love; but perfect love casts out fear: because fear hath torment. He that fears is not made perfect in love.

Ant: Fearfulness

COVENANTS

Pact, promise, agreement, arrangement, bargain, bond, commitment, compact, concordat, contract, convention, deal, deed, stipulation, trust.

God has made several covenants or promised contractual arrangements with human beings. After the Noachian flood, God promised never again to flood the earth and kill all that breathes on it, and gave the rainbow as a sign.

The two main Covenants are known to most people involved with any form of Christian religion, are generally called the Old Covenant, and the New Covenant. Christians now have another covenant as given by Christ of the Mystery

COVETOUSNESS

Greedy; very desirous acquisitive, avaricious, avid, close-fisted, eager, envious, gluttonous, grabby, grasping, greed, green-eyed, grudging, hogging, itchy, jealous, keen, mercenary, piggish, prehensile, rapacious, ravenous, selfish, swinish, voracious, yearning

This world is full of covetousness on every side. It is one of the cancers of character, and is a bother of greed. The basic ten most important suggestions for a happy life include:

Deuteronomy 5:21 KJV Neither shalt thou desire thy neighbour's wife, neither shalt thou covet thy neighbour's house, his field, or his manservant, or his maidservant, his ox, or his ass, or any thing that is thy neighbour's.

Philippians 2:21 KJV For all seek their own, (desires) not the things which are Jesus Christ's.

See: GREED, MONEY

Ant: benevolent, generous, giving

CREATION

All things were created by Yahweh who was and became Christ

John 1:1 In the beginning was the Word, and the Word was with God, and the Word was God. 2 The same was in the beginning with God. 3 All things were made by him; and without him was not any thing made that was made. 4 In him was life; and the life was the light of men. 14 And the Word was made flesh, and dwelt among us, (and we beheld his glory, the glory as of the only begotten of the Father,) full of grace and truth.

John 17:24 KJV Father, I will that they also, whom thou hast given me, be with me where I am; that they may behold my glory, which thou hast given me: for thou lovedst me before the foundation of the world.

CRIME AND PUNISHMENT

Why is there so much crime, and why is it definitely getting worse? Simply because the law is so slow to act, and the punishment handed down is no deterrent.

Ecclesiastes 8:11 KJV Because sentence against an evil work is not executed speedily, therefore the heart of the sons of men is fully set in them to do evil.

Prisons in many cases are a comfortable school for learning wrong-doing.

CREATIVE

Artistic, clever, fertile, gifted, imaginative, ingenious, inspired, inventive, original, productive, stimulating, visionary.

God is our Creator, and we are created in His image, that is we have His characteristics, only in a minute measure. Creativity is part of our makeup, as is design. Developing the skills of creativity in a right way is a Godly pursuit.

One way we can be creative is to work on our 'hearts' and our attitude, but this is a fruitless and hopeless task unless God is involved in the 'work'. So like David, we say:

Psalm 51:10 KJV Create in me a clean heart, O God; and renew a right spirit within me.

But this does not work if we just sit back and ask for a clean heart, we have to work at it, but still to know that it is not ourselves that can achieve this, but that it is God who is doing it.

Philippians 2:13 KJV For it is God which worketh in you both to will and to do of his good pleasure.

Ant: Uncreative, unproductive, unimaginative, inept

DEAD

No longer alive, "asleep", bereft of life, bloodless, breathless, buried, cold, cut off, deceased, defunct, departed, done for, erased, expired, extinct, gone, inanimate, inert, late, lifeless, liquidated, mortified, no more, not existing, out of one's misery, passed away, perished, pushing up daisies, reposing, resting in peace, spiritless, stiff, unanimated, wasted

Two other synonyms of 'dead' in the dictionary are: "gone to meet maker, gone to reward," these are not synonyms, they are false doctrines in common usage. "David, a man after God's own heart" is not in heaven, but is in his grave. Acts 2:29 KJV Men and brethren, let me freely speak unto you of the patriarch David, that he is both dead and buried, and his sepulchre is with us unto this day.

When the breath leaves the body, and the spirit returns to God to be retained until the resurrection, a person is dead. That is unconscious, unaware, and has ceased to exist as an entity, not living a 'floaty' existence in another dimension.

Ant: alive, animated, being, existent, existing, live, living, subsisting

DEBT

Money owed to others, IOU, arrears, commitment, credit, debit, deficit, due, dues, encumbrance, in hock, in the hole, in the red, indebtedness, invoice, liability, manifest, mortgage, note, obligation, outstandings, promissory note, receipt, reckoning, red ink, responsibility.

Proverbs 22:7 KJV The rich ruleth over the poor, and the borrower is servant to the lender.

The prosperity our nation and many other nations enjoyed historically has given way to a system of debt where many countries owe more than they can ever repay. They owe so much that they cannot even afford the interest. This is not the way God wants us to live. Earn, and build by working, save and accumulate wealth, then spend. This is a result of man's greed and a Satanic plot to destroy any chance of happiness for humans.

Romans 13:8 KJV Owe no man any thing, but to love one another: for he that loveth another hath fulfilled the law.

See GREED, MONEY, SURETY

Ant: asset, cash, credit, excess, profit

DECISIVENESS

Definite, absolute, all out, assured, certain, conclusive, crisp, critical, crucial, decided, definitive, determined, fateful, final, firm, flat out, forceful, imperative, intent, positive, resolute, resolved, set, settled, significant, straight out, strong-minded, trenchant.

James 1:8 A double minded man is unstable in all his ways

Ant: Indecisive, indefinite, procrastinating, wavering.

DEDICATION

Faithfulness, loyalty, adherence, allegiance, commitment, devotedness, devotion, diligence, single-mindedness, wholeheartedness

Dedication is one of the hallmarks of the Christian. Loyalty to God, His laws, and commitment and devotion to living according to His plan is the way of life. Impossible for any human being to follow Christ, as the constraints are too narrow, and too difficult. We can only make any degree of success with the help of the indwelling Holy Spirit of God. It is God within us that wills and does it for us, which is what living with Christ in us is all about, but it still requires our active participation and will too.

Psalm 119:4 Thou hast commanded us to keep thy precepts diligently.

Hebrews 11:6 But without faith it is impossible to please him: for he that cometh to God must believe that he is, and that he is a rewarder of them that diligently seek him.

Matthew 25:23 His lord said unto him, Well done, good and faithful servant; thou hast been faithful over a few things, I will make thee ruler over many things: enter thou into the joy of thy lord.

Ant: Disloyalty, offhand, unfaithfulness.

DELIGHT

Enjoyment, happiness, contentment, delectation, ecstasy, enchantment, felicity, fruition, gladness, glee, gratification, hilarity, jollity, joy, joyance, mirth, pleasure, rapture, relish, satisfaction, transport

Psalm 1:2 But his delight is in the law of the LORD; and in his law doth he meditate day and night.

Psalm 112:1 Praise ye the LORD. Blessed is the man that feareth (respects) the LORD, that delighteth greatly in his commandments

Ant: depression, disappointment, dismay, melancholy, misery, pain, sorrow, trouble, unhappiness

DESIRE

Desire can be a good emotion, or a bad and sinful one. It all depends on attitude.

Ant: Coolness, aversion, disinterest, antipathy

DEVOTION

Adherence, allegiance, commitment, consecration, constancy, dedication, faithfulness, fidelity, loyalty, adoration, devoutness, godliness, holiness, piety, prayer, religiousness, reverence, sanctity, spirituality, worship, affection, ardour, attachment, earnestness, fervour, fondness, intensity, love, passion, zeal

Devotion is great love, affection, or admiration for someone, or for beliefs. Devotion is commitment to a particular activity particularly in our love and respect for God.

Ant: carelessness, disregard, inattention, indifference, laxity, laxness, neglect, thoughtlessness, derision, disrespect, impiety, irreverence.

DILIGENCE

Perseverance in carrying out action, careful activity, alertness, application, assiduousness, attention, attentiveness, care, constancy, earnestness, heedfulness, industry, intent, intentness, keenness, laboriousness, perseverance, vigour.

Proverbs 4:23 KJV Keep thy heart (attitude) with all diligence; for out of it are the issues of life.

Proverbs 21:5 KJV The thoughts of the diligent tend only to plenteousness; but of every one that is hasty only to want.

Take care of your assets and your business.

Proverbs 22:29 KJV Seest thou a man diligent in his business? He shall stand before kings; he shall not stand before mean men.

Proverbs 27:23 KJV Be thou diligent to know the state of thy flocks, and look well to thy herds.

Every farmer and every shepherd knows how important this is!

2 Peter 3:13 Nevertheless we, according to his promise, look for new heavens and a new earth, wherein dwelleth righteousness. 14 Wherefore, beloved, seeing that ye look for such things, be diligent that ye may be found of him in peace, without spot, and blameless.

We have to keep our minds on the goal of attaining the Kingdom and eternal life as a gift.

Ant: inactivity, indifference, laziness, lethargy, neglect

Christians are required to be diligent in everything they do in their lives.

DISPUTES

Argument altercation, beef, bickering, bone of contention, brawl, broil, brouhaha, commotion, conflict, contention, controversy, debate, difference of opinion, disagreement, discord, discussion, dissension, disturbance, embroilment, falling-out, feud, fireworks, flare-up, fracas, friction, fuss, hubbub, miff, misunderstanding, polemic, quarrel, row, rumpus, squabble, squall, strife, tiff, uproar, variance, words, wrangle.

There are plenty of alternative words for 'dispute' as we see above. This is probably because they are so common, and for so many different reasons, and under all sorts of circumstances.

Our job as Christians hopefully growing in our spirituality will do all we can to avoid entering into any form of dispute with others. Sometimes this will take a great deal of tact and diplomacy, not to mention patience.

Jesus gave us a three step process for dealing with perceived problems with others.

Matthew 18:15 Moreover if thy brother shall trespass against thee, go and tell him his fault between thee and him alone: if he shall hear thee, thou hast gained thy brother. 16 But if he will not hear thee, then take with thee one or two more, that in the mouth of two or three witnesses every word may be established. 17 And if he shall neglect to hear them, tell it unto the church: but if he neglect to hear the church, let him be unto thee as an heathen man and a publican.

Disputes in summary:

1. Talk to the person about it, and do your best to resolve it.

2. Go to the person with a friend who will witness your willingness to resolve it.

3. If that does not work, then the verse says, "Go to the Church ekklesia" or presumably the "elders" in your community. That might present a problem to those who do not attend any place of worship. So what is the principle? Perhaps go to a counselor, an ombudsman or who will arrive at a decision about the matter. When you go back to the person, and they still will not hear you or be reasonable, then the best plan is to disassociate yourself from them.

Notice, this does not suggest we go to law for a judgment. God gave us ten simple instructions which cover everything about laws governing human behaviour in principle. Jesus combined them in to just two, love God, and your fellow humans. Human lawyers and judges have filled huge buildings with 'new' laws, and case law judgments defining every tiny possibility that can occur. Most of these new laws are completely unnecessary if the Law of God is administered in love.

Getting involved with the law is both complicated and invariably very expensive. There are those who feel strongly that the "law is an ass", and indeed there is a lot of evidence daily to support that suggestion.

Luke 12:58 KJV When thou goest with thine adversary to the magistrate, as thou art in the way, give diligence that thou mayest be delivered from him; lest he hale thee to the judge, and the judge deliver thee to the officer, and the officer cast thee into prison.

The Jewish Bible renders the verse: Luke 12:58 CJB Complete Jewish Bible. If someone brings a lawsuit against you, take pains to settle with him first; otherwise he will take the matter to court, and the judge will turn you over to the bailiff, and the bailiff will throw you in jail.

So think carefully before you go to law!

ANT: agreement, resolution

DIVINATION

Fortune-telling, augury, clairvoyancy, horoscopy, occultism, palmistry, prediction, premonition, prognostication, prophecy, soothsaying.

Deuteronomy 18:10 KJV

There shall not be found among you any one that maketh his son or his daughter to pass through the fire, or that useth divination, or an observer of times, or an enchanter, or a witch

Those who are in touch with "familiar spirits" can use tantalizing, but vague, and usually trivial and useless information to fool people to think that they are in touch with those on the "other side". The beings on the "other side" they are in touch with are not dead people, but wicked spirits, cohorts of Satan the Devil. God forbids any activities in this area.

Daniel 2:27 KJV Daniel answered in the presence of the king, and said, The secret which the king hath demanded cannot the wise men, the astrologers, the magicians, the soothsayers, shew unto the king. Daniel 4:7 KJV Then came in the magicians, the astrologers, the Chaldeans, and the soothsayers: and I told the dream before them; but they did not make known unto me the interpretation thereof.

They talk a lot, and intrigue people with their opinions, which are largely guesses based on vague questions and answers, "Is there someone who is a 'J'?" and so on, but they never reveal real truths of any significance or import. Only just a few shreds of things which are "close enough" to something they have experienced to keep the enquirer mesmerized.

Acts 16:16 And it came to pass, as we went to prayer, a certain damsel possessed with a spirit of divination met us, which brought her masters much gain by soothsaying: 17 The same followed Paul and us, and cried, saying, These men are the servants of the most high God, which shew unto us the way of salvation. 18 And this did she many days. But Paul, being grieved, turned and said to the spirit, I command thee in the name of Jesus Christ to come out of her. And he (the evil spirit) came out the same hour.

Ant: Pray only to God for answers to life's issues.

DIVORCE

Split-up of marriage, annulment, breach, break, breakup, decree nisi, detachment, disparateness, dissociation, dissolution, disunion, division, divorcement, parting of the ways, partition, separation, severance, split

Matthew 5:31 It hath been said, Whosoever shall put away his wife, let him give her a writing of divorcement: 32 But I say unto you, That whosoever shall put away his wife, saving for the cause of fornication, causeth her to commit adultery: and whosoever shall marry her that is divorced committeth adultery.

In the same way as many aspects of the law have been liberalized over the last fifty to sixty years, divorce, once rare and considered non-Biblical, is now taken for normal in over fifty percent of marriages which end in the courts.

Ant: Marriage

DOUBT

Lack of faith, conviction; questioning, agnosticism, ambiguity, apprehension, confusion, demurral, difficulty, diffidence, dilemma, disbelief, discredit, disquiet, distrust, dubiety, dubiousness, faithlessness, faltering, fear, hesitancy, hesitation, incertitude, incredulity, indecision, irresolution, lack of confidence, misgiving, mistrust, perplexity, problem, qualm, quandary, rejection, reluctance, scruple, skepticism, suspense, suspicion, uncertainty, vacillation, wavering

Matthew 21:21 KJV Jesus answered and said unto them, Verily I say unto you, If ye have faith, and doubt not, ye shall not only do this which is done to the fig tree, but also if ye shall say unto this mountain, Be thou removed, and be thou cast into the sea; it shall be done.

Mark 11:23 KJV For verily I say unto you, That whosoever shall say unto this mountain, Be thou removed, and be thou cast into the sea; and shall not doubt in his heart, but shall believe that those things which he saith shall come to pass; he shall have whatsoever he saith

Ant: belief, certainty, confidence, dependence, faith, reliance, trust

DRUNKENNESS

Over indulgence in alcohol is not a godly pursuit. Christ's first miracle was to change water into the best wine, so any notion of abstinence from alcohol is not Christ-like either.

Luke 21:34 And take heed to yourselves, lest at any time your hearts be overcharged with surfeiting, and drunkenness, and cares of this life, and so that day come upon you unawares.

1 Corinthians 6:10 Nor thieves, nor covetous, nor drunkards, nor revilers, nor extortioners, shall inherit the kingdom of God.

Ant: Sobriety, self-control

EDIFIED

Make cultured; develop, acquaint, advance, better, cultivate, edify, educate, elevate, enlighten, ennoble, enrich, ethicize, foster, help forward, humanize, idealize, improve, indoctrinate, inform, instruct, polish, promote, reclaim, refine, spiritualize, tame, uplift

Study to shew thyself approved unto God, a workman that needeth not to be ashamed, rightly dividing the word of truth. 2 Timothy 2:15 KJV

Do not allow others, whether individuals or organizations to presume to tell you what to believe and what not to believe. Allow the Spirit of Truth to lead you.

Howbeit when he, the Spirit of truth, is come, he will guide you into all truth: for he shall not speak of himself; but whatsoever he shall hear, that shall he speak: and he will shew you things to come. John 16:13 KJV

So get it "from the horses' mouth"! Not from the organ grinder or his monkey!!

Ant: Ignorant

ENCOURAGING

Bright, cheerful, cheering, comforting, good, heartening, hopeful, promising, reassuring, rosy, satisfactory, stimulating

Someone who is encouraging gives people support, hope, or confidence.

Ant: daunting, depressing, disappointing, discouraging, disheartening, dispiriting, off-putting, unfavourable, unpropitious.

ENTHUSIASM

c.1600, from M.Fr. enthousiasme (16c.) and directly from L.L. enthusiasmus, from Gk. enthousiasmos "divine inspiration," from enthousiazein "be inspired by a god, be rapt, be in ecstasy," from entheos "divinely inspired by a god," from en "in" (see en- (2)) + theos "god",.ardour, avidity, devotion, eagerness, earnestness, excitement, fervour, interest, keenness, passion, relish, vehemence, warmth, zeal, zest.

So the right sort of enthusiasm is a spiritual gift of God. It is the evidence that God is within us.

Ant: Indolence

FAIR DEALING

I Thessalonians 4:15 See that none render evil for evil unto any man; but ever follow that which is good, both among yourselves, and to all men.

Proverbs 11:1 KJV A false balance is abomination to the LORD: but a just weight is his delight.

Proverbs 20:23 KJV Divers weights are an abomination unto the LORD; and a false balance is not good.

Ant: dishonest dealing

FAITH

Assurance, confidence, conviction, credence, credit, dependence, reliance, trust, belief, creed, allegiance, constancy, faithfulness, fealty, fidelity, loyalty.

Hebrews 11:1 Now faith is the substance of things hoped for, the evidence of things not seen.

Faith is not ethereal, it has substance. That we have Faith at all is the evidence in us of things not seen. The worlds were framed from that which was not seen, i.e. the Power and Spirit of God. See: Belief

Ant: Faithless

FAITHFUL

Loyal, reliable, affectionate, allegiant, ardent, circumspect, confiding, conscientious, constant, dependable, devoted, dutiful, enduring, fast, firm, genuine, honest, honorable, incorruptible, loving, obedient, scrupulous, sincere, staunch, steadfast, steady, straight, sure, true, trustworthy, truthful, unchanging, unswerving, unwavering, upright, veracious

All these word that are synonyms of faithful are indeed aspects of love, and are more basic attributes of our God, who wants us to become like Him. Sadly many of them are losing their place in the common language spoken by many, as mankind waxes worse and worse.

2 Timothy 3:13 But evil men and seducers shall wax worse and worse, deceiving, and being deceived.

Deuteronomy 7:9 KJV Know therefore that the LORD thy God, he is God, the faithful God, which keepeth covenant and mercy with them that love him and keep his commandments to a thousand generations;

Ant: Dishonest, disloyal, false, inconstant, treacherous, unfaithful, unreliable, untrue

FORGIVING

Compassionate, forbearing, humane, lenient, magnanimous, merciful, mild, gentle hearted, tolerant

Matthew 6:14 KJV For if ye forgive men their trespasses, your heavenly Father will also forgive you:

Matthew 6:15 KJV But if ye forgive not men their trespasses, neither will your Father forgive your trespasses.

Luke 6:37 KJV Judge not, and ye shall not be judged: condemn not, and ye shall not be condemned: forgive, and ye shall be forgiven:

Ephesians 4:32 KJV And be ye kind one to another, tenderhearted, forgiving one another, even as God for Christ's sake hath forgiven you.

I Thessalonians 4:15 See that none render evil for evil unto any man; but ever follow that which is good, both among yourselves, and to all men.

See: Judgment

Ant: Unforgiving

FREEDOM

Freedom is the opposite of bondage or restraint and has no reference to the theological concept of free will. Choice is the act of selection or having the power to choose between alternative options. Although we have "free choice" to conduct our lives how we like, in one respect we are forced to choose. We either follow our natural bias and our will towards the opposite of goodness when we are deceitful (to ourselves and others) and desperately wicked by nature; or we choose to go God's way. That choice is forced on us despite our free will.

Matthew 7:21 KJV Not every one that saith unto me, Lord, Lord, shall enter into the kingdom of heaven; but he that doeth the will of my Father which is in heaven.

Romans 7:18 KJV For I know that in me (that is, in my flesh,) dwelleth no good thing: for to will is present with me; but how to perform that which is good I find not.

Having free will is a gift which carries huge responsibility. Our life's work is to develop the desire and the practice to recognize that our task is to set aside our will and to allow the will of the Father to flow through to us through Jesus Christ. Not an easy assignment.

Luke 22:42 KJV Saying, Father, if thou be willing, remove this cup from me: nevertheless not my will, but thine, be done

Matthew 26:39 KJV And he went a little further, and fell on his face, and prayed, saying, O my Father, if it be possible, let this cup pass from me: nevertheless not as I will, but as thou wilt.

We can do nothing of any real value unless it is within the will of the Father for us. See: Choice

John 5:30 KJV I can of mine own self do nothing: as I hear, I judge: and my judgment is just; because I seek not mine own will, but the will of the Father which hath sent me.

Ant: Bondage, slavery

FRIENDLINESS

Affability, amiability, companionability, congeniality, conviviality, geniality, kindliness, neighbourliness, open arms, sociability, warmth

Proverbs 18:24 KJV A man that hath friends must shew himself friendly: and there is a friend that sticketh closer than a brother.

Ant: Hostile, unfriendly

FUTURE

God prophesies the future, but the signs follow.

Isaiah 65:17 KJV For, behold, I create new heavens and a new earth: and the former shall not be remembered, nor come into mind.

GENEROSITY

I Thessalonians 4:15 See that none render evil for evil unto any man; but ever follow that which is good, both among yourselves, and to all men.

Ant: Meanness, greed, stingyness

GENTLE

Amiable, benign, bland, compassionate, dove-like, humane, kind, kindly, lenient, meek, merciful, mild, pacific, peaceful, placid, quiet, soft, sweet-tempered, tender, balmy, calm, clement, easy, light, low, mild, moderate, muted, placid, quiet, serene, slight, smooth, soft, soothing, temperate, tranquil, untroubled, gradual, imperceptible, light, mild, moderate, slight, slow, docile, manageable, placid, tame, tractable, aristocratic, civil, courteous, cultured, elegant, genteel, gentlemanlike, gentlemanly, high-born, ladylike, noble, polished, polite, refined, upper-class, well-born, well-bred

Someone who is gentle is kind, mild, and calm. Gentle actions or movements are performed in a calm and controlled manner, with little force.

Ant: Harsh, aggressive, agitated, unkind, aggressive, cruel, fierce, hard, harsh, heartless, impolite, powerful, rough, savage, sharp, strong, sudden, unkind, unmanageable, violent, wild.

GIFT

Something given freely, for no recompense, award, benefaction, benefit, bequest, bestowal, bonus, dispensation, endowment, favor, gratuity, largesse, legacy, present, provision, reward,

Life itself is a GIFT from God.

The past is history,

The future's a mystery,

Today is a gift,

That is why it is called 'The Present'.

Ecclesiastes 3:13 KJV And also that every man should eat and drink, and enjoy the good of all his labour, it is the gift of God.

Ecclesiastes 5:19 KJV Every man also to whom God hath given riches and wealth, and hath given him power to eat thereof, and to take his portion, and to rejoice in his labour; this is the gift of God.

John 4:10 KJV Jesus answered and said unto her, If thou knewest the gift of God, and who it is that saith to thee, Give me to drink; thou wouldest have asked of him, and he would have given thee living water.

Acts 2:38 KJV Then Peter said unto them, Repent, and be baptized every one of you in the name of Jesus Christ for the remission of sins, and ye shall receive the gift of the Holy Ghost.

Acts 10:45 KJV And they of the circumcision which believed were astonished, as many as came with Peter, because that on the Gentiles also was poured out the gift of the Holy Ghost.

Romans 5:15 KJV But not as the offence, so also is the free gift. For if through the offence of one many be dead, much more the grace of God, and the gift by grace, which is by one man, Jesus Christ, hath abounded unto many.

Romans 6:23 KJV For the wages of sin is death; but the gift of God is eternal life through Jesus Christ our Lord.

Ephesians 2:8 KJV For by grace are ye saved through faith; and that not of yourselves: it is the gift of God:

James 1:17 KJV Every good gift and every perfect gift is from above, and cometh down from the Father of lights, with whom is no variableness, neither shadow of turning.

Ant: Loss, ungifted

GIVING

There are two ways in this world, the GIVE way and the GET way.

Jesus said: Luke 6:38 KJV Give, and it shall be given unto you; good measure, pressed down, and shaken together, and running over, shall men give into your bosom. For with the same measure that ye mete withal it shall be measured to you again.

However, giving has to be done wisely. If by giving too much we impoverish ourselves we might render it impossible to give in the future. Like selling your house and giving it to a charity, may not be wise giving. Most charities when investigated, it seems very little of the donations gathered actually reach the beneficiaries intended by the donors.

"Priming someone's pump" with help in the time of need, someone who shows an otherwise responsible attitude, is a great way to give. On the other hand, giving to someone who will definitely abuse the gift, drink it, gamble it, etc. is not doing them any favours. See: Saving, Money

Ant: Taking, robbing, stealing,

GLORY

Our destination!

GODLESS

The theory of evolution is godless. Romans 1:20 KJV For the invisible things of him from the creation of the world are clearly seen, being understood by the things that are made, even his eternal power and Godhead; so that they are without excuse.

GODLY

2 Corinthians 7:10 KJV For godly sorrow worketh repentance to salvation not to be repented of: but the sorrow of the world worketh death.

Titus 2:12 KJV Teaching us that, denying ungodliness and worldly lusts, we should live soberly, righteously, and godly, in this present world;

2 Timothy 3:12 KJV Yea, and all that will live godly in Christ Jesus shall suffer persecution.

1 Corinthians 10:13 KJV There hath no temptation (or test) taken you but such as is common to man: but God is faithful, who will not suffer you to be tempted above that ye are able; but will with the temptation also make a way to escape, that ye may be able to bear it.

Ant: Ungodly, heathen, pagan

GOSPEL

"Good News!" O.E. godspel "gospel, glad tidings announced by Jesus; one of the four gospels," from god "good" (see good) + spel "story, message" (see spell (n.)); translation of L. bona adnuntiatio, itself a translation of Gk. euangelion "reward for bringing good news."

Synonyms: Actuality, authority, belief, certainty, credo, creed, dogma, faith, last word, scripture, testament, truism, truth, veracity, verity

Exactly what was the Gospel or the "Good News"?

That humankind, thanks to Jesus, has the opportunity to become sons and daughters of the Great God, and live forever!! Then shall the King say unto them on his right hand, Come, ye blessed of my Father, inherit the kingdom prepared for you from the foundation of the world: Matthew 25:34 KJV

Not a lot of people understand that, not in reality. Many in the "Christian" churches might think that they are off to heaven to do nothing when they die, BUT Jesus said: Blessed are the meek: for they shall inherit the earth. Matthew 5:5 KJV Not heaven – the EARTH! And the HUGE concept of being a spirit born child of God is not in the minds of many people. It is just too AWESOME!

John 3:16 God so loved the world, that he gave his only begotten Son, that whosoever believeth in him *should not perish, but have everlasting life.* 17 For God sent not his Son into the world to condemn the world; but that the world through him might be saved.

Most are blinded to this. But as it is written, Eye hath not seen, nor ear heard, neither have entered into the heart of man, the things which God hath prepared for them that love him. 1 Corinthians 2:9 KJV

Matthew 24:14 KJV And this gospel of the kingdom shall be preached in all the world for a witness unto all nations; and then shall the end come.

Ant: False gospel, 'another gospel'

GRACE

Unmerited pardon, free forgiveness, absolution.

Also, in days gone by, many people traditionally and habitually said "grace" before eating.

Sadly this practice is all but defunct. For significance of saying "grace", see Health.

Psalm 84:11 KJV For the LORD God is a sun and shield: the LORD will give grace and glory: no good thing will he withhold from them that walk uprightly.

John 1:14 KJV And the Word was made flesh, and dwelt among us, (and we beheld his glory, the glory as of the only begotten of the Father,) full of grace and truth.

John 1:17 KJV For the law was given by Moses, but grace and truth came by Jesus Christ.

Romans 5:2 KJV By whom also we have access by faith into this grace wherein we stand, and rejoice in hope of the glory of God.

Romans 6:14 KJV For sin shall not have dominion over you: for ye are not under the law, but under grace.

Romans 6:15 KJV What then? Shall we sin, because we are not under the law, but under grace? God forbid.

Romans 11:6 KJV And if by grace, then is it no more of works: otherwise grace is no more grace. But if it be of works, then is it no more grace: otherwise work is no more work.

2 Corinthians 1:2 KJV Grace be to you and peace from God our Father, and from the Lord Jesus Christ.

Ephesians 1:7 KJV In whom we have redemption through his blood, the forgiveness of sins, according to the riches of his grace;

Ephesians 2:5 KJV Even when we were dead in sins, hath quickened us together with Christ, (by grace ye are saved;)

Ephesians 2:8 KJV For by grace are ye saved through faith; and that not of yourselves: it is the gift of God:

Titus 3:7 KJV That being justified by his grace, we should be made heirs according to the hope of eternal life.

Hebrews 4:16 KJV Let us therefore come boldly unto the throne of grace, that we may obtain mercy, and find grace to help in time of need.

Hebrews 10:29 KJV Of how much sorer punishment, suppose ye, shall he be thought worthy, who hath trodden under foot the Son of God, and hath counted the blood of the covenant, wherewith he was sanctified, an unholy thing, and hath done despite unto the Spirit of grace?

1 Peter 3:7 KJV Likewise, ye husbands, dwell with them according to knowledge, giving honour unto the wife, as unto the weaker vessel, and as being heirs together of the grace of life; that your prayers be not hindered

1 Peter 5:10 KJV But the God of all grace, who hath called us unto his eternal glory by Christ Jesus, after that ye have suffered a while, make you perfect, stablish, strengthen, settle you.

2 Peter 3:18 KJV

But grow in grace, and in the knowledge of our Lord and Saviour Jesus Christ. To him be glory both now and for ever. Amen.

Ant: Under Law

GRACIOUS

Kind, giving, accommodating, affable, amiable, amicable, approachable, beneficent, benevolent, benign, benignant, big-hearted, bland, bonhomous, charitable, chivalrous, civil, compassionate, complaisant, congenial, considerate, cordial, courteous, courtly, easy, forthcoming, friendly, gallant, genial, good-hearted, good-natured, hospitable, indulgent, lenient, loving, merciful, mild, obliging, pleasing, polite, sociable, stately, suave, tender, unctuous, urbane, well-mannered. gracious means characterized by charm, good taste, kindness, and generosity of spirit

Psalm 86:15 KJV But thou, O Lord, art a God full of compassion, and gracious, longsuffering, and plenteous in mercy and truth.

Psalm 103:8 KJV The LORD is merciful and gracious, slow to anger, and plenteous in mercy.

Psalm 145:8 KJV The LORD is gracious, and full of compassion; slow to anger, and of great mercy.

Numbers 6:23 Speak unto Aaron and unto his sons, saying, On this wise ye shall bless the children of Israel, saying unto them, 24 The LORD bless thee, and keep thee: 25 The LORD make his face shine upon thee, and be gracious unto thee: 26 The LORD lift up his countenance upon thee, and give thee peace. 27 And they shall put my name upon the children of Israel; and I will bless them.

Ant: discourteous, hateful, mean, nasty, rude, sarcastic, severe, ungiving, ungracious, unkind,

GRATITUDE

Appreciation, gratefulness, indebtedness, obligation, recognition, sense of obligation, thankfulness, thanks. We have been given so much, life in an amazing body, the beauty of the world, and the opportunity for eternal life in God's Kingdom. Too few people show gratitude in life for all the good things they have and that happen to them.

Also, in days gone by, many people traditionally and habitually said "grace" before eating. An attitude of showing gratitude to God in connection with our food is actually vital to the proper digestion of food and the assimilation of the nutrients essential for health. For more significance of saying "grace", see Health.

I Thessalonians 4:18 In every thing give thanks: for this is the will of God in Christ Jesus concerning you

Luke 17: 12 And as he entered into a certain village, there met him ten men that were lepers, which stood afar off: 13 And they lifted up their voices, and said, Jesus, Master, have mercy on us. 14 And when he saw them, he said unto them, Go shew yourselves unto the priests. And it came to pass, that, as they went, they were cleansed. 15 And one of them, when he saw that he was healed, turned back, and with a loud voice glorified God, 16 And fell down on his face at his feet, giving him thanks: and he was a Samaritan. 17 And Jesus answering said, Were there not ten cleansed? but where are the nine?

Gratitude is an important spiritual attitude to develop.

Psalm 136:2 KJV O give thanks unto the God of gods: for his mercy endureth for ever.

Psalm 95:2 KJV Let us come before his presence with thanksgiving, and make a joyful noise unto him with psalms.

Read Psalm 95 | View in parallel

Psalm 100:4 KJV Enter into his gates with thanksgiving, and into his courts with praise: be thankful unto him, and bless his name.

Colossians 4:2 KJV Continue in prayer, and watch in the same with thanksgiving;

Ant: ingratitude, ungratefulness, unthankfulness

GREED

Overwhelming desire for more. Acquisitiveness, avarice, avidity, covetousness, craving, cupidity, eagerness, edacity, excess, gluttony, gormandizing, graspingness, hunger, indulgence, insatiableness, intemperance, longing, piggishness, rapacity, ravenousness, selfishness, the gimmies, voracity.

The overwhelming desire for more is at the root of most human problems. Even those who have more money and possessions than they can ever use want more. See also COVET, DEBT, MONEY

Mark 8:36 KJV For what shall it profit a man, if he shall gain the whole world, and lose his own soul?

Ant: Generosity, giving

HAPPINESS

Beatitude, blessedness, bliss, cheer, cheerfulness, cheeriness, contentment, delight, ecstasy, elation, enjoyment, exuberance, felicity, gaiety, gladness, high spirits, joy, jubilation, light-heartedness, merriment, pleasure, prosperity, satisfaction, wellbeing.

Proverbs 3:13 KJV Happy is the man that findeth wisdom, and the man that getteth understanding.

Romans 14:22 KJV Hast thou faith? have it to thyself before God. Happy is he that condemneth not himself in that thing which he alloweth. (himself to do.)

God does want us to appreciate that we fall short, but the idea of incessantly mumbling "we have left undone those things we ought to have done, and done those things that we ought not to have done, and there is no good in us" without being happy is not The Way.

Romans 12:15 KJV Rejoice with them that do rejoice, and weep with them that weep.

Philippians 4:4 KJV Rejoice in the Lord always: and again I say, Rejoice.

Ant: annoyance, bane, depression, despondency, distress, grief, low spirits, misery, misfortune, sadness, sorrow, unhappiness.

HATE

Abhor, abominate, be hostile to, be repelled by, be sick of, despise, detest, dislike, execrate, have an aversion to, loathe, recoil from, be loath to, be reluctant, be sorry, be unwilling, dislike, feel disinclined, have no stomach for, shrink from.

God Is Love, and God also hates. Prov 6:16 These six things doth the LORD hate: yea, seven are an abomination unto him: 17 A proud look, a lying tongue, and hands that shed innocent blood, 18 An heart that deviseth wicked imaginations, feet that be swift in running to mischief, 19 A false witness that speaketh lies, and he that soweth discord among brethren.

Ant: Love in all its aspects

HEALTH

Physical, mental, and spiritual wellness, constitution, energy, fitness, form, good condition, haleness, hardihood, hardiness, healthfulness, healthiness, lustiness, robustness, soundness, stamina, strength, tone, tonicity, top form, verdure, vigor, well-being, wholeness

God wants us to be healthy, wealthy and happy, and to make the most of ourselves and our life. Especially is this true because a Christian wants Christ to live His life through us as He experiences His own Beingness, and develops ours.

3 John 1:2 KJV Beloved, I wish above all things that thou mayest prosper and be in health, even as thy soul prospereth.

Proverbs 3:5 Trust in the LORD with all thine heart; and lean not unto thine own understanding. 6 In all thy ways acknowledge him, and he shall direct thy paths. 7 Be not wise in thine own eyes: fear the LORD, and depart from evil. 8 It shall be health to thy navel, and marrow to thy bones.

Proverbs 4:20 My son, attend to my words; incline thine ear unto my sayings. 21 Let them not depart from thine eyes; keep them in the midst of thine heart. 22 For they are life unto those that find them, and health to all their flesh. 23 Keep thy heart with all diligence; for out of it are the issues of life.

Our tongues can be used for good and ill.

Proverbs 12:18 KJV There is that speaketh like the piercings of a sword: but the tongue of the wise is health.

Proverbs 16:24 KJV Pleasant words are as an honeycomb, sweet to the soul, and health to the bones.

It does your health good to do charitable acts of kindness, always provided that by doing so you are not drawn into charities where very little of your help ever reaches those who need it most. Better to do what you can for those of your acquaintance who have serious needs they cannot manage themselves. Pump priming is always good if the person throws their efforts into the project as well. Lending to others invariably does them no good. Shakespeare said, "Neither a borrower nor a lender be, for borrowing dulls the edge of husbandry." And often ruins friendships.

Isaiah 58:7 Is it not to deal thy bread to the hungry, and that thou bring the poor that are cast out to thy house? when thou seest the naked, that thou cover him; and that thou hide not thyself from thine own flesh? 8 Then shall thy light break forth as the morning, and thine health shall spring forth speedily: and thy righteousness shall go before thee; the glory of the LORD shall be thy rereward. 9 Then shalt thou call, and the LORD shall answer; thou shalt cry, and he shall say, Here I am.

Ant: disease, illness, infirmity, sickness

HEART

A person's emotions, affection, benevolence, character, compassion, concern, disposition, feeling, humanity, inclination, love, nature, pity, relish, response, sensitivity, sentiment, soul, sympathy, temperament, tenderness, understanding, zest

We reveal what is in our "heart of hearts" when we speak.

Luke 6:45 KJV A good man out of the good treasure of his heart bringeth forth that which is good; and an evil man out of the evil treasure of his heart bringeth forth that which is evil: for of the abundance of the heart his mouth speaketh.

Jeremiah 17:9 The heart is deceitful above all things, and desperately wicked: who can know it? 10 I the LORD search the heart, I try the reins, even to give every man according to his ways, and according to the fruit of his doings.

Deuteronomy 6:5 KJV And thou shalt love the LORD thy God with all thine heart, and with all thy soul, and with all thy might.

Genesis 6:5 KJV And GOD saw that the wickedness of man was great in the earth, and that every imagination of the thoughts of his heart was only evil continually. 6. And it repented the LORD that he had made man on the earth, and it grieved him at his heart.

Deuteronomy 5:29 KJV O that there were such an heart in them, that they would fear me, and keep all my commandments always, that it might be well with them, and with their children for ever!

Proverbs 4:23 Keep thy heart with all diligence; for out of it are the issues of life.

See: Tongue

Ant: Heartless

HUMILITY

Diffidence, humbleness, lack of pride, lowliness, meekness, modesty, self-abasement, servility, submissiveness, unpretentiousness

Matt 23:11 But he that is greatest among you shall be your servant. 12 And whosoever shall exalt himself shall be abased; and he that shall humble himself shall be exalted.

Ant: arrogance, conceit, disdain, haughtiness, pomposity, presumption, pretentiousness, pride, snobbishness, superciliousness, superiority, vanity

Ant: Pride

INDUSTRIOUSNESS

Active, assiduous, busy, conscientious, diligent, energetic, hard-working, laborious, persevering, persistent, productive, purposeful, sedulous, steady, tireless, zealous

Proverbs 14:23 KJV In all labour there is profit: but the talk of the lips tendeth only to penury.

Ant: good-for -nothing, idle, indolent, lackadaisical, lazy, shiftless, slothful

JEW - JEWS

A member of the Semitic people who are notionally descended from the ancient Israelites, are spread throughout the world, and are linked by traditions and loose cultural or religious ties, a person whose religion is Judaism,

The word "jew" does not appear in any of the first English translations made around A.D. 1611 from the original texts which were written in Hebrew, Aramaic and Greek. The word "jew" was coined much later in the 1800's. Several words like "judahite", "Judah", or "Judean" were translated "Jew", "Jews" or "Jewish" in the revised versions of the Bible.

The religious people called "Jews" in the New Testament were not following the principles of the Torah, the first five books of the Bible inspired by God. But rather were "teaching for doctrines the commandments of men" from the Babylonian Talmud which contains material which is very far from being God's inspired Word. It is a text polluted with all the worst of the heathen ideas, idolatry, immorality, sex worship.

This is why Jesus Christ condemned the "Jews" in the strongest terms: John 8:44 KJV Ye are of your father the devil, and the lusts of your father ye will do. He was a murderer from the beginning, and abode not in the truth, because there is no truth in him. When he speaketh a lie, he speaketh of his own: for he is a liar, and the father of it.

"Jews" own or control most of the banks and financial institutions of the world which make their money by usury which is fundamentally against God's Law. The Jewish people throughout history have flagrantly broken one of the principle laws of God which states: Exodus 22:25 KJV If thou lend money to any of my people that is poor by thee, thou shalt not be to him as an usurer, neither shalt thou lay upon him usury.

Jesus was incensed at the practice of the "Jews" using the temple as their office for money changing. John 2:13 And the Jews' passover (the Passover was for all Israel, and later for all mankind, not just the jews.) was at hand, and Jesus went up to Jerusalem, 14 And found in the temple those that sold oxen and sheep and doves, and the changers of money sitting: 15 And when he had made a scourge of small cords, he drove them all out of the temple, and the sheep, and the oxen; and poured out the changers' money, and overthrew the tables; 16 And said unto them that sold doves, Take these things hence; make not my Father's house an house of merchandise.

Money changers have traditionally charged a fee for the work of less than a minute equal to what the money would make in a year at a reasonable rate of interest. They still do. This is usury, which is charging an unreasonable rate of interest, i.e. credit cards. In the parable of the rich man and his servant who buried his money instead of investing it wisely, Jesus said: Matt 25:27 Thou oughtest therefore to have put my money to the exchangers, and then at my coming I should have received mine own with usury. (Strong's 5110 tokos – a reasonable rate of interest which is not usury!) The sub-prime mortgage situation caused financial disaster for millions because the interest was unfairly above the base rate.

"Jews" also control much of the medical profession, the clinics which perform procedures which are very far from godly.

Any slight reference that suggests the mildest criticism of "Jews" will bring forth the judgement that you are being "anti-semitic". The people who practice the worst anti-semitism in the world are the "Jews", the "Israelis" who persecute, murder, and harass the Arabs who are actually their 'brothers', being also sons of Shem, Abraham, and Isaac.

Isaac had two sons, Jacob and Esau. Jacob, who became Israel, who had twelve sons, including Judah whose descendents are "Jews". Esau, Jacob's brother became the peoples we know as Arabs.

The religious Jews of today hate the idea of Christ being the Messiah, and are the enemies of Christendom. Jews claim to be the chosen people of God, and say that Christ blasphemes by claiming to be the Son of God. In doing so, the Jewish people separate themselves from the true God, since Jesus clearly stated in John 14:6 KJV Jesus saith unto him, I am the way, the truth, and the life: no man cometh unto the Father, but by me. So for all their religious machinations, they cut themselves off from the true God.

The Jews, descendants of Judah, Levi, and Benjamin also claim that the country known today as Israel is the land God gave to them through Abraham. They claim to be all that is left of "Israel" who were the twelve tribes which grew out of the children of Jacob whose name was changed to Israel. They claim that all the other Israelites "died out". History does not bear this out, as a careful study will show.

Yet in the book of Revelation in the future the twelve tribes of Israel will exist.

Revelation 7:4 KJV And I heard the number of them which were sealed: and there were sealed an hundred and forty and four thousand of all the tribes of the children of Israel.

1 Corinthians 6:2 KJV Do ye not know that the saints shall judge the world? (in the Kingdom of God) and if the world shall be judged by you, are ye unworthy to judge the smallest matters?

Ant: Gentile

JOY

Great happiness, pleasure, bliss, cheer, comfort, delectation, delight, diversion, ecstasy, elation, exultation, exulting, gaiety, gladness, glee, good humor, gratification, jubilance, liveliness, merriment, mirth, rejoicing, satisfaction, solace, wonder.

Matthew 13:44 KJV Again, the kingdom of heaven is like unto treasure hid in a field; the which when a man hath found, he hideth, and for joy thereof goeth and selleth all that he hath, and buyeth that field.

Matthew 25:21 KJV His lord said unto him, Well done, thou good and faithful servant: thou hast been faithful over a few things, I will make thee ruler over many things: enter thou into the joy of thy lord.

John 15:11 KJV These things have I spoken unto you, that my joy might remain in you, and that your joy might be full.

Psalm 35:9 KJV And my soul shall be joyful in the LORD: it shall rejoice in his salvation.

Ant: sadness, sorrow, unhappiness, woe

JUDGMENT

Acumen, common sense, discernment, discrimination, intelligence, penetration, percipience, perspicacity, prudence, sagacity, sense, shrewdness, taste, understanding, wisdom, arbitration, award, conclusion, decision, decree, determination, finding, order, result, ruling, sentence, verdict, appraisal, assessment, belief, conviction, deduction, diagnosis, estimate, finding, opinion, valuation, view

Luke 6:37 KJV Judge not, and ye shall not be judged: condemn not, and ye shall not be condemned: forgive, and ye shall be forgiven:

John 7:24 KJV Judge not according to the appearance, but judge righteous judgment.

Resurrected saints will judge the world in the Kingdom of God under Christ. 1 Corinthians 6:2 KJV Do ye not know that the saints shall judge the world? and if the world shall be judged by you, are ye unworthy to judge the smallest matters?

Anyone who is put into, or takes a position where they are required to judge others, takes on a huge responsibility. The legal systems in even the more civilized countries are parlous examples of unfair and unjust judgments. They operate in such a way that it is unlikely that true justice will be achieved either in criminal or civil cases. Lawyers in Christ's time were not his favourite people. Luke 11:52 KJV Woe unto you, lawyers! for ye have taken away the key of knowledge: ye entered not in yourselves, and them that were entering in ye hindered.

Matthew 5:45 KJV That ye may be the children of your Father which is in heaven: for he maketh his sun to rise on the evil and on the good, and sendeth rain on the just and on the unjust.

Let us not therefore judge one another any more: but judge this rather, that no man put a stumblingblock or an occasion to fall in his brother's way. Romans 14:13 KJV

Ant: Non-judgemental

KINDNESS

Affection, amiability, beneficence, benevolence, charity, clemency, compassion, decency, fellow-feeling, generosity, gentleness, goodness, goodwill, grace, hospitality, humanity, indulgence, kindliness, magnanimity, patience, philanthropy, tenderness, tolerance, understanding, aid, assistance, benefaction, bounty, favour, generosity, good deed, help, service.

Ephesians 4:32 KJV And be ye kind one to another, tenderhearted, forgiving one another, even as God for Christ's sake hath forgiven you.

Ant: Animosity, callousness, cold-heartedness, cruelty, hard-heartedness, heartlessness, ill will, inhumanity, malevolence, malice, misanthropy, viciousness

KINGDOM

Country, domain, dominion, dynasty, lands, monarchy, nation, principality, province, realm, reign, rule, scepter, sovereignty, sphere, state, territory, throne, tract;

The Kingdom is our goal! Our primary aim in life.

Matthew 6:33 But seek ye first the kingdom of God, and his righteousness; and all these things shall be added unto you.

Although salvation is the gift to all mankind, there are conditions to attain to the Kingdom of God. Although "By Grace you are saved, not of works", works cannot earn us salvation but evil works can prevent us from being in the Kingdom. Paul explains:

1 Corinthians 6:9 Know ye not that the unrighteous shall not inherit the kingdom of God? Be not deceived: neither fornicators, nor idolaters, nor adulterers, nor effeminate, nor abusers of themselves with mankind, 10 Nor thieves, nor covetous, nor drunkards, nor revilers, nor extortioners, shall inherit the kingdom of God. 11 And such were some of you: but ye are washed, but ye are sanctified, but ye are justified in the name of the Lord Jesus, and by the Spirit of our God.

Galatians 5:19 Now the works of the flesh are manifest, which are these; Adultery, fornication, uncleanness, lasciviousness, 20 Idolatry, witchcraft, hatred, variance, emulations, wrath, strife, seditions, heresies, 21 Envyings, murders, drunkenness, revellings, and such like: of the which I tell you before, as I have also told you in time past, that they which do such things shall not inherit the kingdom of God.

So although "works" cannot save you, "the evil works that men do" can drastically affect our future. See: WORKS

Ant: Anarchy

LAW ABIDING

Compliant, dutiful, good, honest, honourable, lawful, obedient, orderly, peaceable, peaceful

Our natural carnal human heart is naturally rebellious towards the laws of God which He gave us to guide us into a life of fulfillment and happiness. So the law says: Deuteronomy 12:8 KJV Ye shall not do after all the things that we do here this day, every man whatsoever is right in his own eyes.

Jeremiah 31:33 KJV But this shall be the covenant that I will make with the house of Israel, (and all humanity) After those days, saith the LORD, I will put my law in their inward parts, and write it in their hearts; and will be their God, and they shall be my people.

During God's Theocratic rule, anyone aspiring to be a king, ruler, or a leader was instructed to write out a copy of God's law so they would become more than familiar with it. If the rulers of this present evil world did this, they would see their responsibilities in a different light, and treat their populations very differently.

Deut 17:18 And it shall be, when he sits upon the throne of his kingdom, that he shall write him a copy of this law in a book out of that which is before the priests the Levites: 19 And it shall be with him, and he shall read therein all the days of his life: that he may learn to fear the LORD his God, to keep all the words of this law and these statutes, to do them: 20 That his heart be not lifted up above his brethren, and that he turn not aside from the commandment, to the right hand, or to the left: to the end that he may prolong his days in his kingdom, he, and his children, in the midst of Israel. (or any other country!)

Ant: Criminal

LIFE AND DEATH

John 14:6 KJV Jesus saith unto him, I am the way, the truth, and the life: no man cometh unto the Father, but by me.

The idea that we go to heaven when we die, or the concept of an ever burning hell (Dante's inferno)They have no basis in the scripture whatsoever. Hell is a notion that were thought up by religions to control and hold people in fear.

Matthew 5:5 KJV Blessed are the meek: for they shall inherit the earth. (After the resurrection when the Kingdom of God is established on earth.)

Psalm 37:11 KJV But the meek shall inherit the earth; and shall delight themselves in the abundance of peace.

John 3:13 KJV And no man hath ascended up to heaven, but he that came down from heaven, even the Son of man which is in heaven.

John 8:53 KJV Art thou greater than our father Abraham, which is dead? and the prophets are dead: whom makest thou thyself?

Acts 2:34 KJV For David is not ascended into the heavens: but he saith himself, The LORD said unto my Lord, Sit thou on my right hand.

Acts 2:29 KJV Men and brethren, let me freely speak unto you of the patriarch David, that he is both dead and buried, and his sepulchre is with us unto this day.

What then is the mechanism of life and death?

Genesis 2:7 KJV And the LORD God formed man of the dust of the ground, and breathed into his nostrils the breath of life; and man became a living soul.

DUST PLUS BREATH = LIVING SOUL

Job 33:4 KJV The Spirit of God hath made me, and the breath of the Almighty hath given me life

DUST MINUS BREATH = DUST

Ecclesiastes 9:5 KJV For the living know that they shall die: but the dead know not any thing, neither have they any more a reward; for the memory of them is forgotten.

Psalm 6:5 KJV For in death there is no remembrance of thee: in the grave who shall give thee thanks?

Ecclesiastes 12:7 KJV Then shall the dust return to the earth as it was: and the spirit shall return unto God who gave it.

The spirit of man has no life without the body. But the person is not in heaven, as the spirit has no consciousness without the body. When the person is resurrected, God creates a new body for the person out of Spirit and re-creates the person by joining the new body with their spirit which He has kept stored in heaven with Him.

The analogy of a tape and a tape recorder, or computer file and a video helps some understand this concept. The music (the spirit) is recorded on the tape cassette or file, but cannot be played without a tape recorder or TV (the body).

See: Spirit

LIGHT

Medium of illumination that makes sight possible, visible radiation, electromagnetic radiation that is capable of causing a visual sensation and has wavelengths from about 380 to about 780 nanometres, electromagnetic radiation that has a wavelength outside this range, esp. ultraviolet radiation, ultraviolet light, the sensation experienced when electromagnetic radiation within the visible spectrum falls on the retina of the eye

1 John 1:5 KJV This then is the message which we have heard of him, and declare unto you, that God is light, and in him is no darkness at all.

God gave us light, the amazing spectrum of beautiful colour, and the eyes to see and enjoy it.

Genesis 1:16 KJV And God made two great lights; the greater light to rule the day, and the lesser light to rule the night: he made the stars also.

2 Corinthians 4:6 KJV For God, who commanded the light to shine out of darkness, hath shined in our hearts, to give the light of the knowledge of the glory of God in the face of Jesus Christ.

John 1:4 KJV In him (Christ) was life; and the life was the light of men. 5 And the light shineth in darkness; and the darkness comprehended it not.

Matthew 6:22 KJV The light of the body is the eye: if therefore thine eye be single, thy whole body shall be full of light.

Matthew 6:23 KJV But if thine eye be evil, thy whole body shall be full of darkness. If therefore the light that is in thee be darkness, how great is that darkness!

Matthew 5:16 KJV Let your light so shine before men, that they may see your good works, and glorify your Father which is in heaven.

Lights make no noise, so our lives should be an example, not our words.

Matthew 5:16 KJV Let your light so shine before men, that they may see your good works, and glorify your Father which is in heaven.

Being in the 'light' is not easy. This world is controlled by invisible powers controlling world governments, the media, the financial systems.

Ephesians 6:12 KJV For we wrestle not against flesh and blood, but against principalities, against powers, against the rulers of the darkness of this world, against spiritual wickedness in high places.

Human beings are in darkness, so they cannot really 'see' the Godlessness of this world.

John 3:19 KJV And this is the condemnation, that light is come into the world, and men loved darkness rather than light, because their deeds were evil.

2 Corinthians 4:4 KJV In whom the god of this world hath blinded the minds of them which believe not, lest the light of the glorious gospel of Christ, who is the image of God, should shine unto them.

Acts 26:18 KJV To open their eyes, and to turn them from darkness to light, and from the power of Satan unto God, that they may receive forgiveness of sins, and inheritance among them which are sanctified by faith that is in me.

1 Peter 2:9 KJV But ye are a chosen generation, a royal priesthood, an holy nation, a peculiar people; that ye should

shew forth the praises of him who hath called you out of darkness into his marvellous light:

Ant: Darkness, godless

LOVING

Affectionate, amorous, ardent, cordial, dear, demonstrative, devoted, doting, fond, friendly, kind, solicitous, tender, warm, warm-hearted

Loving is an attitude of mind and spirit that is motivated by the desire to keep the laws of love.

John 14:15 KJV If ye love me, keep my commandments.

John 15:10 KJV If ye keep my commandments, ye shall abide in my love; even as I have kept my Father's commandments, and abide in his love.

Ant: aloof, cold, contemptuous, cruel, detached, distasteful, hateful, hostile, indifferent, mean, scornful, unconcerned, unloving

LOVING KINDNESS

Is an attribute of God.

Psalm 31:21 KJV Blessed be the LORD: for he hath shewed me his marvellous kindness in a strong city.

Psalm 117:2 KJV For his merciful kindness is great toward us: and the truth of the LORD endureth for ever. Praise ye the LORD.

Ephesians 2:7 KJV That in the ages to come he might shew the exceeding riches of his grace in his kindness toward us through Christ Jesus.

MATURITY

adulthood, full growth, development, experience, matureness, wisdom,

1 Corinthians 13:11 KJV When I was a child, I spake as a child, I understood as a child, I thought as a child: but when I became a man, I put away childish things.

Ant: Immaturity, childishness,

MEDIATOR

Advocate, arbiter, arbitrator, go-between, honest broker, interceder, intermediary, judge, middleman, moderator, negotiator, peacemaker, referee, umpire.

1 Timothy 2:5 KJV For there is one God, and one mediator between God and men, the man Christ Jesus;

Hebrews 8:6 KJV But now hath he obtained a more excellent ministry, by how much also he is the mediator of a better covenant, which was established upon better promises

Hebrews 9:15 KJV And for this cause he is the mediator of the new testament, (or covenant) that by means of death, for the redemption of the transgressions that were under the first testament, they which are called might receive the promise of eternal inheritance.

MEDITATE

Cogitate, consider, contemplate, deliberate, muse, ponder, reflect, ruminate, study, think, consider, contemplate, design, devise, have in mind, intend, mull over, plan, purpose, scheme, think over.

A person who recognizes God as Love, will want to think about the Creator, His laws, and precepts that He has given mankind so we can live a happy, productive, godly life.

Psalm 1:2 But his delight is in the law of the Lord, and in his law doth he meditate day and night.

Antonym: 'Meditation' that takes the form of 'emptying the mind' or concentrating on the endless repetition of a meaningless 'mantra' takes the mind into a state of mental hibernation, but loses the spiritual connection with the Creator.

MEEKNESS

deference, docility, forbearance, gentleness, humbleness, humility, long-suffering, lowliness, mildness, modesty, patience, peacefulness, resignation, softness, submission, submissiveness, acquiescence, compliance

Meekness is NOT weakness, it is a spiritual attitude of humility. This attribute concerns being quiet, amenable and ready to listen to what other people say, and willing to learn. Being willing to learn under all circumstances is a great personal spiritual strength.

Antonym: Knows it all, cannot be told, stuck in opinions.

MERCIFUL

beneficent, benignant, clement, compassionate, forbearing, forgiving, generous, gracious, humane, kind, lenient, liberal, mild, pitying, soft, sparing, sympathetic, tender-hearted

Matthew 5:7 KJV Blessed are the merciful: for they shall obtain mercy.

Ant: cruel, hard-hearted, inhumane, merciless, pitiless, uncompassionate, unfeeling

MIND

Intellect, intelligence, mentality, reason, sense, spirit, understanding, wits, memory, recollection, remembrance

Matthew 22:37 KJV Jesus said unto him, Thou shalt love the Lord thy God with all thy heart, and with all thy soul, and with all thy mind.

Philippians 2:5 Let this mind be in you, which was also in Christ Jesus: 6 Who, being in the form of God, thought it not robbery to be equal with God: 7 But made himself of no reputation, and took upon him the form of a servant, and was made in the likeness of men: 8 And being found in fashion as a man, he humbled himself, and became obedient unto death, even the death of the cross. 9 Wherefore God also hath highly exalted him, and given him a name which is above every name: 10 That at the name of Jesus every knee should bow, of things in heaven, and things in earth, and things under the earth; 11 And that every tongue should confess that Jesus Christ is Lord, to the glory of God the Father.

1 Chronicles 28:9 KJV And thou, Solomon my son, know thou the God of thy father, and serve him with a perfect heart and with a willing mind: for the LORD searcheth all hearts, and understandeth all the imaginations of the thoughts: if thou seek him, he will be found of thee; but if thou forsake him, he will cast thee off for ever.

Isaiah 26:3 KJV Thou wilt keep him in perfect peace, whose mind is stayed on thee: because he trusteth in thee.

Matthew 22:37 KJV Jesus said unto him, Thou shalt love the Lord thy God with all thy heart, and with all thy soul, and with all thy mind.

Mark 12:30 KJV And thou shalt love the Lord thy God with all thy heart, and with all thy soul, and with all thy mind, and with all thy strength: this is the first commandment

Luke 10:27 KJV And he answering said, Thou shalt love the Lord thy God with all thy heart, and with all thy soul, and with all thy strength, and with all thy mind; and thy neighbour as thyself.

Humanistic psychologists and evolutionary ideologies are godless, and lead to people doing what they think is right in their own mind, invariably against and in contradiction of

God's laws. Romans 1:28 KJV And even as they did not like to retain God in their knowledge, God gave them over to a reprobate mind, to do those things which are not convenient;

Our mind is a battle ground where constant warfare is going on either to follow God's way and not the inclination of our own human nature.

Romans 7:23 KJV But I see another law in my members, warring against the law of my mind, and bringing me into captivity to the law of sin which is in my members.

Romans 7:25 KJV I thank God through Jesus Christ our Lord. So then with the mind I myself serve the law of God; but with the flesh the law of sin.

Romans 8:5 KJV For they that are after the flesh do mind the things of the flesh; but they that are after the Spirit the things of the Spirit.

Romans 8:7 KJV Because the carnal mind is enmity against God: for it is not subject to the law of God, neither indeed can be

Romans 12:2 KJV And be not conformed to this world: but be ye transformed by the renewing of your mind, that ye may prove what is that good, and acceptable, and perfect, will of God.

Ephesians 4:23 KJV And be renewed in the spirit of your mind;

Philippians 2:5 KJV Let this mind be in you, which was also in Christ Jesus:

Colossians 3:12 KJV Put on therefore, as the elect of God, holy and beloved, bowels of mercies, kindness, humbleness of mind, meekness, longsuffering;

2 Timothy 1:7 KJV For God hath not given us the spirit of fear; but of power, and of love, and of a sound mind.

Hebrews 8:10 KJV For this is the covenant that I will make with the house of Israel after those days, saith the Lord; I will put my laws into their mind, and write them in their hearts: and I will be to them a God, and they shall be to me a people:

MISCEGENATION

Composite, mixture, amalgam, bastard, combination, compound, cross, crossbreed, half-blood, half-breed, half-caste, miscegenation, mongrel.

Having other Gods than the One Tue God is a pathway to destruction.

Deuteronomy 5:7 Thou shalt have none other gods before me. 8 Thou shalt not make thee any graven image, or any likeness of any thing that is in heaven above, or that is in the earth beneath, or that is in the waters beneath the earth: 9 Thou shalt not bow down thyself unto them, nor serve them: for I the LORD thy God am a jealous God, visiting the iniquity of the fathers upon the children unto the third and fourth generation of them that hate me, 10 And shewing mercy unto thousands of them that love me and keep my commandments.

Nations other than Israel worshipped other gods and had heinous practices like sacrificing children in fire, using illicit sex to worship and so on. They still do. There are many nations in the world who make idols of wood and stone, and bow down to them. Some also have practices which God hates. It is 'modern' to 'accept' that other religions have their place. Not according to the laws God laid down for His special people.

Inter-marriage with other nations is explicitly forbidden because their practices will take Israel's people away from the worship of the One True God. For that reason miscegenation is strictly forbidden, as is the modern determination to establish multi-culturalism as the norm.

Deuteronomy 7:1 When the LORD thy God shall bring thee into the land whither thou goest to possess it, and hath cast out many nations before thee ... 2 And when the LORD thy God shall deliver them before thee; thou shalt smite them, and utterly destroy them; thou shalt make no covenant with them, nor shew mercy unto them: 3 Neither shalt thou make marriages with them; thy daughter thou shalt not give unto his son, nor his daughter shalt thou take unto thy son. 4 For they will turn away thy son from following me, that they may serve other gods: so will the anger of the LORD be kindled against you, and destroy thee suddenly. 5 But thus shall ye deal with them; ye shall destroy their altars, and break down their images, and cut down their groves, and burn their graven images with fire.

God wanted to keep His people racially pure. This sounds like racism, and it is, pure and simple. God wanted to keep the races separate, and Satan wanted to mix them all up, and he has succeeded in huge measure. The effect of miscegenation has resulted in the worship of the true God is being hindered and even prevented in our modern world. It has become politically incorrect to be a God-fearing Christian!

Deuteronomy 7:6 For thou art an holy people unto the LORD thy God: the LORD thy God hath chosen thee to be a special people unto himself, above all people that are upon the face of the earth. 7 The LORD did not set his love upon you, nor choose you, because ye were more in number than any people; for ye were the fewest of all people: 8 But because the LORD loved you, and because he would keep the oath which he had sworn unto your fathers, hath the LORD brought you out with a mighty hand, and redeemed you out of the house of bondmen, from the hand of Pharaoh king of Egypt. 9 Know therefore that the LORD thy God, he is God, the faithful God, which keepeth covenant and mercy with them that love him and keep his commandments to a thousand generations;

Ant: homogeneous, pedigreed, pure, purebred, thoroughbred, unmixed

MONEY

A medium of exchange that functions as legal tender. The official currency, in the form of banknotes, coins, etc., issued by a government or other authority, a particular denomination or form of currency, silver money, property or assets with reference to their realizable value.

Money is NOT the root of all evil. This is a mis-quoted passage in the Bible where it states:

1 Timothy 6:10 For the love of money is the root of all evil: which while some coveted after, they have erred from the faith, and pierced themselves through with many sorrows.

Since Britain and the United States abolished the 'gold standard' and issued paper money, or coins from base metal, money has no intrinsic value whatsoever. Its rate of exchange (or "value") can easily be manipulated by the federal or national banks. The money printed by these organizations is then leased (at interest – or usury) to the appropriate government at a rate of interest which the bankers decide. This leads to a steady or at times violent spiral of inflation, which actually is stealing as inflation makes the money worth less and less. This usually leads to the banks printing more money which has no value.

Almost nobody realizes the these federal banks of the U.S., (the "Fed", Britain (the Bank of England), and the Federal bank of Australia are all privately owned and controlled by the undeclared owners behind the scenes who do not have to reveal their identity. This relatively small number of people basically runs the world's finances.

All this breaks the fundamental laws of God concerning money.

Deuteronomy 25:15 KJV But thou shalt have a perfect and just weight, a perfect and just measure shalt thou have: that thy days may be lengthened in the land which the LORD thy God giveth thee.

Exodus 22:25 KJV If thou lend money to any of my people that is poor by thee, thou shalt not be to him as an usurer, neither shalt thou lay upon him usury.

Leviticus 25:36 KJV Take thou no usury of him, or increase: but fear thy God; that thy brother may live with thee.

Psalm 37:21 KJV The wicked borroweth, and payeth not again: but the righteous sheweth mercy, and giveth.

Proverbs 11:1 KJV A false balance is abomination to the LORD: but a just weight is his delight.

1 Tim 6:10 For the love of money is the (a) root of all evil: which while some coveted after, they have erred from the faith, and pierced themselves through with many sorrows.

There is nothing in this present evil world that can give us any real security.

1 Timothy 6:7 For we brought nothing into this world, and it is certain we can carry nothing out

Matt 6:19 Lay not up for yourselves treasures upon earth, where moth and rust doth corrupt, and where thieves break through and steal: 20 But lay up for yourselves treasures in heaven, where neither moth nor rust doth corrupt, and where thieves do not break through nor steal: 21 For where your treasure is, there will your heart be also.

Proverbs 30:8 Remove far from me vanity and lies: give me neither poverty nor riches; feed me with food convenient for me: 9 Lest I be full, and deny thee, and say, Who is the LORD? or lest I be poor, and steal, and take the name of my God in vain.

On the other hand, it is prudent to use money wisely. In good times, spend carefully, and save long-term. Proverbs 30:25 The ants are a people not strong, yet they prepare their meat in the summer; See Give, Save, Covet, Wealth

An: Destitute, penniless

MYSTERY

Secret, closed book. Up until after the time of Christ in A.D.63, the "mystery" of God's plan had not been revealed to mankind.

Perhaps some of those individuals, like Noah, Abraham, David, etc., with whom God worked more closely with His Spirit may have had glimpses, but that is not clear. The disciples did not understand the "mystery" at all, although they had been told about the Kingdom of God.

Mark 4:11 KJV And he said unto them, Unto you it is given to know the mystery of the kingdom of God: but unto them that are without, all these things are done in parables:

Matthew 13:35 KJV That it might be fulfilled which was spoken by the prophet, saying, I will open my mouth in parables; I will utter things which have been kept secret from the foundation of the world.

Matthew 25:34 KJV Then shall the King say unto them on his right hand, Come, ye blessed of my Father, inherit the kingdom prepared for you from the foundation of the world:

But the time was coming when it would be revealed more clearly.

Romans 11:25 KJV For I would not, brethren, that ye should be ignorant of this mystery, lest ye should be wise in your own conceits; that blindness in part is happened to Israel, until the fullness of the Gentiles be come in.

Romans 16:25 KJV Now to him that is of power to stablish you according to my gospel, and the preaching of Jesus Christ, according to the revelation of the mystery, which was kept secret since the world began,

1 Corinthians 2:7 KJV But we speak the wisdom of God in a mystery, even the hidden wisdom, which God ordained before the world unto our glory:

1 Corinthians 15:51 KJV Behold, I shew you a mystery; We shall not all sleep, but we shall all be changed,

Ephesians 1:9 KJV Having made known unto us the mystery of his will, according to his good pleasure which he hath purposed in himself:

Ephesians 3:3 KJV How that by revelation he made known unto me the mystery; (as I wrote afore in few words, 4 Whereby, when ye read, ye may understand my knowledge in the mystery of Christ)

Ephesians 3:9 KJV And to make all men see what is the fellowship of the mystery, which from the beginning of the world hath been hid in God, who created all things by Jesus Christ:

Colossians 1:26 KJV Even the mystery which hath been hid from ages and from generations, but now is made manifest to his saints:

Colossians 1:27 KJV To whom God would make known what is the riches of the glory of this mystery among the Gentiles; which is Christ in you, the hope of glory

Jesus Christ revealed the fact that the "mystery" concerned the plan for humans to become part of the Family and Kingdom of God, but more detailed information was to come after the coming of the Holy Spirit.

Ephesians 1:4 KJV According as he hath chosen us in him before the foundation of the world, that we should be holy and without blame before him in love

Later "the revelation of the mystery" was given to Peter and Paul, that Gentiles, as well as Israel would be partakers of His Spirit, and that our destiny is to become fully born spirit children of God.

Parables obscured the truth from the masses, then as now, to protect them, because it was not "their time" then and for most people on the earth, it is not "their time" now.

Despite the fact that it has been revealed, the 'mystery' is still a complete "mystery" to most people, even those who claim to be Christians, as they neither know nor appreciate the magnitude of the offer, preferring to hold Biblically unsubstantiated notions of a life in heaven. Still blinded, or what?

Mark 4:10 And when he was alone, they that were about him with the twelve asked of him the parable. 11 And he said unto them, Unto you it is given to know the mystery of the kingdom of God: but unto them that are without, all these things are done in parables: 12 That seeing they may see, and not perceive; and hearing they may hear, and not understand; lest at any time they should be converted, and their sins should be forgiven them.

Many people think that Christianity is for everyone, and should be preached to all. But Jesus said to the contrary. Enlightenment is only given to those who God calls, and when He calls them, and many are called but few are chosen.

Matthew 22:14 KJV For many are called, but few are chosen.

Matthew 7:14 KJV Because strait is the gate, and narrow is the way, which leadeth unto life, and few there be that find it.

Romans 8:28 KJV And we know that all things work together for good to them that love God, to them who are the called according to his purpose.

The institution of marriage pictures the unity, (and ecstasy), we shall have with Christ in the Kingdom. Ephesians 5:32 This is a great mystery: but I speak concerning Christ and the church. Christ is the husband, and the wife is the church. 33 Nevertheless let every one of you in particular so love his wife even as himself; and the wife see that she reverence her husband.

NATURALNESS

artlessness, candidness, frankness, genuineness, ingenuousness, openness, realism, simpleness, simplicity, spontaneousness, unaffectedness, unpretentiousness, unsophisticatedness, unstudiedness, candour, frankness, honesty, sincerity, truthfulness.

Ant: Guile: artfulness, artifice, cleverness, craft, craftiness, cunning, deceit, deception, duplicity, gamesmanship, knavery, ruse, sharp practice, slyness, treachery, trickery, trickiness, wiliness. 1 Peter 2:1 KJV Wherefore laying aside all malice, and all guile, and hypocrisies, and envies, and all evil speakings,

John 1:47 KJV Jesus saw Nathanael coming to him, and saith of him, Behold an Israelite indeed, in whom is no guile!

Ant: Unnatural

OBEDIENCE

accordance, acquiescence, agreement, assent, compliance, conformability, deference, docility, dutifulness, duty, observance, respect, reverence, submission, submissiveness, subservience, tractability

Obedience to God's Law is the Way of life.

John 15:10 KJV If ye keep my commandments, ye shall abide in my love; even as I have kept my Father's commandments, and abide in his love.

John 14:15 KJV If ye love me, keep my commandments.

The projection of a harsh, punishing God is from religions that are influenced and guided by Satan, who have used fear to control the people. For us, the commandments are not harsh 'thou shalt NOT's.

When God made the Old Covenant with Israel, the commandments were first given to carnal people who had no access to God's Spirit, the punishment for breaking them was physical death. Even that penalty did not stop the Israelites from breaking them at every opportunity. Even the daily miracle of being fed with manna, and the recent memory of their miraculous deliverance from Egypt with God's direct intervention did not stop them from breaking the law.

Now we are under the New Covenant, and the commandments have an entirely different "feel" to them, or should have if we believe what Christ told us about them. They are the loving recommendations of a loving God. The reason we learn the law, and keep it, is because we love and appreciate

God, not because we are terrified not to, nor because we fear punishment.

The laws are now of the Spirit, and are therefore more binding on us as Christians than the Old Law. There really are only two commandments, love God, and your neighbour as yourself.

Physical adultery was punishable with death. The new law Jesus gave us intensified that to read, just by looking and lusting after a woman, or man, is to commit adultery in your heart. By coveting, disrespecting parents on our minds, we are breaking the law. Jesus said if we hate anyone in our hearts, we are guilty of murder. So the bar has been raised a great deal higher than with the Israelites of old!

We have to keep our hearts and minds from transgressing the laws of God as we strive to become more like Him. It is of course impossible for a human not to break these spiritual laws, but our death penalty has been removed by the death of Christ on the stake as we live our lives in a constant of ongoing repentance.

Ant: Disobedience, law breaking, sin

PATIENCE

Calmness, composure, cool, equanimity, even temper, forbearance, imperturbability, restraint, serenity, sufferance, tolerance, toleration, constancy, diligence, endurance, fortitude, long-suffering, perseverance, persistence, resignation, stoicism, submission

Luke 21:19 KJV In your patience possess ye your souls.

Romans 5:3 KJV And not only so, but we glory in tribulations also: knowing that tribulation worketh patience 4 And patience, experience; and experience, hope:

Romans 8:25 KJV But if we hope for that we see not, then do we with patience wait for it.

James 1:3 KJV

Knowing this, that the trying of your faith worketh patience.

Hebrews 12:1 KJV Wherefore seeing we also are compassed about with so great a cloud of witnesses, let us lay aside every weight, and the sin which doth so easily beset us, and let us run with patience the race that is set before us,

Ant: Agitation, exasperation, excitement, impatience, irritation, nervousness, passion, restlessness, irresolution, vacillation

PEACE

Harmony, agreement, accord, amity, armistice, cessation, conciliation, concord, friendship, love, neutrality, order, pacification, pacifism, reconciliation, treaty, truce, unanimity, union, unity.

Psalm 119:165 KJV Great peace have they which love thy law: and nothing shall offend them.

Isaiah 26:3 KJV Thou wilt keep him in perfect peace, whose mind is stayed on thee: because he trusteth in thee.

Colossians 3:14 And above all these things put on charity, which is the bond of perfectness. 15 And let the peace of God rule in your hearts, to the which also ye are called in one body; and be ye thankful.

BUT... There will never be peace on this earth despite all efforts to engage in a "peace process" what ever that is. It is certainly not a process that leads to peace! War is the glue that keeps the people of nations focused on their national identity. Wars provide a 'cause' for people to associate themselves with, and feed the human nature's motivation to fight.

Jeremiah 6:13 For from the least of them even unto the greatest of them every one is given to covetousness; and from the prophet even unto the priest every one dealeth falsely. 14 They have healed also the hurt of the daughter of my people slightly, saying, Peace, peace; when there is no peace. 15 Were they ashamed when they had committed abomination? nay, they were not at all ashamed, neither could they blush: therefore they shall fall among them that fall: at the time that I visit them they shall be cast down, saith the LORD.

War will never be banished on this planet until Christ's second coming, and the setting up of the Kingdom of God, and even then there will be wars until peace is finally established.

And Christ warned that being a Christian would put us in opposition to our families and to the world. Christianity is not an easy path! It is not a nicey-nice cosy social club like so many in churchianity 'enjoy'. Following God's law, and doing one's best to be a Christian separates a person from those who have no interest in doing so. It creates disharmony, disunity, and invites criticism from those whose only interests are worldly.

Matthew 10:34 Think not that I am come to send peace on earth: I came not to send peace, but a sword. 35 For I am come to set a man at variance against his father, and the daughter against her mother, and the daughter in law against her mother in law. 36 And a man's foes shall be they of his own household. 37 He that loveth father or mother more than me is not worthy of me: and he that loveth son or daughter more than me is not worthy of me. 38 And he that taketh not his cross, and followeth after me, is not worthy of me. 21 And the brother shall deliver up the brother to death, and the father the child: and the children shall rise up against their parents, and cause them to be put to death

Ant: disagreement, disharmony, fighting, war

POLITE

Affable, civil, complaisant, courteous, deferential, gracious, mannerly, obliging, respectful, well-behaved, well-mannered, civilized, courtly, cultured, elegant, genteel, polished, refined, sophisticated, urbane, well-bred.

Ant: crude, discourteous, ill-mannered, impertinent, impolite, impudent, insulting, rude, uncultured, unrefined

POVERTY

Poverty is not for God loving and fearing people.

See: Prosperity

PRAYER

Asking, pleading, especially with a deity; appeal, application, begging, beseeching, communion, devotion, entreaty, grace, imploration, imploring, invocation, litany, petition, plea, pleading, request, request for help, supplication, worship

Luke 11:2 KJV And he said unto them, When ye pray, say, Our Father which art in heaven, Hallowed be thy name. Thy kingdom come. Thy will be done, as in heaven, so in earth.

Most people pray for "their" will to be done, what "they" want, need, or desire. If we truly believe Jesus instruction, we will pray for God's Will to be done in any matter.

And, God has a plan for our lives, and to pray for things that are not part of His plan may possibly get the answer "no" unless our fervency and clarity and intensity creates a different response from our Father. Daily repetitious pleading is not necessary, but holding the thought and the clear vision in mind of what we want in life is.

Mark 11:24 KJV Therefore I say unto you, What things soever ye desire, when ye pray, believe that ye receive them, and ye shall have them.

Faith that we will receive what we pray for is essential, and even more essential is that we will receive according to our faith as we work consistently towards our goals.

I Thessalonians 4:16 Rejoice evermore. 17 Pray without ceasing.

PRIDE

Self-esteem delight, dignity, ego, ego trip, egoism, egotism, face, gratification, happiness, honor, joy, pleasure, repletion, satisfaction, self-admiration, self-confidence, self-glorification, self-love, self-regard, self-respect, self-satisfaction, self-sufficiency, self-trust, self-worth, sufficiency, humility

There is a good pride, and a bad pride.

Psalm 101:5 KJV Whoso privily slandereth his neighbour, him will I cut off: him that hath an high look and a proud heart will not I suffer

Proverbs 16:5 KJV Every one that is proud in heart is an abomination to the LORD: though hand join in hand, he shall not be unpunished.

Proverbs 16:19 KJV Better it is to be of an humble spirit with the lowly, than to divide the spoil with the proud

Proverbs 28:25 KJV He that is of a proud heart stirreth up strife: but he that putteth his trust in the LORD shall be made fat.

James 4:6 KJV But he giveth more grace. Wherefore he saith, God resisteth the proud, but giveth grace unto the humble.

Ant: Humility, poor in spirit

PROSPERITY

Affluence, good fortune abundance, accomplishment, advantage, arrival, bed of roses, benefit, boom, clover, easy street, expansion, fortune, good, good times, gravy train, growth, increase, interest, life of luxury, luxury, opulence, plenteousness, plenty, prosperousness, riches, success, successfulness, the good life, thriving, velvet, victory, wealth, welfare, well-being

God is totally rich, as everything is His, and was made, and is being made by Him!

Haggai 2:8 KJV The silver is mine, and the gold is mine, saith the LORD of hosts.

God wants all His children to enjoy prosperity. Not all seem to, but there are always reasons why this is so. Poverty can always be traced to broken spiritual and physical laws.

God is faithful in what He says, so if we have serious needs, (and wants!) perhaps some careful self-examination and prayer and focus might point us in a better direction?

3 John 1:2 KJV Beloved, I wish above all things that thou mayest prosper and be in health, even as thy soul prospereth.

Psalm 1:1 Blessed is the man that walketh not in the counsel of the ungodly, nor standeth in the way of sinners, nor sitteth in the seat of the scornful. 2 But his delight is in the law of the LORD; and in his law doth he meditate day and night. 3 And he shall be like a tree planted by the rivers of water, that bringeth forth his fruit in his season; his leaf also shall not wither; and whatsoever he doeth shall prosper.

Thieves and conmen also prosper! Psalm 73:12 KJV Behold, these are the ungodly, who prosper in the world; they increase in riches. Their time of judgment will certainly come.

Inflation is theft. Inflation manipulated by governments and bankers and the financial industry degrades and devalues prosperity, and happens because the financial systems of this world are not in accordance with God's way or His laws. See: Capitalism

Ant: failure, loss, poorness, poverty

PUNCTUAL

Early, exact, in good time, on the dot, on time, precise, prompt, punctilious, seasonable, strict, timely.

Being on time is a function of courtesy and good manners. Being late, "the traffic was awful" etc., and other 'reasons' are just an excuse for being inconsiderate, and not caring that one is wasting someone else's life time, rather than exercising the self-discipline to arrive on time.

Ant: behind, behindhand, belated, delayed, late, overdue, tardy, unpunctual

PURE

Unmixed, genuine, authentic, bright, classic, clear, complete, fair, flawless, lucid, natural, neat, perfect, plain, pure and simple, real, simple, straight, transparent, true, unadulterated, unalloyed, unclouded, undiluted, unmingled.

2 Timothy 2:21 NLT If you keep yourself pure, you will be a utensil God can use for his purpose. Your life will be clean, and you will be ready for the Master to use you for every good work.

Ant: Impure, tainted, filthy

QUESTIONNING

Ask, cross-examine, enquire, examine, investigate, probe, sound out, call into question, cast doubt upon, challenge, controvert, disbelieve, dispute, distrust, doubt, impugn, mistrust, oppose, query, suspect, examination, inquiry, interrogation, investigation.

It is wise to question ideas and concepts, especially when they are commonly held by most people. There is a concept that says, the more people there are that believe something, the less likely it is to be true.

Our natural carnal human heart is deceitful above all things and desperately wicked. We think that everything we do is right. Proverbs 12:15 KJV The way of a fool (who says there is no God) is right in his own eyes: but he that hearkeneth unto counsel is wise. Proverbs 21:2 KJV Every way of a man is right in his own eyes: but the LORD pondereth the hearts.

We can however choose to question our actions, put that nature away, and go God's way. Philippians 2:13 KJV For it is God which worketh in you both to will and to do of his good pleasure.

QUIETNESS

Calm, calmness, hush, peace, placidity, quiescence, quiet, quietude, repose, rest, serenity, silence, still, stillness, tranquillity

Being deliberately quiet sometimes enables us to expand into 'quiet time', which can be a refreshing spiritual experience in this hectic world.

Ant: noisy, cacophony, clangour, din.

RELIGIOUS TITLES

Matt 23:8 But be not ye called Rabbi: for one is your Master, even Christ; and all ye are brethren. 9 And call no man your father (in a religious context) upon the earth: for one is your Father, which is in heaven. 10 Neither be ye called masters: for one is your Master, even Christ

RESPECT

adoration, appreciation, approbation, awe, consideration, courtesy, deference, dignity, esteem, estimation, homage, honour, obeisance, recognition, regard, repute, reverence, testimonial, tribute, veneration, worship.

Romans 2:11 KJV For there is no respect of persons with God.

Everyone is under the same identical rule of law.

We should not have "respect of persons" by deferring to rich and famous, or treating the poor and dirty with disdain, but have respect for all.

James 2:9 KJV But if ye have respect to persons, (favouring or disdaining anyone) ye commit sin, and are convinced (convicted) of the law as transgressors.

Ant: disdain, dishonor, disrespect

RESPONSIVENESS

alive, awake, aware, forthcoming, impressionable, open, perceptive, quick to react, reactive, receptive, sensitive, sharp, susceptible, sympathetic.

Really being "with" someone entails responding actively to the situation at the time. If we have ever been with an unresponsive person, we know how awkward that can be. Part of loving others involves interacting with them as they would wish.

Ant: apathetic, impassive, insensitive, silent, unresponsive, unsympathetic

RIGHTEOUS

Blameless, charitable, commendable, conscientious, creditable, deserving, devoted, devout, dutiful, equitable, ethical, exemplary, fair, faithful, godlike, guiltless, holy, honorable, impartial, innocent, irreproachable, just, laudable, law-abiding, matchless, meritorious, moral, noble, peerless, philanthropic, philanthropic, praiseworthy, punctilious, pure, reverent, right-minded, saintly, scrupulous, sinless, spiritual, sterling, trustworthy, upright, virtuous, worthy

Matthew 5:48 KJV Be ye therefore perfect, even as your Father which is in heaven is perfect.

And be balanced!

Ecclesiastes 7:16 KJV Be not righteous over much; neither make thyself over wise: why shouldest thou destroy thyself?

Romans 3:10 KJV As it is written, There is none righteous, no, not one:

Romans 3:23 KJV For all have sinned, and come short of the glory of God;

Our only hope is through Jesus Christ, who washes our wrongdoings away.

John 6:65 KJV And he said, Therefore said I unto you, that no man can come unto me, except it were given unto him of my Father.

Isaiah 1:18 KJV Come now, and let us reason together, saith the LORD: though your sins be as scarlet, they shall be as white as snow; though they be red like crimson, they shall be as wool.

And we get help in facing the temptations that we meet in life.

1 Corinthians 10:13 KJV There hath no temptation taken you but such as is common to man: but God is faithful, who will not suffer you to be tempted above that ye are able; but will with the temptation also make a way to escape, that ye may be able to bear it.

Ant: law breaking, bad, corrupt, dishonest, immoral, unfair

SANCTIFY

Sanctify, set apart for a Holy purpose, hold in highest esteem, absolve, anoint, bless, cleanse, consecrate, dedicate, glorify, hallow, purify, worship.

John 17:17 KJV Sanctify them through thy truth: thy word is truth.

1 Thessalonians 5:23 KJV And the very God of peace sanctify you wholly; and I pray God your whole spirit and soul and body be preserved blameless unto the coming of our Lord Jesus Christ.

1 Peter 3:15 KJV But sanctify the Lord God in your hearts: and be ready always to give an answer to every man that asketh you a reason of the hope that is in you with meekness and fear:

Ant: Desecrate,

SATAN

The Devil, Angel of Darkness, Antichrist, Apollyon, Beelzebub, Diabolus, King of Hell, Lucifer, Mephistopheles, Prince of Darkness, archfiend, demon, the Evil Spirit

Revelation 12:9 KJV And the great dragon was cast out, that old serpent, called the Devil, and Satan, which deceiveth the whole world: he was cast out into the earth, and his angels were cast out with him.

Many people think that Satan does not exist. In fact, his greatest deception is to have the world think this. We need to realize the existence of the Devil

Jesus was not under any illusion about the existence of Satan:

Luke 4:3 And the devil said unto him, If thou be the Son of God, command this stone that it be made bread. 4 And Jesus answered him, saying, It is written, That man shall not live by bread alone, but by every word of God.

Jesus recognized that Satan, with God's permission, has control of the whole world for this era, otherwise when Satan said Jesus could have all the kingdoms of the world, Jesus would have said that it was not in his power to grant that.

Luke 4:5 And the devil, taking him up into an high mountain, shewed unto him all the kingdoms of the world in a moment of time. 6 And the devil said unto him, All this power will I give thee, and the glory of them: for that is delivered unto me; and to whomsoever I will I give it. (by God!) 7 If thou therefore wilt worship me, all shall be thine. 8 And Jesus answered and said unto him, Get thee behind me, Satan: for it is written, Thou shalt worship the Lord thy God, and him only shalt thou serve

And the great dragon was cast out, that old serpent, called the Devil, and Satan, which deceiveth the whole world: he was cast out into the earth, and his angels were cast out with him. Revelation 12:9 KJV

In whom the god of this world hath blinded the minds of them which believe not, lest the light of the glorious gospel of Christ, who is the image of God, should shine unto them. Corinthians 4:4 KJV

SAVE

See Give, Money, Wealth

SAVED

All humanity will be saved before God makes all in all.

SEARCH

To look for diligently. See also SEEK

John 5:39 KJV Search the scriptures; for in them ye think ye have eternal life: and they are they which testify of me.

SCIENCE

Methodical study of part of material world art, body of knowledge, branch, discipline, education, erudition, information, learning, lore, scholarship, skill, system, technique, wisdom

1 Timothy 6:20 KJV O Timothy, keep that which is committed to thy trust, avoiding profane and vain babblings, and oppositions of science falsely so called:

Romans 1:20 For the invisible things of him from the creation of the world are clearly seen, being understood by the things that are made, even his eternal power and Godhead; so that they are without excuse: 21 Because that, when they knew God, they glorified him not as God, neither were thankful; but became vain in their imaginations, and their foolish heart was darkened. 22 Professing themselves to be wise, they became fools, 23 And changed the glory of the uncorruptible God into an image made like to corruptible man, and to birds, and fourfooted beasts, and creeping things.

SEEK

Be after, follow, go gunning for, go in pursuit of, go in quest of, go in search of, hunt, inquire, look for, pursue, search for, aim, aspire to, attempt, endeavour, essay, strive.

Matthew 6:33 But seek ye first the kingdom of God, and his righteousness; and all these things shall be added unto you. Matthew 7:7 KJV Ask, and it shall be given you; seek, and ye shall find; knock, and it shall be opened unto you:

Isaiah 55:6 Seek ye the LORD while he may be found, call ye upon him while he is near: 7 Let the wicked forsake his way, and the unrighteous man his thoughts: and let him return unto the LORD, and he will have mercy upon him; and to our God, for he will abundantly pardon.

See: Conduct

SELFLESSNESS

Someone is selfless because they care about other people more than themselves.

John 15:13 KJV Greater love hath no man than this, that a man lay down his life for his friends.

And to balance that thought, we are commanded to love our neighbour AS ourselves, which means that we need to take care of our self-esteem. That does not extend to vanity and self-aggrandisement.

Ant: Selfishness, me, my

SERENITY

Clear, calm, peaceful. Remaining serene, especially in the face of difficulties is not always easy, but it is an attitude worth cultivating. It puts others at ease.

Ant: Agitated, angry

SEX

Sexual activity is a gift of God, but only to be used in the context of marriage. The sex act is actually one of the most spiritual things humans can engage in, as it represents the type of joy and ecstasy we shall experience when we are united with the God Family. It is impossible to approach a place selling newspapers or magazines without being exposed to pictures that are designed to excite lustful thoughts. It is a tragedy to observe pubescent young girls dressed provocatively, shamelessly displaying their bodies, inviting men to think of them as sex objects.

Ant: Pure physical loving when a man and wife coalesce.

SPIRIT

Air, breath, life, life force, psyche, soul, vital spark, attitude, character, complexion, disposition, essence, humour, outlook, quality, temper, temperament, animation, ardour, backbone, courage, dauntlessness, earnestness, energy, enterprise, enthusiasm, fire, force, gameness, grit, life, liveliness, mettle, resolution, sparkle, stoutheartedness, vigour, warmth, zest, motivation, resolution, resolve, will, willpower, essence, intent, intention, meaning, purport, purpose, sense, substance, feelings, frame of mind, humour, mood, morale.

John 4:24 KJV God is a Spirit: and they that worship him must worship him in spirit and in truth.

Job 32:8 KJV But there is a spirit in man: and the inspiration of the Almighty giveth them understanding

SPIRIT IN MAN

Zechariah 12:1 KJV The burden of the word of the LORD for Israel, saith the LORD, which stretcheth forth the heavens, and layeth the foundation of the earth, and formeth the spirit of man within him.

Ecclesiastes 8:8 KJV There is no man that hath power over the spirit to retain the spirit; neither hath he power in the day of death: and there is no discharge in that war; neither shall wickedness deliver those that are given to it.

Ecclesiastes 12:7 KJV Then shall the dust return to the earth as it was: and the spirit shall return unto God who gave it.

Ecclesiastes 3:21 KJV Who knoweth the spirit of man that goeth upward, and the spirit of the beast that goeth downward to the earth? The 'spirit' of animal life goes down into the earth, indicating that once dead, there is no further use for it.

But the 'spirit in man' goes upwards to God for Him to store it until it is time for a resurrection for that individual. The 'spirit in man' cannot have any life or consciousness without a body, but the essence of the person is stored like a tape or DVD until it is reunited with a new body which will have all the characteristics of the original person. See: Life & Death

SPIRIT ESSENCE

Spirit essence is the power of God, which pervades the universes and everything there is, and is the "stuff" of which everything was and is made, it creates energy, enables life, and it is that which sustains all. Every atom is 99.999999999% empty space with a nucleus and at least one other particle, moving endlessly in a predetermined pattern, which gives it its form and existence, all powered by God's essence.

Hebrews 11:3 Through faith we understand that the worlds were framed by the Word of God, so that things which are seen were not made of things which do appear.

Everything we can see of Creation was made by God out of a material that we cannot see. That material is Spirit Essence.

Creation was brought about by God through the God of the Old Testament who was called Yahweh who became the One we call Jesus, or more accurately Yashua. Our Elder Brother is the Christ, the Messiah, our Saviour.

Hebrews 1:1 God, (Yahweh) who at sundry times and in divers manners spake in time past unto the fathers by the prophets, 2 Hath in these last days spoken unto us by his Son, whom he hath appointed heir of all things, by whom also he made the worlds;

Jesus Christ was the Creative Power of God, through Whom the Father made all things

Hebrews 1:3 Who)Yahweh) being the brightness of His (the Father's) glory, and the express image of His (the Father's) person, and upholding (sustaining) all things by the Word of His (the Father's) power.

John 1:1 In the beginning was the Word (Yahweh), and the Word was with God, and the Word (Yahweh) was God. 2 The same was in the beginning with God.

This is the a mystery because we cannot perceive One when more than one is described, but there is only ONE GOD, and to make that comprehensible to us, it is useful to describe God as one "Family". Yahweh was not a separate God, but the manner is which God expressed Himself and organized Himself to effect creation.

God said: "Let US". Genesis 1:26 KJV And God said, Let us make man in our image, after our likeness: and let them have dominion over the fish of the sea, and over the fowl of the air, and over the cattle, and over all the earth, and over every creeping thing that creepeth upon the earth.

John 1:3 All things were made by Him (by Jesus Christ); and without Him was not any thing made that was made.

John 1:4 In Him (God) was life; It was God that infused His Creation with the gift of "LIFE". Nothing can exist without God's Spirit Essence, and nothing can have Life without that Essence.

God is Light. So God was able to create Light for us to see and enjoy.

1 John 1:5 KJV This then is the message which we have heard of him, and declare unto you, that God is light, and in him is no darkness at all.

In the final analysis, when God is All in All, and His throne is the Earth, there will be no time, there will be no need for the sun or moon. Revelation 21:23 KJV And the city had no need of the sun, neither of the moon, to shine in it: for the glory of God did lighten it, and the Lamb is the light thereof.

John 1:4b and the life was the light of men. 5 And the light shineth in darkness; and the darkness comprehended it not.

Hebrews 11:1 Now faith is the substance of things hoped for, the evidence of things not seen.

SPIRITUAL

Religious, otherworldly, devotional, divine, holy, metaphysical, nonmaterial, nonphysical, pure, sacred.

Are religious people spiritual? There is only one standard of spirituality, and that is provided by God in His Word to us. There is no other source of true spirituality. That is why this book is written as it is, using quotations from God's Word to authenticate the meaning of each word. So a person's spirituality could be assessed by observing the degree to which they live their lives according to the spiritual laws given to us in the Bible by God directly inspiring His Words to be written down by His appointed servants.

The author has studied the Bible for over half a century, and has never come across any religious organization that follows implicitly, and whose doctrines or teachings do not contradict in any way, the teachings of the Bible and Jesus Christ. All religions are man-made. Human beings are fallible, and are not basically spiritual, so they construct organizations to control and manipulate what their followers think and believe.

Ant: Profane

One of the definitions for 'spiritual' given by dictionaries is 'metaphysical'. The "new age" movement is metaphysical in nature and in ideologies, but are they truly spiritual. No, they not truly spiritual, they are counterfeit beliefs and practices that are the opposite of true spirituality.

Metaphysical: abstract, abstruse, bodiless, deep, difficult, discarnate, esoteric, eternal, fundamental, high-flown, ideal, immaterial, impalpable, incorporeal, insubstantial, intangible, intellectual, jesuitic, mystical, nonmaterial, nonphysical, numinous, oversubtle, philosophical, preternatural, profound, recondite, spiritual, superhuman, superior, supermundane, supernatural, suprahuman, supramundane, supranatural, theoretical, transcendental, unearthly, unfleshly, universal, unphysical, unreal, unsubstantial

Ant: concrete, material, objective, physical, real, solid, substantial

Ant: Earthy, irreligious, irreverent, physical, profane, unspiritual

STRENGTH

Stamina, mental or physical, backbone, courage, durability, energy, firmness, force, fortitude, hardiness, health, healthiness, might, potency, power, robustness, security, soundness, stability, stableness, stalwartness, steadiness, substance, tenacity, toughness, vigor, vitality,

Isaiah 40:29 He giveth power to the faint; and to them that have no might he increaseth strength. 30 Even the youths shall faint and be weary, and the young men shall utterly fall: 31 But they that wait upon the LORD shall renew their strength; they shall mount up with wings as eagles; they shall run, and not be weary; and they shall walk, and not faint.

Ant: Weakness

STRIVE

Aim, assay, attempt, bear down, contend, do one's best, do one's utmost, drive, endeavor, essay, fight, go after, go all out, go the limit, labor, leave no stone unturned, make every effort, struggle, sweat, tackle, take on, toil, try hard, work

Luke 13:24 KJV Strive to enter in at the strait gate: for many, I say unto you, will seek to enter in, and shall not be able.

Strive towards godliness and righteousness, but not with people, and certainly not about religious or theological matters.

2 Timothy 2:14 KJV Of these things put them in remembrance, charging them before the Lord that they strive not about words to no profit, but to the subverting of the hearers.

2 Timothy 2:24 KJV And the servant of the Lord must not strive; but be gentle unto all men, apt to teach, patient,

Ant: Indolence, lazyness

STUDY

To apply the mind to the learning or understanding of (a subject), esp. by reading to study languages, to investigate or examine, as by observation, research, etc., to look at minutely; scrutinize, to give much careful or critical thought to, to take a course in, to meditate on or contemplate; reflect.

We live in an era of excess information. This current incredible increase in knowledge was foretold hundreds of years before Christ, and predicted to occur at the end of the age. Daniel 12:4 KJV But thou, O Daniel, shut up the words, and seal the book, even to the time of the end: many shall run to and fro, and knowledge shall be increased.

Never before in mankind's history have so many "run to and fro" in planes, trains, and automobiles, and yet... bombarded from every side by unbelievable quantities of knowledge, the world is full of unhappiness, wars, disease, and human misery. Why?

Because it is not the right sort of knowledge! Hosea 4:6 KJV My people are destroyed for lack of knowledge: because thou hast rejected knowledge, I will also reject thee, that thou shall be no priest to me: seeing thou hast forgotten the law of thy God, I will also forget thy children. So our so-called civilizations slide into the abyss of law breaking and depravity.

We need to get back to the right knowledge individually and collectively, only available in the Bible. Luke 4:4 KJV And Jesus answered him, saying, It is written that man shall not live by bread alone, but by every word of God.

2Tim 2:15 Study (God's word) to shew thyself approved unto God, a workman that needeth not to be ashamed, rightly dividing the word of truth. We need to feed on the real information, and the vital truths for our spiritual nourishment as much as we need physical food every day.

SURETY

Pledge bail, guarantee, guaranty, guarantor, security

We might be tempted to want to help out a friend or relative by standing surety or guarantor for them. This can put a person in financial jeopardy from which they might never recover. Best avoided.

Proverbs 6:1 My son, if thou be surety for thy friend, if thou hast stricken thy hand with a stranger, 2 Thou art snared with the words of thy mouth, thou art taken with the words of thy mouth. 3 Do this now, my son, and deliver thyself, when thou art come into the hand of thy friend; go, humble thyself, and make sure thy friend. 4 Give not sleep to thine eyes, nor slumber to thine eyelids. 5 Deliver thyself as a roe from the hand of the hunter, and as a bird from the hand of the fowler.

Proverbs 11:15 KJV He that is surety for a stranger shall smart for it: and he that hateth suretiship is sure.

Proverbs 17:18 KJV A man void of understanding striketh hands, and becometh surety in the presence of his friend.

SWEARING

Bad language, blasphemy, cursing, foul language, profanity.

Matt 5:34 But I say unto you, Swear not at all; neither by heaven; for it is God's throne: 35 Nor by the earth; for it is his footstool: neither by Jerusalem; for it is the city of the great King. 36 Neither shalt thou swear by thy head, because thou canst not make one hair white or black. 37 But let your communication be, Yea, yea; Nay, nay: for whatsoever is more than these cometh of evil.

TEMPTATION

Lure, attraction, allurement, appeal, attractiveness, bait, blandishment, coaxing, come-on, decoy, draw, enticement, fancy, fascination, hankering, inducement, inveiglement, invitation, provocation, pull, seducement, seduction, snare, tantalization, trap, yen.

Our human nature has a bias against obedience. This creates a pull towards toward the attractions of this world which inveigle us to want to follow Satan's way. Here is a promise to fall back on when we feel we are likely to give in to temptation. God tempts no man, so when temptations do come, we know where they are coming from.

1 Corinthians 10:13 There hath no temptation taken you but such as is common to man: but God is faithful, who will not suffer you to be tempted above that ye are able; but will with the temptation also make a way to escape, that ye may be able to bear it.

Ant: Repulsion, moral strength.

THINK, THOUGHTS

Believe, conceive, conclude, consider, deem, determine, esteem, estimate, imagine, judge, reckon, regard, suppose, surmise, brood, cerebrate, cogitate, consider, contemplate, deliberate, have in mind, meditate, mull over, muse, ponder, rack one's brains, reason, reflect, revolve, ruminate, turn over in one's mind, weigh up, call to mind, recall, recollect, remember, anticipate, envisage, expect, foresee, imagine, plan for, presume, suppose

John 5:39 KJV Search the scriptures; for in them ye think ye have eternal life: and they are they which testify of me.

Philippians 4:8 KJV Finally, brethren, whatsoever things are true, whatsoever things are honest, whatsoever things are just, whatsoever things are pure, whatsoever things are lovely, whatsoever things are of good report; if there be any virtue, and if there be any praise, think on these things.

We think about God and His plan for us, but we are limited. We cannot think like He does!

Isaiah 55:8 KJV For my thoughts are not your thoughts, neither are your ways my ways, saith the LORD.

Isaiah 55:9 KJV For as the heavens are higher than the earth, so are my ways higher than your ways, and my thoughts than your thoughts.

Although God's mind is so far above ours, nevertheless we can have His mind and His Spirit in us.

Psalm 94:11 KJV

The LORD knoweth the thoughts of man, that they are vanity.

Matthew 6:25 Therefore I say unto you, Take no thought for your life, (Heb. do not be anxious for your soul) what ye shall eat, or what ye shall drink; nor yet for your body, what ye shall put on. Is not the life more than meat, and the body than raiment? 27 Which of you by taking (Heb. anxious) thought can add one cubit unto his stature? 28. And why take ye (Heb. anxious) thought for raiment? Consider the lilies of the field, how they grow; they toil not, neither do they spin: 31. Therefore take no (Heb. anxious) thought, saying, What shall we eat? or, What shall we drink? or, Wherewithal shall we be clothed? 34. Take therefore no (Heb. Anxious) thought for the morrow: for the morrow shall take thought (Heb. Be anxious) for the things of itself. Sufficient unto the day is the evil thereof.

2 Corinthians 10:5 KJV Casting down imaginations, and every high thing that exalteth itself against the knowledge of God, and bringing into captivity every thought to the obedience of Christ;

Ecclesiastes 8:17 KJV Then I beheld all the work of God, that a man cannot find out the work that is done under the sun: because though a man labour to seek it out, yet he shall not find it; yea further; though a wise (?) man (scientists!) think to know it, yet shall he not be able to find it.

Romans 12:3 KJV For I say, through the grace given unto me, to every man that is among you, not to think of himself more highly than he ought to think; but to think soberly, according as God hath dealt to every man the measure of faith.

We are not what we think, but what we think we are. (or become!)

Proverbs 23:7 KJV For as he thinketh in his heart, so is he:

TONGUE

It is our inner being, our heart that rules the tongue. This creates the need for constant vigilance in what we think about for without realizing we will reveal our inner thoughts when we use the tongue.

Luke 6:45 KJV A good man out of the good treasure of his heart bringeth forth that which is good; and an evil man out of the evil treasure of his heart bringeth forth that which is evil: for of the abundance of the heart his mouth speaketh.

James 1:26 KJV If any man among you seem to be religious, and bridleth not his tongue, but deceiveth his own heart, this man's religion is vain.

James 3:5 KJV Even so the tongue is a little member, and boasteth great things. Behold, how great a matter a little fire kindleth!

James 3:6 KJV And the tongue is a fire, a world of iniquity: so is the tongue among our members, that it defileth the whole body, and setteth on fire the course of nature; and it is set on fire of hell.

James 3:8 KJV But the tongue can no man tame; it is an unruly evil, full of deadly poison.

1 Peter 3:10 KJV For he that will love life, and see good days, let him refrain his tongue from evil, and his lips that they speak no guile:

Proverbs 29:11 KJV A fool uttereth all his mind: but a wise man keepeth it in till afterwards.

Proverbs 12:18 KJV There is that speaketh like the piercings of a sword: but the tongue of the wise is health.

Proverbs 16:24 KJV Pleasant words are as an honeycomb, sweet to the soul, and health to the bones.

TRUSTWORTHY

Dependable, ethical, honest, honourable, level-headed, mature, principled, reliable, reputable, responsible, righteous, sensible, staunch, steadfast, to be trusted, true, trusty, truthful, upright.

As unpalatable as most people might find the truth about human nature, it is summed up in Jeremiah 17:9 The heart is deceitful above all things, and desperately wicked: who can know it? Unaware of this fact, most are unable to fight against the tendency to conduct themselves in the opposite of trustworthy. Hence the antonyms.

Ant: Deceitful, dishonest, disloyal, irresponsible, treacherous, undependable, unethical, unprincipled, unreliable, untrustworthy

TRUTH

Reality, validity, accuracy, actuality, authenticity, certainty, correctness, exactitude, exactness, fact, facts, factualism, factuality, factualness, genuineness, gospel truth, gospel, honest truth, infallibility, legitimacy, maxim, naked truth, perfection, picture, plain talk, precision, principle, rectitude, rightness, scoop, score, trueness, truism, truthfulness, unvarnished truth, veracity, verisimilitude, verity, whole story

Jesus Christ, the Son of God is the Word of Truth.

John 17:17 KJV Sanctify them through thy truth: thy word is truth.

John 16:13 KJV Howbeit when he, the Spirit of truth, is come, he will guide you into all truth: for he shall not speak of himself; but whatsoever he shall hear, that shall he speak: and he will shew you things to come.

Ant: falsehood, invention, untruth

URBANE

Civil, civilized, cosmopolitan, courteous, cultivated, cultured, debonair, elegant, mannerly, polished, refined, smooth, sophisticated, suave, well-bred, well-mannered

Ant: Boorish, discourteous, gauche, impolite, rude, uncivilized, uncouth, uncultured.

VANITY

All is empty, vanity and a striving after wind, unless it is of God in us.

VISION

Perception, farsightedness, foresight, imagination, insight, concept, conception, daydream, dream, idea, ideal, image, mental picture.

What is the vision that inspires us as we go through life? The vision of eternal life as God's children is our ultimate goal.

Proverbs 29:18 KJV Where there is no vision, the people perish: but he that keepeth the law, happy is he.

The Kingdom of God and eternal life is that vision we need to keep in mind and strive for. Matthew 6:33 KJV But seek ye first the kingdom of God, and his righteousness; and all these things shall be added unto you.

Ant: Visionless, no forward perceptions.

WATCHFULNESS

Alertness, attention, attentiveness, caution, cautiousness, circumspection, heedfulness, vigilance, wariness.

Being aware of the goings on in this world is an important part of our conduct. It is wise to be ignorant of current affairs, natural events, weather, the dangers of public disorder and so on. Many people are involved in car accidents, when more care might have avoided it. Thousands ignore warnings of floods and wild weather to their cost. Others could have fled before the awful events of wars came upon them.

Matthew 24:43 KJV But know this, that if the goodman of the house had known in what watch the thief would come, he would have watched, and would not have suffered his house to be broken up.

Matthew 25:13 KJV Watch therefore, for ye know neither the day nor the hour wherein the Son of man cometh.

Ant: Unaware, carelessness, heedlessness, inattention, indiscretion, irresponsibility, neglect, recklessness, thoughtlessness.

WAY OF LIFE

John 14:6 KJV Jesus saith unto him, I am the way, the truth, and the life: no man cometh unto the Father, but by me.

WEALTH

Money, resources, abundance, affluence, assets, belongings, bounty, cache, capital, cash, commodities, copiousness, cornucopia, estate, fortune, funds, gold, goods, hoard, holdings, lap of luxury, lucre, luxuriance, luxury, means, opulence, plenty, possessions, profusion, property, prosperity, prosperousness, revenue, riches, richness, security, stocks and bonds, store, substance, substantiality, treasure, worth.

God wants His people to be prosperous and enjoy the good things of life.

3 John 1:2 KJV Beloved, I wish above all things that thou mayest prosper and be in health, even as thy soul prospereth

But the pursuit of riches is a snare that takes the mind off Godly things, and the real values. Often for the rich, there can never be enough.

Matthew 6:21 KJV For where your treasure is, there will your heart be also.

Matthew 6:19 KJV Lay not up for yourselves treasures upon earth, where moth and rust doth corrupt, and where thieves break through and steal. 20. But lay up for yourselves treasures in heaven, where neither moth nor rust doth corrupt, and where thieves do not break through nor steal:

Proverbs 18:11 KJV The rich man's wealth is his strong city, and as an high wall in his own conceit. (But)

Matthew 19:24 KJV And again I say unto you, It is easier for a camel to go through the eye of a needle, than for a rich man to enter into the kingdom of God.

Ant: lack, need, poverty, want

WILL

personal choice, aim, attitude, character, conviction, craving, decision, decisiveness, decree, design, desire, determination, discipline, discretion, disposition, feeling, heart's desire, inclination, intention, liking, longing, mind, option, passion, power, preference, prerogative, purpose, resolution, resolve, self-control, self-discipline, self-restraint, temperament, urge, volition, willfulness, willpower, wish, wishes, yearning.

Matthew 7:21 KJV Not every one that saith unto me, Lord, Lord, shall enter into the kingdom of heaven; but he that doeth the will of my Father which is in heaven.

Matthew 12:50 KJV For whosoever shall do the will of my Father which is in heaven, the same is my brother, and sister, and mother.

Matthew 18:14 KJV Even so it is not the will of your Father which is in heaven, that one of these little ones should perish.

John 4:34 KJV Jesus saith unto them, My meat is to do the will of him that sent me, and to finish his work.

We in truth can do nothing worthwhile of ourselves, our entire lives are governed and led by God. It is His will that we should attempt to ascertain and get in harmony with.

John 5:30 KJV I can of mine own self do nothing: as I hear, I judge: and my judgment is just; because I seek not mine own will, but the will of the Father which hath sent me.

Philippians 2:13 KJV For it is God which worketh in you both to will and to do of his good pleasure.

We, as Jesus lived, are here to do God's Will.

John 6:38 KJV For I came down from heaven, not to do mine own will, but the will of him that sent me.

It is God's Will that all humans given to Christ by the Father are intended to achieve Sonship.

John 6:39 KJV And this is the Father's will which hath sent me, that of all which he hath given me I should lose nothing, but should raise it up again at the last day.

John 6:40 KJV And this is the will of him that sent me, that every one which seeth the Son, and believeth on him, may have everlasting life: and I will raise him up at the last day.

John 17:24 KJV Father, I will that they also, whom thou hast given me, be with me where I am; that they may behold my glory, which thou hast given me: for thou lovedst me before the foundation of the world.

Romans 12:2 KJV And be not conformed to this world: but be ye transformed by the renewing of your mind, that ye may prove what is that good, and acceptable, and perfect, will of God.

Galatians 1:4 KJV Who gave himself for our sins, that he might deliver us from this present evil world, according to the will of God and our Father:

1 Thessalonians 5:18 KJV In every thing give thanks: for this is the will of God in Christ Jesus concerning you.

1 Timothy 2:1 I exhort therefore, that, first of all, supplications, prayers, intercessions, and giving of thanks, be made for all men; 2 For kings, and for all that are in authority; that we may lead a quiet and peaceable life in all godliness and honesty. 3 For this is good and acceptable in the sight of God our Saviour; 4 Who will have all men to be saved, and to come unto the knowledge of the truth.

Hebrews 10:36 KJV For ye have need of patience, that, after ye have done the will of God, ye might receive the promise.

1 John 2:17 KJV And the world passeth away, and the lust thereof: but he that doeth the will of God abideth for ever.

See: CHOICE and FREE WILL

WISDOM – in Greek and Hebrew is a feminine attribute

Astuteness, circumspection, comprehension, discernment, enlightenment, erudition, foresight, insight, intelligence, judgment, judiciousness, knowledge, learning, penetration, prudence, reason, sagacity, sapience, sense, sound judgment, understanding.

Proverbs 9:10 KJV The fear (awe, respect) of the LORD is the beginning of wisdom: and the knowledge of the holy is understanding.

I Timothy 3:15 For jealousy and selfishness are not God's kind of wisdom. Such things are earthly, unspiritual, and motivated by the Devil. 16 For wherever there is jealousy and selfish ambition, there you will find disorder and every kind of evil. 17 But the wisdom that comes from heaven is first of all pure. It is also peace loving, gentle at all times, and willing to yield to others. It is full of mercy and good deeds. It shows no partiality and is always sincere. 18 And those who are peacemakers will plant seeds of peace and reap a harvest of goodness.

Ecclesiastes 8:1 KJV Who is as the wise man? and who knoweth the interpretation of a thing? a man's wisdom maketh his face to shine, and the boldness of his face shall be changed. Wisdom changes your facial appearance.

Matthew 10:16 Behold, I send you forth as sheep in the midst of wolves: be ye therefore wise as serpents, and harmless as doves.

1 Corinthians 1:19 KJV For it is written, I will destroy the wisdom of the wise, and will bring to nothing the understanding of the prudent.

1 Corinthians 1:20 KJV Where is the wise? where is the scribe? where is the disputer of this world? hath not God made foolish the wisdom of this world?

1 Corinthians 3:19 KJV For the wisdom of this world is foolishness with God. For it is written, He taketh the wise in their own craftiness.

Psalm 111:10 KJV The fear (awe, respect) of the LORD is the beginning of wisdom: a good understanding have all they that do his commandments: his praise endureth for ever.

Proverbs 1:7 KJV The fear (awe respect) of the LORD is the beginning of knowledge: but fools despise wisdom and instruction.

Ant: Ignorance, stupidity, foolishness

WORK

Labour, effort, elbow grease, endeavor, exertion, industry, job, performance, production, task, toil, travail, undertaking.

People say they are doing the work of God when they preach and attempt to spread the gospel, but what did Christ say?

John 6:28 Then said they unto him, What shall we do, that we might work the works of God? 29 Jesus answered and said unto them, This is the work of God, that ye believe on him whom he hath sent.

Believing in Jesus Christ as being the Son of God, and our Saviour is The WORK! Our day to day work should be a source of joy and pleasure.

Proverbs 14:23 KJV In all labour there is profit: but the talk of the lips tendeth only to penury. (hardship, being penniless.)

Proverbs 23:4 KJV Labour not to be rich: cease from thine own wisdom. For many rich people, there is never enough.

Ecclesiastes 3:13 KJV And also that every man should eat and drink, and enjoy the good of all his labour, it is the gift of God.

Ecclesiastes 5:18 KJV Behold that which I have seen: it is good and comely for one to eat and to drink, and to enjoy the good of all his labour that he taketh under the sun all the days of his life, which God giveth him: for it is his portion.

Ecclesiastes 5:19 KJV Every man also to whom God hath given riches and wealth, and hath given him power to eat thereof, and to take his portion, and to rejoice in his labour; this is the gift of God.

Proverbs 10:5 KJV He that gathereth in summer is a wise son: but he that sleepeth in harvest is a son that causeth shame.

Ant: entertainment, fun, pastime. The rewards after work!

WORKS

Labour, attempt, commission, effort, endeavor, exertion, functioning, industry, job, performance, striving, struggle, toil, travail, undertaking.

Galatians 2:16 KJV Knowing that a man is not justified by the works of the law, but by the faith of Jesus Christ, even we have believed in Jesus Christ, that we might be justified by the faith of Christ, and not by the works of the law: for by the works of the law shall no flesh be justified

Titus 3:5 KJV Not by works of righteousness which we have done, but according to his mercy he saved us, by the washing of regeneration, and renewing of the Holy Ghost;

We are not saved by works. But we can spoil our future if we give in to evil works, and may even miss out on the Kingdom Phase when Christ returns. See: KINGDOM

WORLD - WORLDLINESS

Worldly is used to describe things relating to the ordinary activities of life, rather than to spiritual things. Carnal, earthly, fleshly, lay, mundane, physical, profane, secular, sublunary, temporal, terrestrial, avaricious, covetous, grasping, greedy, materialistic, selfish, worldly-minded, blasé, cosmopolitan, experienced, knowing, politic, sophisticated, urbane, well versed in the ways of the world, worldly-wise.

1 John 2:15 KJV Love not the world, neither the things that are in the world. If any man love the world, the love of the Father is not in him.

Matthew 13:22 KJV He also that received seed among the thorns is he that heareth the word; and the care of this world, and the deceitfulness of riches, choke the word, and he becometh unfruitful.

Matthew 16:26 KJV For what is a man profited, if he shall gain the whole world, and lose his own soul? or what shall a man give in exchange for his soul?

John 12:25 KJV He that loveth his life shall lose it; and he that hateth his life in this world shall keep it unto life eternal.

John 15:19 KJV If ye were of the world, the world would love his own: but because ye are not of the world, but I have chosen you out of the world, therefore the world hateth you.

Romans 12:2 KJV And be not conformed to this world: but be ye transformed by the renewing of your mind, that ye may prove what is that good, and acceptable, and perfect, will of God.

1 Corinthians 3:18 KJV Let no man deceive himself. If any man among you seemeth to be wise in this world, let him become a fool, that he may be wise.

1 Corinthians 3:19 KJV For the wisdom of this world is foolishness with God. For it is written, He taketh the wise in their own craftiness.

2 Corinthians 4:4 KJV In whom the god of this world hath blinded the minds of them which believe not, lest the light of the glorious gospel of Christ, who is the image of God, should shine unto them.

1 Corinthians 3:19 KJV For the wisdom of this world is foolishness with God. For it is written, He taketh the wise in their own craftiness.

1 Corinthians 1:27 KJV But God hath chosen the foolish things of the world to confound the wise; and God hath chosen the weak things of the world to confound the things which are mighty;

1 Corinthians 2:12 KJV Now we have received, not the spirit of the world, but the spirit which is of God; that we might know the things that are freely given to us of God.

Romans 12:2 KJV And be not conformed to this world: but be ye transformed by the renewing of your mind, that ye may prove what is that good, and acceptable, and perfect, will of God.

Galatians 1:4 KJV Who gave himself for our sins, that he might deliver us from this present evil world, according to the will of God and our Father:

Once we know God in measure we no longer find the 'world' desirable.

Ephesians 2:2 KJV Wherein in time past ye walked according to the course of this world, according to the prince of the power of the air, the spirit that now worketh in the children of disobedience:

This world is controlled almost entirely by Satan the god of this present evil world, yet under God's watchful eye. Governments, rulers of every sort, the powerful in finance and banks are all influenced by Satan the Devil. We have to wrestle not to be drawn into the machinations of this present evil world.

Ephesians 6:12 KJV For we wrestle not against flesh and blood, but against principalities, against powers, against the rulers of the darkness of this world, against spiritual wickedness in high places.

Colossians 2:8 KJV Beware lest any man spoil you through philosophy and vain deceit, after the tradition of men, after the rudiments of the world, and not after Christ.

Titus 2:12 KJV Teaching us that, denying ungodliness and worldly lusts, we should live soberly, righteously, and godly, in this present world;

James 4:4 KJV Ye adulterers and adulteresses, know ye not that the friendship of the world is enmity with God? whosoever therefore will be a friend of the world is the enemy of God.

1 John 2:15 KJV Love not the world, neither the things that are in the world. If any man love the world, the love of the Father is not in him.

1 John 2:16 KJV For all that is in the world, the lust of the flesh, and the lust of the eyes, and the pride of life, is not of the Father, but is of the world.

We are warned about the way people of the world will be in the latter years.

2 Timothy 3:1 This know also, that in the last days perilous times shall come. 2 For men shall be lovers of their own selves, covetous, boasters, proud, blasphemers, disobedient to parents, unthankful, unholy, 3 Without natural affection, trucebreakers, false accusers, incontinent, fierce, despisers of those that are good, 4 Traitors, heady, high-minded, lovers of pleasures more than lovers of God; 5 Having a form of godliness, but denying the power thereof: from such turn away. 6 For of this sort are they which creep into houses, and lead captive silly women laden with sins, led away with divers lusts, 7 Ever learning, and never able to come to the knowledge of the truth…

And in our time right now, the 'Me' Generation, the 'Millennials', that just about sums it up!

Ant: Divine, ethereal, heavenly, immaterial, non-corporeal, spiritual, transcendental, unworldly, moral, non-materialistic, unworldly, ingenuous, innocent, naive, unsophisticated, unworldly.

X-RAY VISION

The study of God's Words given for us gives us an insight of this present evil world. It gives us a type of x-ray vision that can see past and through what seems to be reality for most, the superficial activities of the world of humans, enabling us with the "eyes to see" what God is doing here on earth, and what His plans are for those that love Him.

1 Corinthians 2:9 KJV But as it is written, Eye hath not seen, nor ear heard, neither have entered into the heart of man, the things which God hath prepared for them that love him.

Only if God opens someone's eyes and gives them the gift of x-ray sight, can we even begin to have any idea of what is ahead for us.

YEARNING

To ache, covet, crave, desire, eat one's heart out over, hanker, have a yen for hunger, itch, languish, long, lust, pant, pine, set one's heart upon, would give one's eyeteeth for.

This is how those who have the Spirit of God feel about the prospect of this present evil world being superceded by the establishment of the Kingdom of God and Christ's rule on this earth.

Revelation 21:4 KJV And God shall wipe away all tears from their eyes; and there shall be no more death, neither sorrow, nor crying, neither shall there be any more pain: for the former things are passed away.

Isaiah 65:17 KJV For, behold, I create new heavens and a new earth: and the former shall not be remembered, nor come into mind.

Ant: Lack of zeal

ZEAL

Ardour, devotion, eagerness, earnestness, enthusiasm, fanaticism, fervency, fervour, fire, gusto, keenness, militancy, passion, spirit, verve, warmth, zest

Isaiah 9:7 KJV Of the increase of his government and peace there shall be no end, upon the throne of David, and upon his kingdom, to order it, and to establish it with judgment and with justice from henceforth even for ever. The zeal of the LORD of hosts will perform this.

Ant: Apathy. The sin of sloth, the attitude of lacking in the desire to act on anything.

www.ingramcontent.com/pod-product-compliance
Lightning Source LLC
Chambersburg PA
CBHW070536010526
44118CB00012B/1147